Responding to the Terrorist Threat

Pergamon Titles of Related Interest

Alexander/Gleason   BEHAVIORAL PERSPECTIVES ON TERRORISM
Amos   THE PALESTINIAN RESISTANCE
Rapoport/Alexander   THE MORALITY OF TERRORISM

Related Journals*

LONG RANGE PLANNING
WORLD DEVELOPMENT

*Free specimen copies available upon request.

 PERGAMON POLICY STUDIES ON INTERNATIONAL POLITICS

Responding to the Terrorist Threat
Security and Crisis Management

Edited by
Richard H. Shultz Jr.
Stephen Sloan

Pergamon Press
NEW YORK • OXFORD • TORONTO • SYDNEY • PARIS • FRANKFURT

Pergamon Press Offices:

U.S.A.	Pergamon Press Inc., Maxwell House, Fairview Park, Elmsford, New York 10523, U.S.A.
U.K.	Pergamon Press Ltd., Headington Hill Hall, Oxford OX3 OBW, England
CANADA	Pergamon of Canada, Ltd., Suite 104, 150 Consumers Road, Willowdale, Ontario M2J 1P9, Canada
AUSTRALIA	Pergamon Press (Aust.) Pty. Ltd., P.O. Box 544, Potts Point, NSW 2011, Australia
FRANCE	Pergamon Press SARL, 24 rue des Ecoles, 75240 Paris, Cedex 05, France
FEDERAL REPUBLIC OF GERMANY	Pergamon Press GmbH, Hammerweg 6, Postfach 1305, 6242 Kronberg/Taunus, Federal Republic of Germany

Library of Congress Cataloging in Publication Data
Main entry under title:

Responding to the terrorist threat.

(Pergamon policy studies on international politics)
1. Terrorism—Addresses, essays, lectures.
2. Terrorism—Prevention—Addresses, essays, lectures.
I. Shultz, Richard H., 1947-   II. Sloan, Stephen.
III. Series.
HV6431.R47 1980   303.6'2   80-36812
ISBN 0-08-025106-4

Printed in the United States of America

We respectfully dedicate this book to our parents.

Contents

CHAPTER

Acknowledgments

We would like to take this opportunity to thank those who contributed articles to this book. We appreciate their cooperation, and acknowledge the importance of their contributions. In many cases this work was undertaken in the author's free time, when he was not involved in dealing professionally with operational and research and development issues. We would also like to thank Captain Ed Meech for special consultation on the issues of hostage-taking and hostage behavior. Finally we would like to thank our spouses, Carol Kachadoorian and Roberta Raider Sloan, for their support and encouragement in completing this study.

Richard H. Shultz, Jr.
DeKalb, Illinois

Stephen Sloan
Norman, Oklahoma

1 International Terrorism: The Nature of the Threat

Richard H. Shultz, Jr.
Stephen Sloan

Although various scholars trace the origins of political terrorism to the French Reign of Terror (1793-94), such tactics have maintained a trenchant position in the political calculus within and between nations throughout recorded history. However, since the late 1960s there has been a marked increase in the phenomenon of domestic, international, and transnational terrorism, and current estimates predict that the magnitude of these developments will continue in the future. Predictably, these developments have generated an unprecedented interest in political terrorism, which has manifested itself in a proliferation of books, articles, congressional hearings and reports, conferences, and media exposes. Yet, while this literature offers a wide range of useful insights into the root causes, logic, and characteristic attributes of political terrorism, as well as a substantial number of case studies, the overall thrust is too narrowly focused on the terrorist. We fully agree with S.D. Vestermark that for those with operational responsibilities or the task of developing concrete response policies, the usefulness of the literature on terrorism is limited by its overemphasis on "defining new and exotic terrorist possibilities, and in exploring the various legal and philosophical dilemmas in defining the 'terrorist' . . . Such displays implicitly affirm how 'terrible' the problem of terrorism really is - without offering solutions." (1)

It is these "solutions" or, rather, governmental responses to terrorism that are the concern of this book, which brings together individuals from the governmental and law enforcement communities as well as the private security and academic sectors who have been involved in either an operational or research and development capacity with limiting or deterring terrorist actions. But before we turn our attention to these policies, a brief overview of the nature of contemporary political terrorism will be undertaken, in order to indicate why various antiterrorist policies have been adopted.

1

DEFINING POLITICAL TERRORISM

A plethora of definitions has been proposed for the concept "political terrorism." However, for the sake of parsimony we intend to bypass this semantic confusion, and suggest that political terrorism be understood in the following terms:

> Political terrorism may be defined as the threat and/or use of extranormal forms of political violence, in varying degrees, with the objective of achieving certain political objectives/goals. Such goals constitute the long range and short term objectives that the group or movement seeks to obtain. These will differ from group to group. Such action generally is intended to influence the behavior and attitudes of certain targeted groups much wider than the immediate victims. However, influencing behavior is not necessarily the only aim of terrorist acts. The ramifications of political terrorism may or may not extend beyond national boundaries. (2)

Political terrorism so defined can be divided into four specific categories based on its location and perpetrators: international, transnational, domestic, and state terrorism. (3) International terrorism is an action initiated by an individual or group controlled by a nation-state that occurs outside that state. Transnational terrorism is an action in the international arena initiated by an individual or group that is not controlled by a nation-state. Domestic terrorism is an action initiated by an individual or group of nationals within its own nation-state. Finally, state terrorism consists of actions conducted by a nation-state within its own borders. In this study we shall be concerned with the first three variants.

WHO ARE THE TERRORISTS?

The current wave of international, transnational, and domestic terrorism appears to be the result of a series of unassociated political developments, in conjunction with terrorist awareness of the advantages and vulnerabilities of recent technological advances. Among these political developments, the 1969-70 decision on the part of certain Palestinian factions to move the focus of their attacks outside Israel was an important tactical change. The reasons for this shift stemmed from the failure of guerrilla warfare along Israel's borders, as well as of strikes within Israel and the occupied territories. According to Bard O'Neill, this failure was the result of a combination of factors that included "sound Israeli counterinsurgency practices, a poor physical environment, insurgent disunity, organizational deficiencies, and differences within the Arab States." (4) Therefore an international campaign of terrorism against Israel was initiated during this period, and has gone through a series of subsequent stages since. (5)

Also during the later 1960s, rural insurgency movements in Latin America that had been inspired by the success of the Cuban revolution suffered serious setbacks. In Brazil, Uruguay, Guatemala, Colombia, Peru, and Bolivia the rural guerrillas were either defeated or limited to remote mountainous regions. The death of Che Guevara in Bolivia in 1967 symbolized the at least temporary failure of the Cuban model. (6) In the aftermath of these events the insurgents moved to urban areas, where they believed the struggle would expand and have more impact. (7) As a result, in the late 1960s urban guerrilla warfare intensified in a number of Latin American countries, including Uruguay, Brazil, Guatemala, and Argentina. However, unlike the rural variation, urban guerrilla strategy tended to exclude the development of a political infrastructure and mobilization of the masses, and instead focused on tactical factors. According to Jenkins,

> Urban guerrilla warfare led almost automatically to the use of terrorist tactics. Bombings of political property and other symbolic targets, spectacular bank robberies, attacks on government officials and wealthy businessmen, political kidnappings, audaciously carried out in the heart of the enemy camp are amplified by city communications facilities. Rural guerrillas might win battles nobody would ever hear of, but dramatic acts of violence in a major city win national, perhaps international, attention. It was an easy slide from killing or kidnapping local officials to killing or kidnapping foreign diplomats. (8)

While urban guerrilla terrorism has not resulted in the overthrow of any Latin American government, terrorist tactics continue to be employed against both domestic political structures and representatives of foreign corporations and governments, as well as transnationally.

The third important political development contributing to the current wave of terrorism can be traced to the radical student movements of the 1960s. With the war in Vietnam, one catalyst, universities in the United States, Western Europe, Japan, Latin America, and the Middle East came to be characterized by widespread anti-American, anti-Establishment movements. Although these university-based movements were rapidly declining by 1970, Jenkins accurately notes that from them evolved "a number of radical, violence-prone groups, such as the Angry Brigade in Great Britain, the Red Army Faction in Germany, and the United Red Army of Japan. Some of these groups adopted terrorist tactics." (9) This was certainly true of West European, Japanese, and Latin American groups.

Finally, at the political level it should be noted that the upsurge in terrorism is also attributable to war-punctuated regional conflicts (in addition to the aforementioned Middle East situation) that have affected the interests of a number of nations and are attended by particularly deep-seated bitterness and frustration.

In addition to these political developments, the impact of technology on terrorist capabilities has also contributed to the proliferation of terrorism, with respect to targets, weapons, mobility, and tactical communications. And certain analysts argue that potential terrorists have only begun to tap these possibilities.

Types of Terrorist Groups

Terrorist groups can be categorized on the basis of a number of factors that include motivation, objectives, size, constituency, and outside support. Generally speaking, all terrorist groups seek to realize one or more of the following objectives: promote and advertise their existence and goals; build group morale and sympathy; undermine the sense of order in their targets; provoke countermeasures; and financially subsidize their movement.

More specifically, politically motivated terrorist groups might be divided into the following five categories. First, ethnic separatist movements seeking independence from an incumbent power. These vary in size, ideology, and outside aid; examples would include the Moro National Liberation Front and the Eritrean Liberation Front. Second, nationalist movements, which are very similar to separatist movements except that their constituencies and resources tend to be larger. They also tend to be led by a prominent political figure, such as Yasser Arafat or Ben Bella, in contrast to clandestine groups, where anonymity of the leadership tends to be the rule. The Palestinian movement is an example of a nationalist cause. A third type is the ideological extremist group. While most of these groups are leftist, including variations of Marxism and anarchism, there are also fascist and other right-wing elements in this category. Examples might include the West German Baader-Meinhof gang, the Japanese Red Army, and the Italian Armed Proletarian Nuclei. This category can be subdivided into those moderate elements who employ terrorist tactics against predominant governmental, industrial, and upper-class targets, and those more enigmatic elements that see destruction as a means of curing all societal ills. For such groups, terrorism itself becomes an ideology of sorts. A fourth kind of group that may occasionally resort to terrorism is the issue-oriented interest group. (10) Frustrated with peaceful methods, such groups employ terrorism in a calculated manner to effect changes in the existing political regime. Finally, there are those sociopathic individuals and groups who mount terrorist attacks in the name of some political end, which only serves as a pretext for sociopathic behavior. (However, such groups are not nearly as common as the other four types).

While such categorizations are useful, in actuality various terrorist groups may fall into more than one of these categories. Additionally, it should be noted that such groups do not necessarily exist independently of each other, but may cooperate in a variety of ways, including joint training centers, operations, weapons caches, and coordinating councils. (11)

Individual Terrorist Profile

While a tremendous number of studies have been published on the structure, organization, weaponry, financing, strategy, and tactics of terrorist groups, little work has appeared concerning the types of individuals that engage in such actions.   While a few studies have attributed terrorist behavior to various psychological attributes, (12) there have been almost no studies of the correlations in social origin, political philosophy, education, age, and family background of individuals engaged in terrorism.   The work of Russell and Miller is the exception to this gap in the literature. (13) Using data on more than 350 terrorist cadre and leaders from some 18 revolutionary groups known to specialize in terrorism, the two researchers identify common characteristics under eight category headings.   Based on this data the authors draw the following composite, "into which," they argue, "fit the great majority of those terrorists . . . examined." (14)   To summarize, terrorists have been largely single men in their early to mid-twenties, with some university education, (if not a college degree).   Women terrorists have played primarily support roles, except in the case of the West German groups and occasionally in the Irish Republican Army, the Popular Front for the Liberation of Palestine, and the Japanese Red Army.

As for social and economic factors, "terrorists come from affluent, urban, middle-class families, many of whom enjoy considerable social prestige.   Like their fathers, many of the older terrorists have been trained for the professions." (15)   Most acquired an anarchist or Marxist perspective while attending college, and it was also at that time that they were recruited.

Recent trends show certain changes in this composite.   For instance, "in a number of countries, including Argentina, West Germany, Iran, Northern Ireland and Spain, urban terrorist groups . . . are recruiting younger and younger adherents." (16)   Additionally, increasing numbers are being drawn from those with vocational training backgrounds.

While a step in the right direction, Russell and Miller's analysis concerns a topic deserving of additional research attention.

CURRENT TRENDS IN TERRORISM:
A QUANTITATIVE OVERVIEW

Of the several attempts to investigate empirically and compile incident data on political terrorism, the most comprehensive was that created by Edward Mickolus: International Terrorism: Attributes of Terrorist Events, or ITERATE. (17)   The ITERATE data system contains information drawn from over 200 sources for the years 1968 to 1978, with each event coded for 107 distinct variables.   The figures on political terrorism presented in the following tables are taken from the Central Intelligence Agency annual research study International Terrorism in

1978, whose data is drawn from the ITERATE system. (18)

Table 1.1 presents summary statistics on the various types of terrorist attacks for the years 1968 to 1978. The diversity and frequency of incidents during this period can be noted by examining the various categories.

Certain trends in terrorist attacks during the period can be discerned. First of all, hijacking has declined since its peak years of 1969 to 1972, while barricade-hostage incidents began to tail off after 1975 (probably due to new security measures), only to increase in 1978. Kidnapping has been a frequently employed tactic, ranging from 22 to 37 incidents annually for the years 1973 to 1978. Bombing in various forms (letter, incendiary, explosive) has been the most persistently used tactic, peaking in 1974, and is probably the most difficult terrorist action to prevent. Finally, armed attacks and assassinations have steadily increased (with moderate fluctuation) during the 1968-78 period. In sum, the variation is not very great in terms of total terrorist incidents during the past few years; the same trends have persisted.

During the same 1968-78 period, table 1.2 shows, West Europe suffered the largest percentage of incidents (38.1 percent), with Latin America second (26.6 percent) and the Middle East third (16.1 percent). But since 1976 West Europe has had significantly more incidents than did Latin America and the Middle East, both of which had been experiencing a decline in incidents until 1978. Incidents in the United States peaked in 1975, and have been declining since then. The geographic distribution of international terrorist incidents by the specific category of attack is shown in table 1.3.

As was noted in table 1.1, various forms of bombing dominate all the regional areas. However, if we focus on the four regions showing the greatest number of incidents (Western Europe, Middle East, Latin America, North America), important differences in choice of targets are apparent. For instance, kidnappings have been much more frequent in Latin America than in the other three regions. On the other hand, assassinations have occurred most frequently in Western Europe, with Latin America a close second. Theft and sniping have been most prevalent in Latin America, while armed attacks are more common in the Middle East, and barricade-hostage incidents in Western Europe. Finally, the number of hijackings is very similar for the Middle East, Latin America, and Western Europe, with Asia ranking fourth. One important regional change not apparent in these summary statistics concerns the geographic locus of terrorism in Latin America. According to the CIA's 1978 report, "while violence has declined in its historic arena - the Southern Cone - it has increased in Central America, most notably in Guatemala, El Salvador, and Nicaragua." (19) Additionally, 1978 brought setbacks to some European and Palestinian terrorist organizations. The CIA report notes that "West German radicals . . . suffered severe setbacks when various of their members were arrested," while Fatah engaged in a "feud with Iraq and the Black June Organization," and the Popular Front for the Liberation of

TABLE 1.1. International Terrorist Incidents by Category of Attacks

	1968	1969	1970	1971	1972	1973	1974	1975	1976	1977	1978	Total [1]
Kidnapping	1	3	32	17	11	37	25	38	30	22	27	243 (8.0)
Barricade-hostage	0	0	5	1	3	8	9	14	4	5	11	60 (2.0)
Letter bombing	3	4	3	1	92	22	16	3	11	2	5	162 (5.3)
Incendiary bombing	12	22	53	30	15	31	37	20	91	57	69	437 (14.4)
Explosive bombing	67	97	104	115	106	136	239	169	176	131	133	1,473 (48.4)
Armed attack	11	13	8	8	9	10	21	11	21	14	36	162 (5.3)
Hijacking [2]	3	11	21	9	14	6	8	4	6	8	2	92 (3.0)
Assassination	7	4	46	12	10	18	12	20	48	23	29	199 (6.5)
Theft, break-in	3	7	22	10	1	0	8	8	5	0	12	76 (2.5)
Sniping	3	2	7	3	4	3	3	9	14	6	9	63 (2.1)
Other actions [3]	1	3	11	0	4	4	4	1	7	11	20	76 (2.5)

1   Figures in parentheses are percentages of the total accounted for by
    each category of attack.

2   Includes hijackings of means of air, sea, or land transport, but
    excludes numerous nonterrorist hijackings.

3   Includes occupation of facilities without hostage seizure, shootouts
    with police, and sabotage.

TABLE 1.2. Geographic Distribution of International Terrorist Incidents

Target	1968	1969	1970	1971	1972	1973	1974	1975	1976	1977	1978	Total*	
North America	35	7	23	24	18	18	38	51	37	23	19	293	(9.7)
Latin America	41	71	113	70	49	80	124	48	105	46	61	808	(26.6)
Western Europe	16	31	58	38	112	141	151	109	179	129	166	1,130	(38.1)
USSR/Eastern Europe	0	1	1	2	1	0	1	2	0	2	3	12	(0.1)
Sub-Saharan Africa	0	7	8	4	4	4	9	18	16	20	24	114	(3.7)
Middle East and North Africa	18	32	60	52	35	21	47	56	62	48	61	492	(16.1)
Asia	1	12	19	24	43	10	11	13	14	8	16	171	(5.6)
Oceania	0	5	1	2	3	1	1	0	0	3	3	19	(0.6)
Transregional	0	0	0	0	4	0	0	0	0	0	0	4	(0.1)
Total	111	166	282	216	269	275	382	297	413	279	353	3,043	

* Figures in parentheses are percentages of the total accounted for by each region.

8

TABLE 1.3. Geographic Distribution of International Terrorist Incidents, 1968-78, by Category of Attack

	North America	Latin America	Western Europe	USSR/ Eastern Europe	Sub-Saharan Africa	Middle East/North Africa	Asia	Oceania	Trans-regional	Total
Kidnapping	2	133	23	0	39	33	11	2	0	243
Barricade-hostage	6	11	23	0	2	15	3	0	0	60
Letter bombing	14	9	78	0	14	6	37	0	4	162
Incendiary bombing	29	69	249	2	4	52	28	4	0	437
Explosive bombing	198	388	575	7	10	237	46	12	0	1,437
Armed attack	2	33	34	1	21	58	13	0	0	162
Hijacking [1]	5	22	19	0	7	24	15	0	0	92
Assassination	15	56	69	0	15	31	12	1	0	199
Theft, break-in	3	44	13	0	0	14	2	0	0	76
Sniping	11	28	8	1	1	11	3	0	0	63
Other actions [2]	8	15	39	1	1	11	1	0	0	76
Total	293	808	1,130	12	114	492	171	19	4	3,043

1 Includes hijackings by means of air, sea, or land transport, but excludes numerous nonterrorist hijackings.

2 Includes occupation of facilities without hostage seizure, shootouts with police, and sabotage.

9

Palestine (PFLP) lost its noted planner and organizer of terrorist incidents, Wadi Haddad. (20)   Finally, little was heard from the Japanese Red Army.

During the 1968-78 period U.S. citizens and property have frequently been targets of terrorist attacks. In fact, the year 1978 was marked by an increase in such attacks over 1977, as table 1.4 demonstrates. Attacks against U.S. diplomatic personnel reached a high in 1970, followed by a significant decline through 1976 and then a modest increase over the next two years. This decline may or may not be in part attributable to the official U.S. "no ransom" policy, whose effectiveness is very difficult to determine. Attacks on U.S. private citizens, on the other hand, rose steadily through 1976, with a decline in 1977, and then an increase in 1978. This increase was partly due to the vulnerability of private citizens traveling abroad. Although there has been some fluctuation during the 1968-78 period, both U.S. military officials and property and U.S. business executives and facilities have been frequently attacked.

From table 1.5, which portrays terrorist attacks on U.S. citizens or property on the basis of geographic distribution, we can see the effects of strong regional animosity toward those U.S. officials and corporate representatives who are seen as symbols of Western power and wealth. Latin America has traditionally been an area where anti-United States sentiments run deep, and this is reflected in the large number of terrorist attacks against U.S. citizens or property in Latin America, as against in other world regions. While bombings continue to be the most frequently employed tactic, kidnappings, assassinations, theft/break-ins, and sniping are also frequently used in Latin America. Following Latin America, Western Europe and the Middle East are a distant second and third.

Finally, table 1.6 presents the same data tabulated according to attacks against U.S. citizens or property for the years 1968 to 1978.

In addition to the information in these tables, ITERATE and other data sources provide conclusive evidence concerning domestic and transnational terrorist cooperation and coordination, type of weapons employed, and the regional diffusion of terrorist activities. With respect to the first point, it is known that various terrorist groups have cooperated in coordinating activities that include training, weapons exchange, joint operations, and the creation of coordinating bodies. Of all these, joint operations have received the most publicity. The most spectacular of these operations were:

May 1972:   Japanese Red Army (JRA), PFLP, and German collaboration in an attack on Lod Airport in Israel.

July 1973: PFLP, JRA, and Latin American cooperation in hijacking a Japanese Airlines 747 in Europe.

January 1974:   PFLP/JRA operation against Shell Oil facilities in Singapore.

September 1974: JRA, PFLP, and Baader-Meinhof collaboration in an assault on the French embassy in The Hague.

TABLE 1.4. International Terrorist Attacks on U.S. Citizens or Property, by Category of Target

Target	1968	1969	1970	1971	1972	1973	1974	1975	1976	1977	1978	Total*
U.S. diplomatic officials or property	12	17	52	51	22	19	12	12	12	21	22	252 (19.8)
U.S. military officials or property	4	2	38	36	11	12	12	9	33	40	30	197 (15.5)
Other U.S. government officials or property	26	32	57	21	20	10	16	14	2	7	2	207 (16.3)
U.S. business facilities or executives	6	35	24	40	44	51	86	42	52	33	47	460 (36.2)
U.S. private citizens	3	7	17	5	12	10	13	27	26	13	21	154 (12.2)
Total	51	93	188	153	109	102	139	104	125	84	122	1,270

* Figures in parentheses are percentages of the total accounted for by each category of target.

11

TABLE 1.5. Geographic Distribution of International Terrorist Attacks On U.S. Citizens or Property, by Category of Attack

	North America	Latin America	Western Europe	USSR Eastern Europe	Sub-Saharan Africa	Middle East/North Africa	Asia	Oceania	Total
Kidnapping	0	58	1	0	14	19	3	0	95
Barricade-hostage	3	2	1	0	0	6	1	0	13
Letter bombing	3	2	1	0	2	0	4	0	12
Incendiary bombing	6	60	130	1	3	41	21	4	266
Explosive bombing	65	257	174	0	4	116	36	3	655
Armed attack	0	17	12	0	3	14	8	0	54
Hijacking [1]	5	5	11	0	0	3	10	0	34
Assassination	2	23	5	0	5	14	5	0	54
Theft, break-in	0	28	5	0	0	7	0	0	41
Sniping	0	15	3	1	0	6	3	0	28
Other actions [2]	0	7	2	1	0	8	1	0	19
Total	84	474	245	3	31	234	93	7	1,271

1 Includes hijackings of means of air or land transport, but excludes numerous nonterrorist hijackings, many of which involved U.S. aircraft.

2 Includes occupation of facilities without hostage seizure, shootouts with police, and sabotage.

TABLE 1.6. International Terrorist Attacks on U.S. Citizens or Property, by Category of Attack

	1968	1969	1970	1971	1972	1973	1974	1975	1976	1977	1978	Total [1]
Kidnapping	1	2	17	9	2	20	8	20	7	4	5	95 (7.5)
Barricade-hostage	0	0	3	0	1	2	2	1	1	3	0	13 (1.0)
Letter bombing	2	1	2	0	3	0	1	0	2	1	0	12 (1.0)
Incendiary bombing	12	18	40	26	13	19	25	4	36	24	49	266 (20.9)
Explosive bombing	30	58	77	93	73	52	90	63	44	35	40	655 (51.5)
Armed attack	1	4	3	4	6	6	5	3	8	3	11	54 (4.2)
Hijacking [2]	0	4	12	3	4	0	0	2	5	4	0	34 (2.8)
Assassination	3	2	9	2	2	3	2	7	13	5	6	54 (4.2)
Theft, break-in	0	3	15	8	0	0	3	3	1	0	8	41 (3.2)
Sniping	2	1	5	2	2	0	3	1	5	4	3	28 (2.3)
Other actions [3]	0	0	5	6	3	0	0	0	3	1	1	19 (1.5)
Total	51	93	188	153	109	102	139	104	125	84	123	1,271

1 Figures in parentheses are percentages of the total accounted for by each category of attack.

2 Includes hijackings of means of air, sea, or land transport, but excludes numerous nonterrorist hijackings, many of which involved U.S. aircraft.

3 Includes occupation of facilities without hostage seizure, shootouts with police, and sabotage.

January 1975: PFLP/German/"Carlos" cooperation in an attempted attack against El Al aircraft at Orly Airport in Paris.

December 1975: "Carlos" collaborates with Germans and Palestinians in the assault on the OPEC ministerial conference in Vienna.

June 1976: A PFLP/Latin American/German effort culminates in Entebbe. (21)

A less publicized but equally important point of cooperation between domestic and transnational terrorist groups is in the area of training. Since 1968, it has been the Palestinians who have provided most of the terrorist training. The PFLP has maintained training camps throughout the Middle East, including ones in Lebanon (Tal Za'atar camp), the People's Democratic Republic of (South) Yemen (Camp Khayat), and Iraq (Abu Ali Iyad camp). Among the groups receiving training are the Japanese Red Army, the German Baader-Meinhof gang and Red Army Faction, the Dutch "Red Help," and the Irish Republican Army (IRA), as well as elements from Turkey, Iran, and Latin America. Data also exists on weapons disbursement and the creation of joint terrorist coordinating councils. Perhaps the most alarming example of the former was the discovery of Soviet hand-held, heat-seeking, ground-to-air missiles in the hands of terrorists near the Rome airport in 1974, (23) and the 1977 arrest of two West Germans at the Nairobi airport with surface-to-air (SAM-7) missiles. (24) The Latin American-based Revolutionary Coordinating Council (JCR) was the first important development in this type of terrorist cooperation. Consisting of leaders from the People's Revolutionary Army (ERP) in Argentina, the Bolivian National Liberation Army (ELN), the Uruguayan Tupamaros, and the Movement of the Revolutionary Left (MIR) in Chile, this body has distributed funds and weapons and provided training for many Latin American groups.

A final form of cooperation that should be noted is that between terrorist groups and established governments. Such governments may provide terrorist groups with funds, weapons, training, and safe-havens, and may employ them for surrogate operations. The Soviets and Cubans, in particular, have been involved in such activities for some time. Currently the Libyans are very active in channeling money and arms to groups including the Black September Organization, the Carlos group, the PFLP, JRA, IRA, and Baader-Meinhof. Other countries that have either supported terrorist groups in the past or currently do so, to varying degrees, are Iraq, South Yemen, Somalia, Algeria, Syria, North Korea, and Uganda.

With regard to the diffusion of terrorism throughout the world, Edward Heyman presents important evidence suggesting that the advantageous nature of terrorist tactics for small, disgruntled elements has not gone unnoticed. (25) Building on the adage by Jenkins that "Terrorism works - sometimes," (26) Heyman empirically shows how the successful employment of such tactics, in conjunction with other critical factors, has resulted in the spread of this activity both within and between the different world regions.

While the aggregate data presented above gives the reader important insights into the phenomena of domestic, transnational, and international terrorism, a word of caution concerning the interpretation of aggregate data, however, is necessary. The year 1975, for instance, shows a marked decline in the number of annual casualties - including terrorists, police, and foreign and domestic noncombatants - due to terrorist incidents (624) when compared with 1974 (1,311). Logically, this might be taken as an encouraging development. But, as a recent study by Brian Jenkins of the Rand Corporation illustrates, such year-to-year analysis can be quite misleading. Comparing 1970 with 1972 Rand figures, Jenkins notes that while 1972 had a smaller number of total incidents, a potentially encouraging indicator, it was during that year that two of the most shocking incidents - Lod Airport and Munich - occurred. (27)   Similarly, if we focus only on the 1975 decline in terrorist activities, Jenkins points out, we would overlook the fact that 1975 was labeled the "year of the terrorist" due to a series of shocking incidents. (28) Furthermore, the downturn in 1975 was followed by a marked increase in incidents in 1976, which was in turn followed by a decline in 1977 and another increase in 1978. The point of all of this is that the impact and ramifications of political terrorism go well beyond the mere total number of incidents. It is the fear and alarm terrorism can create that may be the most devastating element. On this point, Jenkins accurately notes that terrorists are "judged not by their actual numbers or violent accomplishments, but by the effect these have on their audience. Since most terrorist groups are actually small, the violence must be all the more dramatic, deliberately shocking." (29)

THE CASE FOR A MULTIPLE RESPONSE APPROACH

What the above evidence suggests is that over the last decade the international system has experienced a significant proliferation of terrorist incidents. Terrorism has diffused within and between world regions, as various terrorist groups have proven to be diverse and innovative in their choice of targets, tactics, and weaponry. And what is ironic is that terrorist groups have really only scratched the surface in terms of their choice of targets, tactics, and weapons. Reflecting this point, Russell, Banker, and Miller of the Office of Special Investigations, U.S. Air Force have recently stated "that terrorists, with minor exceptions . . . have not been 'terribly' creative to date. The potential, yet untapped, for this operational creativity lies in modern technology." (30) Certainly this is true in terms of potential weapons and targets available to terrorist groups. With respect to weaponry, the possibilities available include chemical and biological weapons, nuclear weapons and materials, man-portable, precision-guided munitions, and a wide range of newly developed special infantry weapons. (31) In terms of new targets the possibilities are numerous, and certainly include supertankers, natural gas pipelines, the transportation system for liquified gas, and various communication systems, to name only a few.

Confronted with increasing and often grimly imaginative threats to public order, U.S. policymakers and law enforcement authorities must move in a variety of directions to limit or deter terrorist effectiveness. It is to these programs that we now turn.

NOTES

(1) S.D. Vestermark, SURGE - The Sustained Response Group (Gaithersburg, Md.: International Association of Chiefs of Police, 1977), pp. 7-8.

(2) Richard Shultz, "Conceptualizing Political Terrorism: A Typology," Journal of International Affairs, Spring/Summer 1978, p. 8.

(3) The categorization presented here is borrowed in part from Edward Mickolus, "Statistical Approaches to the Study of Terrorism," in Terrorism: Interdisciplinary Perspective, ed. Yonah Alexander and Maxwell Finger (New York: McGraw-Hill, 1977), pp. 209-69; and David Milbank, International and Transnational Terrorism: Diagnosis and Prognosis (Washington, D.C.: Central Intelligence Agency, 1976).

(4) Bard O'Neill, "Toward a Typology of Political Terrorism: The Palestinian Resistance Movement," Journal of International Affairs, Spring/Summer 1978, p. 25.

(5) Ibid., pp. 25-28.

(6) We use the term "temporary" because of the recent events in Nicaragua.

(7) See Brian Jenkins, The Five Stages of Urban Guerrilla Warfare (Santa Monica, Calif.: Rand, 1974).

(8) Brian Jenkins, "International Terrorism: Trends and Potentialities," in U.S. Senate, Committee on Governmental Affairs, "An Act to Combat International Terrorism," 95th Cong. 2d sess., 1978, p. 8.

(9) Ibid., p. 17.

(10) This point is drawn from Charles Russell, Leon Banker, and Bowman Miller, "Out-Inventing the Terrorist," in U.S. Senate, Committee on Governmental Affairs, "An Act to Combat International Terrorism," 95th Cong., 2d sess., 1978, pp. 869-70.

(11) This point will be discussed below. Useful sources on this issue include Charles Russell, "Transnational Terrorism," Air University Review, January-February, 1976, p. 26-35; and Edward Heyman, Monitoring The Diffusion of Transnational Terrorism (Gaithersburg, Md.: International Association of Chiefs of Police, 1979).

(12) For instance, see Thomas Strentz, "The Terrorist Organizational Profile: A Psychological Evaluation," in U.S. Senate, "An Act to Combat Terrorism," pp. 757-85.

(13) Charles Russell and Bowman Miller, "Profile of a Terrorist," Military Review, August 1977, pp. 21-35. Data files on this and other terrorist factors are currently being developed by the Defense Advanced Research Projects Agency. However, this material is all classified.

(14) Russell and Miller, "Profile of a Terrorist," p. 33.

(15) Ibid., pp. 33-34.

(16) Ibid.

(17) Edward Mickolus, International Terrorism: Attributes of Terrorist Events Data (Ann Arbor: 1976).

(18) International Terrorism in 1978 (Washington, D.C.: Central Intelligence Agency, 1979). Tables are from pp. 7-11.

(19) Ibid., p. 1.

(20) Ibid., pp. 2-3.

(21) Russell, Banker, and Miller, "Out-Inventing the Terrorist," p. 832.

(22) Ibid., pp. 828-29.

(23) Brian Jenkins, International Terrorism: A New Kind of Warfare (Santa Monica, Calif.: Rand, 1974), pp. 7-8.

(24) Washington Post, November 6, 1977, pp. C1-5.

(25) See Heyman, Monitoring the Diffusion of Transnational Terrorism (Gaithersburg, MD.: International Association of Chiefs of Police, 1979).

(26) Brian Jenkins, Terrorism Works - Sometimes (Santa Monica, Calif.: Rand, 1974).

(27) The data drawn from ITERATE show 1972 to have a lower number of incidents also, if letterbombs are excluded.

(28) Brian Jenkins, "International Terrorism: Trends and Potentialities," Journal of International Affairs, Spring/Summer 1978, p. 119.

(29) Jenkins, International Terrorism: A New Kind of Warfare, p. 4.

(30) Russell, Banker, and Miller, "Out-Inventing the Terrorist," p. 837.

(31) See Jenkins, "International Terrorism: Trends and Potentialities," pp. 55-83.

2 The State of the Operational Art: A Critical Review of Anti-terrorist Programs

Richard H. Shultz, Jr.

In the previous chapter's discussion of the nature and ramifications of the domestic, international, and transnational variations of political terrorism, it was asserted that while the locus of such behavior would continue to be the urban-metropolitan area, the tactical repertoire of the terrorist could become even more innovatively destructive. In sum, the tactical principles laid down by Abraham Guillen, the theorist of urban guerrilla terrorism, in the 1960s will continue to be practiced in the 1980s:

> Today the epicenter of the revolutionary war must be in the great urban zones . . . What is important is not to win space, but to destroy the enemy and to endure longer . . . to eat the enemy bit by bit, and through brief and surprise encounters of encirclement and annihilation to live off the enemy's arms, munitions and paramilitary effects. (1)

By selecting the urban area as the arena of combat, the terrorist will continue to ensure a wide variety of targets to select from, as well as ready access to funds, weapons, and other logistical supports. In fact, for those charged with the responsibility of responding to such threats, the number of potential targets may appear to be virtually unlimited. And when this is coupled with the increased technical skills now available in the terrorist inventory, the prevention or limitation of future terrorist actions seems quite problematic.

However, while the solutions to the terrorist threat are complex and not easily devised, terrorism is absolutely intolerable, and it is imperative that governments that have been targeted for terrorist strikes mobilize their law enforcement, national security, and civil preparedness machinery to effectively respond to such crises. We concur with the authors of Terrorism - Threat, Reality, Response that "one of government's most important jobs, therefore, is to 'out-invent' terrorists, assessing as yet unexploited possibilities and counter-measures." (2) In this chapter we will critically examine how effective U.S. policymakers and law enforcement authorities have been in devising such policies to limit or deter terrorist activities.

The study will group various operational and research and develop-ment programs devised over the last decade by a number of different U.S. government agencies and law enforcement authorities, as well as by those in the private and academic sectors, into eight specific categories.

1. The protection of American corporate representatives and govern-ment personnel, as well as corporate complexes and governmental installations, in foreign countries.

2. Programs aimed at preventing the hijacking and/or sabotage of aircraft.

3. The development of negotiating teams and strategies to be employed in hostage-barricade situations.

4. The development of tactical response forces.

5. Security systems designed to protect vital installations against theft, sabotage, or seizure.

6. The organization of federal and state networks designed to facilitate cooperation in establishing contingency plans, crisis management techniques, and other policies.

7. Research and development projects.

8. International programs aimed at curbing terrorism through interna-tional cooperation.

The purpose will be to review these programs, identifying both successes and shortcomings, and to suggest future directions in antiterrorist strategy. Hopefully, this review will be both a more sanguine and a more critical assessment of antiterrorist programs than currently exists in the operational literature, which, heavily involved in the dynamics of organizational self-defense, is characterized by obliquity and a false sense of self-assuredness. This study will show that there is no single panacea or "quick fix" for curbing political terrorism, and that while those charged with the responsibility of "responding to terrorism" have achieved certain tactical successes, a great deal of work in developing effective countermeasures remains to be completed. The chapter will also present a brief synopsis of each of the articles contained in this volume at the end of the sections on the appropriate "response" categories.

PRIVATE SECURITY MANAGEMENT:
CORPORATE EXECUTIVE PROTECTION

Since the late 1960s shift from rural insurgency strategy to an urban guerrilla approach, (3) the private corporations and their executive personnel have frequently been kidnapped and held for exorbitant ransoms. Carlos Marighella, the Brazilian theorist of urban guerrilla terrorism, specifically identifies the corporate executive as a highly vulnerable target in his Mini-Manual of the Urban Guerrilla. (4) After identifying the potential advantages of corporate kidnappings, Marighella presents a "by the numbers" series of steps for successfully planning and executing such seizures. The attractiveness of this tactic can be seen in the statistical data presented in the previous chapter. The reasons for this are primarily twofold: first, such actions create a great deal of public exposure for the terrorist group, and second, it provides them with large amounts of ransom money that can be used to expand the scope of their activities. While it is uncertain how much ransom money kidnappings have netted various terrorist groups, data gathered by Charles A. Russell for Risks International, Inc. indicates that in excess of $145 million was paid out for the almost nine years between January 1, 1970 and November 1, 1978. (5) In 1973 alone, the Ejercito Revolucionarios del Pueblo or People's Revolutionary Army (ERP) extracted over $20 million in ransom. (6) While the kidnapping of foreign corporate executives has been especially popular in Latin America, terrorist groups in other geographical regions have also successfully utilized these tactics. And given the short-run benefits (ransom and publicity), as well as the willingness of the business community to acquiesce, the future kidnapping of vulnerable corporate executives can be expected.

In addition to American corporate executives, U.S. diplomatic and other government personnel assigned abroad have also been targeted by terrorist groups. But in these cases ransom has not been limited to money, but has also included the release of imprisoned revolutionaries. (7) As in the case of kidnappings of corporate executives, the seizing of diplomatic personnel has created a great deal of notoriety for the group involved. Unlike the corporations, however, the U.S. government has not been so willing to comply with ransom demands. Taking the position that yielding only encourages more demands, the United States has taken a strict "no ransom" position, (8) even when other governments have not been as firm.

This apparent vulnerability of the corporate executive abroad inevitably raises the question, Can corporate executives protect themselves against attack? The view from the private security field, as expressed by Paul Shaw, the editor of Assets Protection (a magazine for professionals in business and government security and investigation) is that through the testing and evolution of vulnerability assessment and security program development the private security sector can "determine credible threats and build effective countermeasures." (9) Based on this view, the private security sector has undergone a significant growth in the area of executive protection in the last several years. One recent estimate notes that the annual total cost to U.S. firms for the "provision of private services ranges from two to three billion," with an estimated 12 percent growth rate. (10) Of course, a large part of this is directed at providing security against crime. Nevertheless, with the rise in political kidnappings, more and more is being spent on security aimed at protecting executives from terrorists.

The prototype of the private security agency is the Burns International Security Services, Inc. According to the director of its International Investigation Bureau, Burns has taken a variety of approaches in assisting U.S. corporations located in foreign countries. (11) Perhaps the most familiar function is that of direct protection of corporate executives and their offices. However, Burns has also developed other procedures for assisting corporations and their executive personnel. For instance, the firm has conducted seminars for executives and corporate security directors that provide plans and programs to assist the business community in averting terrorist tactics. Burns has also developed a "Security Handbook for Businessmen Overseas," and an "Industrial Defense Against Civil Disturbances, Bombings, Sabotage" handbook. (12) Another highly regarded publication on terrorist preventive measures available from the private security sector is T.J. Walsh and R.J. Healy's "Protection of Assets Manual." (13)

In addition to private security firms, the FBI, the Law Enforcement Assistance Administration (LEAA), and other government agencies have been involved in developing preventive strategies aimed at providing security for the executive and his or her family at the office, at home, and while traveling. According to the LEAA's Private Security Advisory Council, these strategies "are intended to help minimize the risk of such attacks by providing a 'before-the-fact' awareness of those preventive actions which can be taken to reduce or deter attack." (14) The LEAA committee, in addition to establishing a cooperative way for security professionals from the transportation, utility, petroleum, and other industries to interact with representatives from the law enforcement community, developed a "Terrorist Crimes Countermeasures Guide" and other publications pertaining to terrorism and corporate security. (15) Similar programs have been developed to prepare and protect American government officials and diplomats, as well as military personnel, stationed overseas; in the case of the former, the Foreign Service Institute is involved in personnel security preparation, while the different military service branches have instituted various measures. This was the result of a May 1976 Department of Defense directive (2000,12), which instructed each of the services to establish "programs for the protection of permanently assigned and visiting personnel at overseas installations." (16)

Preventive Security Planning

Even though the corporate executive has been a convenient target, vulnerable to kidnapping and ransom, the thrust of private security programs suggests that "there is a great deal businessmen can do to protect themselves." (17) The main thrust is on prevention by denying the terrorist access to suitable targets.   More specifically, the preventive security approach has a threefold focus: to deny unauthorized individuals entry; to detect those who do gain entrance past perimeter security; and to develop a security system whose effectiveness deters potential terrorists. (18)

The basis of an effective preventive security program includes the utilization of various protective systems (alarm systems, closed circuit monitoring, sensors, and so on) to raise barriers and harden targets, as well as proper planning and design. What follows is a brief overview-summary of various security plans that have been designed for corporate executive and installation protection. While the treatment is cursory, it does incorporate the basic principles of executive protection as identified by Shaw: "analysis of terrorist threats to, and vulnerabilities of the organization"; "analysis of security measures"; "creation of the executive protection program"; and "periodic testing and program reassessment." (19)

These preventive security programs can be divided into three functional areas: one, office-installation security; two, residential security; and three, security while traveling. Given that U.S. corporate headquarters in foreign countries have frequently been targets of terrorist attacks, and given the visibility of such installations, security measures must be stringently implemented.   Fundamental security practices pertaining to perimeter access, visitor screening, mail and package screening, executive office locations, control of sensitive personnel information, and other recently developed physical protective measures are of the utmost importance.   Moreover, they must be integrated into the overall security program designed for insuring office-plant security. (20) Such plans begin by stressing the need to control office-plant accessibility, especially routes to executive offices. Here a variety of newly developed security systems and devices can be utilized, including remote monitoring systems, special lock systems, ingressed doors able to withstand high impact, and other technical security systems that can control both access routes and outer perimeters from unauthorized intrusion. To enhance this program it is suggested that identification badges with photographs and handwriting samples be issued to all employees (automated card readers are highly recommended), and that all local employees be closely screened by corporate security officers before they are hired. Other important "barrier" procedures include special doors and locks for all communications, electrical, and other technical equipment; a system of concealed and unobtrusive alarms (vibration detectors, buried line sensors, video systems); and, if intrusion does occur, an interior "safe room" that is fireproof and equipped with an impenetrable door and lock system, communications equipment, first aid, and other supplies. The importance of a "safe room" can be seen in the recent siege of the American embassy by Islamic fanatics in Pakistan. Although most of the embassy was gutted by fire, those who remained in the "safe room" survived the ordeal. Finally, all incoming mail should be screened by explosive-detecting equipment, and publicity concerning important corporate officials who are likely kidnapping targets should be kept to a minimum.

Improving the level of protection against terrorist attacks at the residences of corporate executives is a much more formidable problem. These dwellings are rarely constructed with protective security in mind and therefore are quite susceptible to penetration. Nevertheless, while the residential area is vulnerable, security procedures and equipment can greatly lower the vulnerability to intrusion. Prior to occupying a home, the executive should have it surveyed by corporate security personnel to determine its vulnerability and the steps that should be taken to guarantee security. In residential protection, primary emphasis is given to the utilization of intrusion alarm systems, remote duress signaling devices, exterior lighting, installation of special doors and window guards, electronic monitoring systems, and the use of security guards. It is also recommended that the executive and his or her family be instructed in security awareness techniques. While such procedures appear to be rather mundane, they can greatly lower the risk of intrusion. (21) To help, there are various awareness films, including the two highly recommended ones offered for sale or rental by Motorola Teleprograms, "Executive Decision" and "Personal and Family Security."

Perhaps the greatest vulnerability to terrorist strikes occurs while the potential victim is in transit, usually between home and place of business. However, this type of strike also requires a significant degree of planning by the terrorist group. Since these attacks depend on the terrorists' ability to acquire precise information concerning daily travel routines, the executive can enhance security by varying daily habits. In addition, preventive and emergency driving techniques, driving alertness, the use of intrusion and emergency alarms, and other special auto modifications are also recommended to minimize the risk of a successful seizure. Finally, a variety of special measures is suggested to protect the executive during commercial and private air travel.

While all of these programs are important, once security programs are instituted it is important that the corporation security staff carry out comprehensive vulnerability assessments at specific intervals. If a successful seizure does occur, the professional security firms recommend procedures to be followed by both the executive's firm and family to minimize the possibility of personal harm as well as increase the possibility of ultimate capture of the terrorists. For the kidnapped executive, rules of behavior to be followed for dealing with his or her captors are recommended during security awareness training. An inclusive summary of these rules, which were derived from previous hostage experiences, can be found in a recently published article by Brooks McClure entitled "Hostage Survival." (22)

Yet while there appears to be a rather extensive array of programs to protect the American corporate executive in foreign countries, the overall effectiveness of such procedures is hard to determine. Although there is a great deal of speculation, and some information on individual cases, a thorough assessment does not currently exist. However, given the high probability that these attacks will continue in the future, the private security sector must continue to take the initiative in instituting successful preventive programs. In line with this need, the article in this volume by Harry Pizer, a security official with a major international airline, addresses a number of issues involved in developing and operationalizing a corporate executive protection plan. Bringing his extensive personal experience to bear on his analysis, Pizer presents a very interesting discussion not only of the problems involved in the preparation of the corporate executive protection plan, but the procedures to be followed if the plan breaks down and a kidnapping occurs.

AVIATION SECURITY: PROGRAMS AND PROCEDURES

During the last years of the 1960s the hijacking of aircraft became an increasingly popular terrorist tactic. As the motivating rationale for hijacking became more revolutionary, the tactics employed intensified. (23) Perhaps the single most shocking example of this change in motivation was the September 1970 simultaneous hijacking and subsequent destruction of four airliners by Palestinian guerrillas. As a result of the politicization of hijacking, the number of seizures grew rapidly in the early 1970s, as is shown in the statistical data presented in the previous chapter.

It quickly became apparent to both the Federal Aviation Administration (FAA) and the airlines that programs and procedures had to be developed to insure the safety of and public confidence in air travel. The pages that follow will review the physical security measures that have resulted in a significant decline in successful airplane seizures since 1972. In fact, in no other area has the terrorist challenge been dealt with so effectively. And it is in this area of preventive physical security, and not that of international agreements (which will be discussed in a latter section), that the major developments have taken place.

The theme of the physical security approach, according to one criminologist, is based on the criminal prevention model. According to William Minor, "The prevention model . . . is one of 'mechanical' . . . prevention. In this form of prevention . . . obstacles are placed in the way of the potential offender so that it becomes difficult or impossible to commit an offense." (24) This is different from the criminal deterrence model, which focuses on the individual's motivation and seeks to create a situation in which the costs of failure deter an attempt to commit a crime. Minor argues that this is "effective only for instrumental offenses committed by those with a high stake in conformity." (25) In the case of politically motivated hijackings, individuals tend to be strongly ideological and emotionally charged. (26) For such individuals, societal norms and conformity, as well as the threat of punishment, are not very relevant. Defense against such determined and potentially well-armed terrorists required the development of the appropriate technologies to deny them access.

Physical Security Procedures

In 1969 the Congress directed the FAA to study the hijacking problem and develop effective countermeasures. Initial efforts proceeded in three directions. One, FAA psychologists studied the characteristics of hijackers in order to develop a behavioral profile. Two, the feasibility of using armed security personnel on airplanes was examined. And three, electronics experts examined airline operations to determine how mechanical detection systems could be utilized.

With regard to the behavioral profile, D. Evan W. Pickrel identified 35 characteristics common to previous hijackers. (27) From this a profile test was developed and employed by specially trained airline personnel to identify potential hijackers. (28) According to FAA officials, the "behavioral profile . . . identified less than two percent of the traveling public in need of close scrutiny." (29) As the technique was refined the percentage was lowered to one-half of one percent. (30) While the initial enthusiasm for the profile was high, a number of drawbacks quickly became apparent. According to Harry Murphy, director of security of the Air Transport Association, these included easy access to the details of the profile, human error due to the arduousness of the task, and the fact that not all hijackers fit the profile. (31)

With respect to the sky marshals program, deputy U.S. marshals were trained and assigned to duty on commercial airliners. Initially 400 air marshals were assigned, but this was quickly expanded to 1,500. Dressed as businessmen, they were armed and charged with taking all steps necessary to restrain hijackers. It is difficult to evaluate the air marshal program, due to its brief existence (1970-72); it was dropped on the grounds that inflight gun battles would be potentially more costly than complying with hijacker demands.

Given these deficiencies in the behavioral profile and sky marshal programs, the security focus shifted almost exclusively to preboarding prevention through the technical refinement of passenger and baggage screening detection equipment. Initially, there was opposition by certain airlines to the screening of all passengers. In December 1972, however, the FAA issued emergency rules requiring 100 percent screening of all passengers, to take place at the corridor access point to several boarding gates. (32) Thus preventive security was to be achieved through reliance on technology. The system employed inspects an individual and his or her baggage in a matter of seconds, with little inconvenience to the passenger. The electronic system for screening passengers consists of a magnetic field that, when disturbed by ferrous or nonferrous metal, activates an alarm. The X-ray system for baggage is connected to a television display screen monitored by a security official. The interpretation of X-ray shadowgraphs of large volumes of luggage is tedious and has proven to be unreliable. Research is presently being directed toward the development of an X-ray device that will activate an audio alarm if a suspicious device is detected. (33) In terms of effectiveness, FAA figures for the January 1976-June 1978 period show 6,905 firearms detected, resulting in 2,098 arrests. (34) Of course, most of these individuals were not hijackers. However, a review of individual cases by the FAA reveals that 12 of those detected had intended to hijack an aircraft.

Where the system appears to break down is when the hijacker uses explosives rather than a firearm. Recent incidents show that security screening points can be penetrated in this fashion. Among the efforts to develop an effective device to detect explosives during screening, the most promising item is a "sniffing" device that can detect the gases or vapors that explosives emit. This device extracts a sample of air from a case or bag and passes it through an ion capture system. If the vapor of an explosive is detected an alarm sounds. A more advanced detection device, the Rapidex, "combines the X-ray system with explosive detection . . . the system is said to be capable of finding even the most carefully concealed weapons and explosives." (35) While such equipment is currently under development, to date the only explosive detection devices employed are the K-9 detection devices. Although effective in searching an aircraft, they are of little use at mass points of entry to boarding gates, and are very expensive and difficult to manage. Another potential technique for combating the use of explosives is tagging them with distinctive and readily detectable chemicals at the time of manufacture. This would make identification of terrorists easier, if mandatory tagging were implemented.

In addition to passenger screening, the threat of sabotage may necessitate the screening of cargo and baggage to be stored on the aircraft. Metal detectors, however, would seem to have limited utility for screening cargo because of the large amount of metal present in innocent cargo. In view of the frequency with which terrorists use explosives, research and development on better detectors is imperative. The fact of potential entry to the aircraft from points other than the passenger gate has resulted in the need to improve control and monitoring of the airfield. To ensure the security of airfield perimeters, seismic sensors, beam systems, and closed-circuit television are currently employed. The types of early warning systems currently used by the United States in monitoring the Sinai could be converted to detect airport perimeter intrusions. (36)

Finally, the FAA, the Air Transport Association, and the airlines have also moved in directions other than technological developments to improve security. This includes the special training, on a continuing basis, of airport security personnel in prevention techniques, and intelligence sharing, seminar and workshop interchanges, and other forms of cooperation. (37)

In sum, the airlines and the FAA have moved in a number of directions to prevent hijacking in the United States. While problems still exist in certain areas, the record exhibits significant improvements in the United States. Unfortunately, such improvements have not been uniformly implemented by other countries.

HOSTAGE-BARRICADE NEGOTIATING PROCEDURES

In the years since the September 1972 incident at the Munich Olympics, many hostage-takings have been committed by a number of terrorist groups. These have taken various forms, such as airplane hijacking, kidnapping of diplomats or corporate executives, and the seizure of embassies or other facilities with the intention of holding their staffs for ransom or the release of other terrorists. Here we are concerned with only one variation of the hostage-taking strategy common to each of these: the hostage-barricade scenario. One analyst has described this in terms of the following attributes:

> The barricade-hostage scenario produces the first situation-type in which a nation or corporation may find itself faced with the question of negotiating for hostages. In it we find terrorists seizing one or more hostages but making no attempt to leave the scene of the crime. Negotiations are carried on with the perpetrators themselves effectively being held hostage, unable to leave the scene when they choose. This situation frequently climaxes an incident in which the seizure of hostages is not the terrorists' primary aim . . . (38)

A major policy issue facing the U.S. government since Munich has centered specifically on how the United States should respond to international hostage-barricade situations where Americans are involved. Proposals have been advanced spanning a continuum from "no ransom negotiations" to what amounts to capitulation to terrorist demands. The official U.S. position that emerged from this debate was that of "no ransom negotiations." (39) However, this hard-line position came under heavy criticism from various sources, including members of the State Department, in the aftermath of the March 1973 kidnapping and subsequent murder of three American diplomats in Khartoum. (40) A full-scale review of the event by the Working Group of the Special Cabinet Committee to Combat Terrorism, working in conjunction with analysts from the Rand Corporation, raised serious questions about this hard-line approach. (41)

While this remains the official U.S. position for hostage-barricade situations that occur outside United States borders, as in the current impasse in Iran, in domestic circumstances law enforcement officials have adopted a strategy of negotiations. Although this has been characterized by a few law enforcement officials as a "soft-line" approach, the consensus of the law enforcement community is that negotiating strategies enhance response effectiveness. (42)   Furthermore, as Cooper points out, flexibility and softness are not synonymous; flexibility can range from its most permissive form, that of leaving all doors open, to that of a hard bargaining position. (43)

The decision to develop negotiating strategies emerged in the aftermath of the Munich events, according to Francis Bolz, coordinator of the New York City Police Department's Hostage Negotiating Team.

> Because of these events and the possibility of similar confrontations taking place in New York City, the United Nations capital . . . Chief Simon Eisdorfer, the Commanding Officer of the Special Operations Division . . . called together representatives of the Police Academy, the Patrol Division, the Emergency Service Unit, the Detective Bureau, and Dr. Harvey Schlossberg of the Psychological Services Section . . . A set of guidelines was developed that sought to eliminate any impulsive or uncoordinated actions which might unnecessarily cost human lives. (44)

The primary objective of this approach is the preservation of the lives of the hostages: the principal course of action to achieve this is based on bargaining-negotiating tactics. Often referred to as the "New York Plan," this approach, according to Bolz, seeks to involve the hostage-taker "in a form of therapy to alleviate the anxiety and tensions that the captor is experiencing." (45)   From this perspective, a hostage-barricade situation requires a team approach. Theoretically such teams are functionally oriented, and generally consist of a group commander, a negotiating group trained in bargaining skills (with a knowledge of human behavior and motivation), and a tactical operations unit trained to respond militarily. In addition to basic preparation for each of the sections, such teams are involved in contingency planning and training simulations. According to Conrad Hassel of the FBI National Academy, a member of the National Advisory Committee Task Force on Disorder and Terrorism,

> The hallmark of any police reaction in a kidnap/hostage situation must be the blending of tactical response and behavioral know-how. This requires the development of team tactics . . . It requires expertise in weapons use, deployment, and instant communications; and it requires the use of behavioral experts coordinated by cool-headed and professional leadership. The phenomenon of the hostage situation has had the positive effect of bringing together the professional expertise of law enforcement and the behavioral sciences . . . and has led to sophisticated training programs . . . (46)

The negotiating policy has become the accepted approach for dealing with domestic hostage-barricade situations. (47) Of course, if negotiations fail the team approach provides the capabilities for shifting to violence-oriented tactics. The remainder of this section will examine the selection and preparation of negotiating teams.

Selection and Preparation

As a result of the stress placed on negotiating tactics, special personnel selection and training procedures have been developed. With respect to the selection of personnel, various law enforcement agencies have identified the type of characteristics that individuals chosen for hostage-negotiation training should possess. Among the New York Police Department's selection criteria for its Detective Bureau Hostage Negotiating teams are: (1) volunteers only; (2) good physical condition; (3) mature; (4) good speaking voice; (5) skilled interrogator; and (6) the ability to speak a foreign language. (48) The most inclusive list of characteristics, compiled by Miron and Goldstein, include interpersonal sensitivity; tolerance for ambiguity; positive self-concept; low authoritarianism; interviewing experience; experience in stressful situations; verbal skills; flexibility; belief in the power of verbal persuasion; conciliation, compromise, and bargaining skills; maturity; good physical condition; and a familiarity with the ideology of the perpetrator if a terrorist is involved. (49) To assist in this selection process, different law enforcement agencies, such as the New York State Police, have developed a battery of psychological tests to be administered to prospective negotiators. (50)

The curriculum for negotiating team preparation has been developed by various law enforcement agencies, as well as at special training schools. Among law enforcement agencies, the New York City Police Department, which maintains the nation's largest hostage negotiating squad, conducts one of the most intensive training programs for squad members. (51) In addition to physical conditioning and training in the use of firearms, electronics equipment, and special vehicles, trainees receive "intensive psychological training to prepare team members to analyze various situations and develop strategies using psychological techniques rather than force." (52) Among the psychological topics of instruction are theories of negotiation; the role(s) of the negotiator; role playing; psychological and physiological evaluation; crisis intervention and stress management; and contingency planning-strategy development. The New York police also periodically conduct a Hostage Confrontation Seminar to inform officials from other law enforcement agencies about new techniques and procedures. Similarly, the Los Angeles County Sheriff's Department has a 64-hour hostage-negotiation training program, and other major metropolitan police departments conduct similar programs.

In addition, special training courses and seminars are conducted by federal and state agencies. For example, in April 1976 the FBI established a Terrorist Research and Management Staff (now known as the Special Operations and Research Staff) at its National Academy in Quantico, Virginia. Among the topics of research and instruction is hostage-negotiations. At the state level the California Specialized Training Institute (CSTI) directed by the State Military Department runs a five-day political terrorism seminar for government and law enforcement personnel, (53) whose topics include hostage-barricade situations. And both New York and Illinois State Police Departments conduct hostage-negotiating programs.

Research on hostage-negotiating is being conducted in both the private and academic sectors, as well as at the government level. For example, in the private sector, part of the Rand Corporation's terrorism research project has been devoted to the issues of hostage-negotiation (54) and hostage survival. (55) Ketron, a systems analysis-operations research firm, has also been involved in the development of political hostage gaming. (56) In academia, a number of individuals are involved in both operational and research and development programs. For instance, Stephen Sloan has for some time been operationally involved in conducting training simulations with military and police personnel, as well as for a major airline. (57) Abraham Miller, in conjunction with the National Institute of Law Enforcement and Criminal Justice, has been involved in interviewing both domestic and foreign law enforcement personnel concerned with hostage-negotiating, and among his published studies is a superb analysis of the March 1977 Hanafi Muslim incident. (58) Finally, Murray Miron and Arnold Goldstein have developed various methods for training law enforcement personnel for hostage-negotiating situations. (59)

Strategies For Hostage-Negotiating

To begin with, it should be recognized that a generalized hostage-negotiating strategy applicable in all situations is not possible; to differing degrees, each situation exhibits unique characteristics. Nevertheless, various studies categorizing hostage situations in order to develop a repertoire of situational responses have been undertaken. John Stratton, an associate of the CSTI connected with the antiterrorism courses, identifies three general categories of hostage-takers: (1) social, political, or religious crusaders; (2) criminals; and (3) the mentally ill. (60) Mickolus presents a more detailed categorization that includes:

Group Type	Examples
Separatists, irredentists	Basques, Eritreans, IRA, Corsicans
Fedayeen	PFLP, Black September, Al Saiqa
Ultraleft anarchists	Japanese Red Army, Baader-Meinhof gang

Latin guerrillas	People's Liberation Army, Montoneros, National Liberation Action
Criminal gangs	Mafia; groups who publicly cloak their actions in political rhetoric, but whose real purpose is personal gain.
Psychotic individuals	The security guard who seized the Israeli embassy in South Africa in 1975.
Hoaxes	Brian Lea's kidnapping in Uganda. (61)

The specific repertoires developed by law enforcement agencies for negotiating with the different types of hostage-takers identified above are not readily available in the public literature. Recently, the question of whether various law enforcement agencies have in fact developed negotiating strategies to deal with the politically motivated hostage-taker has been raised by Miller. In analyzing the Hanafi case he notes,

> Not that the police had been unprepared for such encounters, but the strategy and tactics of police operations in dealing with hostage negotiations had never before been implemented when the captors had been ideologically organized and motivated. No one knows whether in the face of ideologically motivated terrorists the carefully orchestrated procedures of police negotiation techniques would work. No one really wanted to find out. (62)

Interestingly, Miller concludes that "the strategy and tactics used in dealing with criminal hostage takers might not be altogether inapplicable to situations in which the captors are ideologically motivated terrorists." (63)

While we cannot examine the specific repertoires, important aspects common to these strategies can be identified. (64) Perhaps the factor that has received the most emphasis is time. Stratton notes that "developing the communication and relationship needed between the law enforcement official and the perpetrators in order to negotiate takes time . . . the establishment of communication and rapport . . . is of utmost importance and develops only by careful nurturance." (65) In addition, adequate time allows the securing of the area, and the identification of and gathering of information about the terrorist(s) and the hostages. By reducing tension and anxiety on the part of the hostage-taker, time also is on the side of the hostages. According to Cully, the more time the hostage-taker spends with the captives, "the less likely he is to take the hostages' life, because they become acquainted and develop feelings for one another." (66) Commonly referred to as "transference" in the psychological literature, this is an important aspect of the hostage-negotiating procedures developed by Schlossberg of the New York Police Department's Psychological Services Bureau. (67)

A second important factor is the style and approach of the negotiator. Generally, the literature suggests that a properly trained and experienced law enforcement official, not of high rank, with access to consultation from a behavioral scientist and other officials, be chosen. Selection is critical, for the negotiator will become the link between the authorities and the hostage-taker. It is important that a favorable-supportive relationship be established and that the hostage-taker come to trust the negotiator. The low-rank stipulation is important for a number of reasons. First, an authority figure can create anxiety; second, a low-rank official can more easily play the role of a neutral and friend; third, he can more easily say no; and finally, it makes "on the spot" decisions by the negotiator impossible, allowing for more flexibility in responding. In terms of a specific style, Miron and Goldstein identify three potential options: "win-lose battler," "equalizer," and "soft-bargainer." They opt for the "equalizer," because it entails a problem-solving-compromising approach. (68) Other important factors that must be considered in formulating a negotiating strategy are (1) truthfulness versus dishonesty in negotiating; (2) the presentation of suggestions and alternatives to hostage-takers; (3) responding to hostage-taker requests; (4) handling ultimatums and deadlines; and (5) procedures to follow if the terrorist begins to execute hostages. (69)

This volume contains three articles concerned with different aspects of the hostage-taking scenario. Clive C. Aston, drawing on an operational analysis of 91 terrorist sieges that have occurred in Western Europe during the last decade, identifies five distinct clusters of operationally restrictive variables that must be considered and will inevitably limit a government's response options. Once these restrictive factors are understood, the author believes, Western governments can more effectively plan their response procedures for future incidents. Abraham Miller's paper moves beyond the actual hostage situation to examine some of the psychological consequences of having been exposed to the stress of captivity. Using material from personal interviews and recent observations from the emerging literature on victimization, Miller analyzes the psychological consequences of victimization both during and after captivity. Particular attention is given to the concept of transference. In conclusion, Miller suggests the need for change in public policy toward victims of hostage situations. Finally, Stephen Sloan presents a detailed analysis of the use of simulation techniques in preparing law enforcement and military personnel to effectively respond to hostage-taking incidents. Based on ten simulations he has conducted with such authorities, Sloan's chapter discusses reoccurring behavioral and administrative patterns that hamper the successful resolution of such incidents. In addition to raising serious policy questions about the type of training and contingency planning currently taking place. Sloan presents valuable information for those who must respond to hostage-taking situations.

SPECIAL WEAPONS AND TACTICS UNITS

Although the response to the threat of terrorist acts has taken a variety
of forms, the media, enamored of direct action, have paid an inordinate
amount of attention to the development of specialized police and
military units. These units, most commonly known as Special Weapons
and Tactics (SWAT) teams, have even been portrayed (inaccurately) in
the television series "SWAT." The explanation for this publicity can be
traced, in part, to the "get tough with terrorism" approach adopted by
the United States and other Western nations in the aftermath of the
Munich Olympics massacre, a hard-line approach centering on the
development of special weapons and tactics units to combat various
terrorist tactics.   Probably the primary grounds for the media's
fascination with such units were two spectacular rescues of victims of
skyjackings. The first occurred in July 1976, when Israeli commandos
(Saiyeret) flew over 2,000 miles to Ugadna to rescue 104 hostages on an
Air France jet that had been hijacked to Entebbe by Palestinian and
West German terrorists. In addition to demonstrating that terrorists
are not invulnerable to counterattack, the exercise demonstrated the
potential for coordination and cooperation in combating such actions.
The   second   rescue   was   carried   out   by   the   West   German
Grenzschuzgruppe-9 (Border Patrol Group 9) in October 1977. After a
110-hour chase, the West German team, headed by Colonel Ulrich
Wegener, rescued 82 passengers and four crew members of a hijacked
Lufthansa jet in Mogadishu, Somalia.
    In the aftermath of Entebbe and Mogadishu, the U.S. Defense
Department moved to develop a similar special strike force to be
employed outside the United States against terrorists who commit
hijackings and other criminal acts.   At the heart of this force are
specially trained units drawn from nine U.S. Army Special Forces
battalions; each unit consists of 252 men. Five of these battalions are
located at Fort Bragg, North Carolina ("Project Blue Light"), two are at
Fort Devens, Massachusetts, and single units are assigned to the Canal
Zone and West Germany. Additional units are assigned to support these
forces in more complex counterterrorist operations.   These include
elements from the U.S.   Army Rangers, Navy Seals, and Marine
reconnaissance and amphibious units. The Air Force provides special
airlift capabilities. These units are all part of the recently announced
110,000-man force designated by Secretary of Defense Harold Brown
for use in those types of conflicts the Pentagon currently refers to as
"limited contingencies" or "low-intensity" situations. Such situations,
according to one expert, may be divided into the following categories:

1. Rescue Missions

    A. To rescue U.S. citizens caught up in another nation's civil strife.

    B. Antiterrorist operations to rescue hostages, preempt the
       destruction of important facilities or resources, or retake them
       from terrorists.

2. Military Incursions

A. Seizure, protection, or recapture of important assets that are threatened or held by hostile military forces.

B. Intervention between combatants in a civil war, rebellion, or coup d'etat.

C. Commitment of forces to help turn back an invasion. (70)

The effectiveness of these units cannot be determined, since they have yet to be employed. The 252-man units are deployable with current strategic airlift capabilities, but in the case of larger and more prolonged actions, such as the retaking and protection of vital facilities or resources against terrorist attack, serious questions have been raised about the United States' ability to deploy and maintain such forces at a distant location. Perhaps one explanation of the Carter administration's unwillingness to deploy in the Iranian hostage-taking crisis was a recognition of the limitations of such U.S. military capabilities.

In addition to the United States, West Germany, and Israel, 11 other countries are known to have developed commando units for use against terrorist groups: Britain, France, Switzerland, Belgium, Denmark, Italy, the Netherlands, Norway, Austria, Egypt, and Indonesia. The effectiveness of most of these units, as in the case of the United States, is not determinable because they have not yet been used. Of those which have been employed, the French and Dutch conducted effective operations, while the Egyptians demonstrated in the 1978 incident on Cyprus that such operations are not guaranteed to work. (71)

While the few situations in which these units were actually deployed occurred outside their national borders, in most cases they may also be employed against domestic terrorist incidents. However, in the United States the specialized military units are legally available only for overseas operations, unless the President chooses to exercise a waiver of the posse comitatus act. (72) In order to deal with domestic incidents the United States has experienced a proliferation of special weapons and tactics teams at the federal, state, and metropolitan levels. The quality of these units may vary markedly, from the well-trained and well-equipped teams of the New York City Police Department and the Los Angeles County Sheriff's Department, to other local forces which receive only marginal preparation in the more rudimentary aspects of special tactics and weapons. The more professional units are armed with heavier weapons, receive more detailed tactical training, and have available to them the most sophisticated equipment to combat heavily armed criminals and terrorists in barricade and other situations. One critic notes that while "it appears that every department throughout the country, irrespective of size and need," has sought to develop a specialized response unit, "few have had the need, budget, talent, or training facilities to maintain such a unit." In order to eliminate these less qualified units, an interesting but jurisdictionally complicated solution is proposed.

With various forms of political terrorism on the rise, internationally and domestically, there is little doubt that SWAT-type units are vital and necessary . . . However, SWAT teams are not vital to the police programs of every city. Under mutual aid and assistance agreements, the services of such units can be obtained from neighboring metropolises or, in the case of violation of federal law, from the FBI. (73)

Training and Preparation

The training and preparation of tactical units will vary according to whether they are to be domestically or internationally deployed. The role definition of domestic tactical units is generally part of the team approach discussed in the previous section. According to one official, in dealing with hostage-takers, barricaded individuals, and other "special threat" situations, it was determined that a threat can only be neutralized by the rapid application of contingency plans by trained personnel. "This personnel should consist of an on-scene commander, a tactical operations officer and unit, and a negotiating team." (74) Only in a few instances are the negotiators members of the tactical unit, the consensus being that the negotiations must be conducted by completely neutral individuals. According to Miller, this is the approach advanced by the highly successful New York Police Department chief negotiator Frank Bolz and is also the position of Lieutenant Richard Klapp, head negotiator for the San Francisco Police Department. (75)

Both within law enforcement departments and publicly there has been a predisposition to consider tactical teams elite units that operate separately from the rest of the police department. Officially this is repudiated and, according to one special operations unit commander who advocates the team or systems approach, would greatly inhibit effectiveness.

The systems approach [is] one in which any given police function is viewed not as separate and distinct from all other police functions but as part of an interrelated series of activities mutually dependent on one another. It treats the police agency as a whole entity . . . the SWAT unit being one of those components. Many police agencies adopting the systems approach have effectively integrated the SWAT unit with other department units and functions . . . Special weapons and tactics teams are not unique . . . To consider them as such results in several negative effects . . . the systems approach greatly reduces and frequently eliminates these difficulties. (76)

However, in actuality, according to a recently published study of a number of the more prominent metropolitan police special weapons and tactics units, this approach is not always followed. According to the author of the study,

One of the problems that appears to ensue from having an excellent special weapons operation where negotiations are part of the team and under its direct tactical control is that the training emphasis appears to be primarily on the weapons component of the team mission . . . there is another aspect of the special weapons operation that appears to reinforce the deemphasis on negotiations. At the bottom line . . . even many experienced and sophisticated police negotiators believe that for the overwhelming majority of their experiences . . . the primary role of the negotiator is invariably and eventually to convince the subject that if he comes out, he will not be harmed . . . The problem is to convince him that the awesome array of force will not be used against him if he surrenders . . . To some highly placed police officials, hostage negotiations is not even perceived as demanding a special set of skills. (77)

In terms of specific expertise, special units require extensive specialized preparation. Therefore, stringent criteria are, theoretically, followed in selecting personnel. Generally, individuals chosen possess excellent physical condition and good eyesight, and law enforcement experience, with prior paramilitary training and combat experience desirable; and they volunteer. (78) Of course, these requirements vary depending on the organizations. How closely these qualifications are followed is hard to determine, given the lack of data.

There also appears to be variance in the training programs for specialized units. The program of one California police agency consists of 60 hours of exposure to: "specialized uniform equipment; specialized weaponry; chemical agents and their use; approach, entry, and search and arrest techniques; physical training and conditioning; and hostage negotiation techniques. This basic training is supplemented by ongoing training sessions." (79) Other programs are much more rigorous. However, no domestic units appear to receive the rigorous training of the West German Border Patrol Group 9, which is widely considered the best of the antiterrorist teams. (80) According to one account,

They are put through a two-day battery of physical and psychological tests, followed by six months physical training . . . those that remain must become proficient in swimming, diving, and mountain climbing. Among other special training: 140 hours of karate. The men spend up to four hours a day practicing with weapons that range from Smith & Wesson .38-cal. revolvers to a variety of machine guns and other automatic weapons . . . they study the tactics of terrorist organizations . . . They specifically train in a wide range of Lufthansa aircraft, including the Boeing 737. (81)

Whether the U.S. Special Forces units receive such extensive preparation is not certain, but it is known that these units cooperate with the West German and Israeli units.

In terms of composition, the five-man team appears to be the most common organization among domestic tactical units. Trained together and deployed together, these units have four distinctive roles: marksman, observer, scout, and rear guard. Each member of the unit is crosstrained in the others' specialties. In addition, the unit will have a team leader who tactically deploys and directs the team. (82)

To summarize, the domestic SWAT team is intended to operate as a finely tuned infantry squad, capable of bringing overwhelming tactical firepower against an individual or small group. In terms of role definition, it is to operate in conjunction with other elements of the law enforcement agency, including hostage-negotiating teams. How true this is nationally is uncertain, but based on evidence cited above it is certain that uniform acceptance does not currently exist. The international special forces units appear to be much more sophisticated than their domestic counterparts. Given the scope of their role, this is to be expected. Their additional requirements include (1) prior rehearsal of contemplated operations; (2) the use of detailed area studies to provide background data on target areas; (3) skilled intelligence analysis that can be rapidly utilized; (4) utilization of other specialists (for example, medical and communications experts); and (5) availability of long-range transport aircraft and other special equipment. (83) But as was noted above, their effectiveness remains to be demonstrated.

SECURITY OF NUCLEAR FACILITIES
AND VITAL INDUSTRIAL INSTALLATIONS

The proposition that it is "only a matter of time before a terrorist group goes nuclear" has received considerable news media attention. Specifically, this concern has focused on two potential problem areas: the sabotage or seizure of a nuclear weapons or energy facility, and the acquisition (through theft or otherwise) of nuclear material and construction of a crude device that has some probability of working. While this concern has been widely articulated in the popular literature, (84) it has also received serious attention in scientific publications. For instance, Krieger, in an article in the Bulletin of the Atomic Scientists, writes that "the question is not whether the worst will happen, but where and how." (85) Likewise, Willrich and Taylor, two qualified experts, argued in a 1974 report to the Energy Policy Project of the Ford Foundation that nuclear weapons are relatively easy to construct if the required materials are obtained. With respect to the acquisition of materials, they noted that that too was quite possible, given the facility safeguards systems employed at that time. (86)

During the high point of debate over these claims in the mid-1970s, Brian Jenkins and the Rand Corporation suggested that some of this literature had gone beyond "alerting the public to potential threats," and has either "inadvertently or deliberately exaggerated the terrorist threat." (87) However, a forthcoming Rand report has revised its earlier position, moving closer to the Krieger view. (88)

While a segment of this publicly expressed concern is only conjectural, there is sufficient evidence to suggest the need for improved security measures. In the first place, nuclear facilities have been the target of attacks. Flood has identified ten such incidents that occurred in France, the United States, and Argentina during the 1969-75 period. The facilities involved were nuclear reactors and the nature of the attacks ranged from shooting at guards and the placement of explosives to the overrunning of a nearly completed reactor station in Argentina by ERP guerrillas. (89)   A second cause for concern is the disturbing amount of missing or unaccounted for nuclear fuel materials. Rosenbaum, a consultant to the General Accounting Office, states that "more than 50 tons of nuclear materials . . . cannot be accounted for by the 34 uranium and plutonium processing plants in the country . . . the government is unable to find at least 6,000 pounds of material of weapons grade." (90) A recent estimate puts this figure at 7,152 pounds of bomb-grade material. (91) While Rosenbaum notes this "does not prove that any material has been taken," it is still cause for concern. Finally, there are the problems surrounding continued nuclear proliferation, which only enhances the danger of theft, sabotage, or seizure, especially in states with subnational or revolutionary elements that are opposed to the established order. In light of these developments, the safeguarding of nuclear facilities is imperative. In the following pages, the vulnerability of these facilities is considered.

A potentially alluring target for terrorist sabotage or seizure would be an operational weapon.   However, such facilities are generally considered impregnable. For example, Krieger concludes that "stealing an assembled weapon . . . would be the most difficult and least likely route for terrorists to achieve a nuclear weapons capability . . . there are sophisticated lock systems on weapons themselves." (92) In addition to lock systems on weapons, sites are protected by various other barriers, electronic surveillance equipment, on-site guards, and off-site guards that harden the perimeters of such targets. Norton likewise notes that "seizing a complete device would require a sizable quasi-military force with adequate weaponry, sophisticated mobility and an adequate intelligence gathering apparatus." (93) Furthermore, even if a device were seized, it would be very difficult if not impossible to activate due to permissive-action-link (PAL) security systems, which prevent the weapon from detonating in a nuclear mode or from being successfully disassembled to remove the nuclear material. Because of the fail-safe nature of the PAL system, the possibility of seizure or theft of an operational weapon seems quite remote. (94)   In spite of these extensive security measures, the U.S. Department of Defense has, in the wake of the proliferation of terrorism, recently allocated $360 million to upgrade nuclear weapons security systems. (95)

While seizure or theft of an operational weapon seems improbable, the possibility that a nuclear device could be furnished to a terrorist group by another nation-state has increasingly become an issue of serious concern, given that there are states that actively and directly support terrorists (especially Libya and Iraq). (96)

The nuclear industry provides terrorists with a variety of potential targets throughout the nuclear fuel cycle process. This cycle, involving several facilities that provide nuclear reactors with fuel and dispose of their waste materials, includes conversion, enrichment, fuel fabrication, and fuel assembly plants where uranium or plutonium is transformed into reactor fuel, and reprocessing plants where residual uranium or plutonium is separated from spent fuel. The literature identifies the nuclear fuel cycle as the most likely target for theft, sabotage, or seizure. According to Norton, there are two potential routes terrorists might follow: "the theft of fissionable material (that is, weapons grade material which may be used directly for a fission explosive device without resort to complex isotope separation procedures or chemical processing) or material usable subsequent to chemical processing or isotope separation." (97) In the first case, a device could be devised by a team of physicists using unclassified information. However, procuring such material would be quite difficult for, as Norton explains, it is "simply . . . not readily available . . . there is not a commercial reactor in current or projected use which utilizes weapons grade material." (98) Such materials are available only at weapons fabrication points, which are under security measures similar to those employed at nuclear weapons sites. Thus the potential for theft is remote.

The more realistic target, and the focal point of the Willrich and Taylor report, is the theft of materials from some point during the reactor fuel cycle. It is here that the thrust of the debate over terrorist acquisition of a nuclear capability has centered. While there are technical and physical barriers protecting this process, the basis of the argument is that shortcomings in the security barriers, security patrols, alarm systems, and automatic detection devices make theft quite possible. (99) Once the material is acquired, a device can be readily constructed. Are such installations vulnerable to penetration? Recent reports by both Rand and Congress's Office of Technology Assessment warn that a moderately large group of commandos could raid scores of sites and capture radioactive materials. (100)   An additional point of potential seizure is during the transport of nuclear materials and weapons. To improve security during transport, a special truck fleet has been created by the Department of Defense that uses very sophisticated mobile security systems and is used to transport weapons-grade material as well as nuclear bombs and warheads. (101) Similar precautions do not appear to be taken in the transport of non-weapons-grade nuclear material and nuclear waste.

While these latest charges of safeguards system vulnerability have not been officially denied, earlier charges of a similar nature were challenged by those associated with nuclear reactor development. According to Meyer et al., "There are many obstacles that must be overcome by a saboteur in his endeavor to construct a workable nuclear device." (102) With regard to these obstacles, a report by the Nuclear Fuel Cycle Program Staff of Sandia Laboratories outlines the protective characteristics of commercial nuclear power plants, concluding that these systems "greatly increase the difficulty of releasing radioactivity by sabotage," or of theft. (103) These protective systems include:

1. The "defense in depth" concept of reactor plant design.

2. The massive structure of the plant, which protects critical components from external attack.

3. The safety design basis of the plant, which emphasizes system reliability, flexibility, redundancy, and protection against common-made failures.

4. Engineered safety features, which are added to the basic system to cope with abnormal operations or accidents. (104)

Meyer et al. likewise support the effectiveness of "management schemes: including measurement procedures designed to detect and prevent diversion, and the physical security systems." (105) With regard to physical security systems, studies by Ney and Jones present detailed illustrations of the structure and effectiveness of these systems. (106)

Finally, these professionals challenge the assertion that once nuclear materials are acquired, a crude device can easily be constructed. The "build your own bomb" reasoning is based on the availability of the necessary instructional information in the "open literature." But according to one analyst,

> Stealing the low-enriched uranium either prior to fuel fabrication or in pellet form in the fuel rods would still leave the thief with the awesome task of enrichment. Even if this monetary and technical barrier could be overcome, the enrichment process requires a facility of such scale that it would be hard to camouflage for the several months that the process requires, not to mention the construction time in preparation for enrichment. (107)

In spite of such arguments, the Department of Energy has developed Nuclear Emergency Search Teams (NEST) to conduct searches for missing nuclear materials, as well as to locate and disarm potential terrorist attempts to employ nuclear devices. Thus far they have answered four calls, all of them hoaxes. (108)

In sum, the U.S. government has been very concerned with the possibility of nuclear terrorism and has taken a number of steps to ensure the security of nuclear facilities and weapons. The effectiveness of these systems is difficult to determine, given that we have yet to experience a terrorist assault on nuclear weapons or energy security systems. The hasty conclusion that this in itself proves the effectiveness of these systems is quickly dispelled in the article by Robert Mullen, "Subnational Threats to Civil Nuclear Facilities and Safeguards Institutions," which appears in this volume. According to Mullen, the relative attractiveness of nuclear fuel cycle facilities to subnationals for purposes of acquiring fissile material or sensitive technology, or as potential sabotage targets, is a function of variable numbers of factors which depends to some extent upon political and social climates, and to some extent upon the technologies of fuel cycle processes and the safeguards implemented to protect them.   Basing himself on these premises, Mullen examines the subnational threats to fuel cycle facilities within two broad categories: one, the potential for these facilities to be used for illicit purposes, and two, their potential as targets of sabotage.   In his conclusion, he suggests ways to mitigate what is perceived to be the range of subnational threats not now addressed adequately by safeguards institutions.

Industrial Installations - Mass Destruction Devices

In addition to the sabotage or seizure of nuclear facilities, the terrorist has the option of attacking a number of vital facilities that are not nearly as well defended.   A case in point is the natural gas and oil industries.   According to a recent assessment by Maynard Stephens, the principal scientist for energy projects at the Gulf South Research Institute,

> Established petroleum and natural gas operations, their pipeline interstices and associated tankage and storage are the most attractive targets of dissent.   But there is no part of the industry that is immune to being seriously damaged by someone who has a little knowledge of it or makes an effort to learn its frailties. (109)

Given that 75 percent of this nation's energy is furnished by oil and natural gas, it is clear how devastating a coordinated terrorist strike would be to the operation of the nation itself.   Other potentially attractive targets include communications networks, various government agencies and installations, and centers of commerce and trade.   In many instances these are as vulnerable as the oil and natural gas industries, and consequently require extensive security improvements.

Finally, if terrorists seek to employ mass destruction devices, they are not limited to nuclear ones.   Mullen notes that a wide range of potential chemical and biological weapons are available for use in various sabotage or blackmail scenarios.   And unlike nuclear materials, the materials necessary for the creation of biological or chemical weapons are much more easily acquired and constructed. (110)   And at the conventional weapons level, the terrorist has available a number of recently developed, sophisticated devices, such as man-portable precision-guided weapons, that can be employed in similar scenarios. (111)

U.S. ORGANIZATIONAL RESPONSE NETWORK: CONTINGENCY PLANNING, CRISIS MANAGEMENT, EMERGENCY PREPAREDNESS

In the final analysis, an effective and cohesive counterterrorism program in the United States will require the development of federal, state, and local cooperation, based on formal interagency planning and management, as well as clear lines of responsibility and authority. Such an organizational network would facilitate the development of crossagency contingency planning, preestablished lines of authority, crisis management techniques and routines, and emergency preparedness programs designed to improve the United States' ability to respond effectively. As Kupperman and Trent explain, however, these developments have not occurred.

> Typically, authority for dealing with various aspects of a terrorist incident is dispersed over a number of government departments and jurisdictions in a manner well suited to handling day-to-day concerns but that may impede efforts to deal with a crisis . . . the details of present organizational arrangements are more elaborate than illuminating. They are steeped in statutory and bureaucratic precedent rather than tuned to meet the external threat. (112)

Concurring with this criticism is the recently released report of the National Advisory Commission on Criminal Justice Standards and Goals on Disorders and Terrorism. (113) Given the proliferation of terrorist incidents during the last ten years, it is quite bewildering that a structured response network that integrates federal, state, and metropolitan authorities has not been initiated. The fact that very positive developments have occurred to parry specific terrorist tactics only makes this situation more perplexing.

The initial attempt to develop a formally structured interagency response occurred in the aftermath of the terrorist strike during the 1972 Munich Olympics. At that time President Nixon directed Secretary of State Kissinger to establish and chair a Cabinet Committee to Combat Terrorism. According to the president, the committee was to determine "the most effective means to prevent terrorism here and abroad." (114) The cabinet committee consisted of the secretaries of state (chairman), defense, treasury, and transportation; the attorney general; the U.S. ambassador to the United Nations; the directors of the FBI and CIA; and the president's assistants for national security and domestic affairs. However, it was the cabinet committee's working group that directed the interagency efforts. This group was composed of senior representatives from the agencies represented in the cabinet committee, as well as members from a number of other agencies. (115) According to Lewis Hoffacker, the first chairman of the working group under Kissinger, it was the working group that was "in constant contact as issues arise and incidents occur . . . this interagency effort has been extremely active . . . in responding to the continuing threat from a variety of organizations or individuals seeking to strike at us at home and abroad." (116) Functionally, the working group was to be involved in a number of specific tasks that included (1) crisis warning and management; (2) contingency and prevention planning; (3) establishment of federal, state, and local collaboration among agencies involved with terrorist incidents; (4) collection and compilation of information on all aspects of terrorism, to be utilized in policy planning and crisis management; and (5) promotion of multilateral conventions and co-operation. (117)

By the time the Carter administration entered office the response system that had developed over the previous four years had come under intense criticism. As a result, in 1977 President Carter initiated an extensive review of U.S. policy and procedures for responding to terrorist strikes that resulted in important organizational changes. (118) Under this reorganization it was determined that "within the National Security Council (NSC) its Special Coordinating Committee (SCC) would function as the primary liaison between the council and the government's planning and operating elements responsible for countering acts of terrorism." (119) This system was devised to manage response to international terrorist incidents, as well as to produce contingency plans and incident management schemes. Within the Special Coordinating Committee the following division of responsibility exists:

> Contingency planning and coordination issues are handled by a working group on terrorism and its executive committee, which are chaired by the State Department, with a Justice Department official serving as the vice chairman for both. The Executive Committee has representation from the Departments of State, Defense, Justice, the CIA, and the NSC staff. The working group has been divided into various functional subgroups dealing with policy and planning issues (research and development, security policy contingency planning and crisis management, public relations, and international initiatives). (120)

Actual international incident management responsibility has been delegated to the State Department (Office for Combating Terrorism). The effectiveness of this system is hard to determine. However, during the 1978 Senate hearings on the "Act to Combat International Terrorism," certain criticisms were voiced.

> There still are overlapping jurisdictions and no clear-cut lines of authority. During the course of the committee's long investigation several sources expressed the opinion that antiterrorism policy has not been given a high enough priority within the administration. The criticism has also been made that the orientation of the Working Group is toward "ad hoc incident response", rather than to broader policy formulation and implementation. In addition, at present several agencies conduct independent and overlapping research . . . the Working Group does not appear to have the authority to better combine and direct interagency resources on this question. (121)

If interagency coordinating problems exist at this level, the situation becomes more complex when those agencies concerned with domestic terrorism at the federal, state, and local levels become involved. Given

all the departments and agencies that could potentially become
involved, it is little wonder that jurisdictional and organizational
bottlenecks occur. (122)   Bell, in the following examples, accurately
portrays the problems involved.

> In New York City unless a federal statute has been violated, thereby
> involving the FBI, the local police are responsible for law enforce-
> ment.   Even in a federal matter, like the Croation incident, the
> Federal Aviation Administration and/or the State Department may
> be responsible rather than the FBI.   Plans for emergency readiness
> are even more chaotic: for example, in 1977 in the United States,
> 175 interagency committees and groups would be involved in the
> case of a nuclear terrorist incident. (123)

In terms of an organizational structure for managing domestic terrorist
incidents, at the federal level the Justice Department, supported by the
FBI, has primary responsibility.   The Justice Department is concerned
with actual incident management, while the FBI's Special Operations
and Research Staff (SOARS) is responsible for research and contingency
planning.   While this seems straightforward, it should be noted that
there are 26 federal agencies that might have direct or indirect
responsibility for involvement in responding to a terrorist incident.
Even more serious problems arise in terms of incident management
when federal, state, and local jurisdictional authority is unclear.   The
seriousness of this problem was outlined in a recent "Evaluation of the
United States Counter-Terrorism Response Capability."

> The State, county, and local police response against terrorists is a
> more difficult item to grasp.   Current problems concerning these
> agencies complicate the possibility of a timely response.   Decen-
> tralized police agencies, unclear jurisdictional lines, and constantly
> varying levels of sophistication, training, and equipment undermine
> the total response capability . . . These problems are most obvious in
> discussions of intelligence gathering, specialization, and clear lines
> of authority. (124)

Unfortunately, these jurisdictional conflicts remain, and must be
resolved if effective coordination and management is to occur.   An
examination of any one of a number of incidents that took place in the
United States over the last five years, especially hostage-barricade
situations, will demonstrate how serious these coordination and jurisdictional problems can be.   In the previously mentioned article by Stephen
Sloan, contained in a later chapter of this book, these problems of
coordination and management, as well as the issues of training and
contingency planning, are discussed in the context of hostage-taking
incidents.

Thus new organizational structures and procedures that cut across
agencies and government levels to establish a unified and coordinated
response system have yet to be established.   The result, according to

the National Advisory Committee on Criminal Justice Standards and Goals, is an enduring "confusion and/or disagreement over the division of responsibility . . . which can prove fatal to the effectiveness of combined operations when time is of the essence and seriously damaging when it is not." (125) To improve this situation the National Advisory Committee, in its final report, made a series of recommendations that would result in the development of an effective coordinated division of responsibility, at the federal, state, and local levels, through formal specification of agency functions. According to the report,

> In tactical operations, investigations, or non-incident-related law enforcement activities involving extraordinary violence, it is essential to achieve an effective division of functions among all . . . agencies permitted to cooperate by applicable laws. Such division of functions should be governed by formal interagency agreement.
>
> 1. Wherever laws do not clearly stipulate jurisdictional authority . . . every . . . agency should negotiate understandings on the division of responsibility . . .
>
> 2. Where exclusive jurisdiction . . . is vested by law in federal, state, or local law enforcement, agencies . . . where jurisdiction is vested should initiate discussions . . . to determine the extent and nature of support . . .
>
> 3. Where an . . . agency . . . is aware of an omission or inconsistency in the definition or division of agency responsibilities . . . it should initiate discussions to remedy the deficiency.
>
> 4. When any . . . operation involving the cooperation of . . . agencies at differing levels of government is . . . commenced, planned definitions and divisions of functions should be confirmed. (126)

The previously mentioned "Act to Combat International Terrorism" makes quite similar recommendations, and specifies the need to greatly improve federal, state, and local interagency incident coordination and management, as well as cooperation in training programs, special research projects, intelligence gathering, and related endeavors. Whether such developments are undertaken remains to be seen.

RESEARCH AND DEVELOPMENT: APPROACHES TO INFORMATION MANAGEMENT AND APPLICATIONS

Basic and applied research on the various aspects of political terrorism have spawned an enormous body of literatures that cannot be synthesized within the confines of this section. However, in one of the later chapters of this volume Mickolus, Heyman, and Schlotter present an extensive survey of terrorism research in which they identify major themes, directions, and approaches. In the present part of this chapter our examination will be limited primarily to research and development on effective approaches to information/intelligence management.

The importance of good intelligence cannot be overstated. According to one authoritative source, "The assembly and dissemination of accurate and timely knowledge of terrorist activities and plans is probably the most useful countermeasure against terrorism. Intelligence may enable us to prevent some attacks . . . Good intelligence permits concentration of expensive defenses on likely targets." (127) In recognition of the fact that an effective government response to terrorist actions would be greatly enhanced if decision-makers had access to reliable intelligence data, a number of projects have been initiated to develop sophisticated information systems. Among the more comprehensive of these data systems is International Terrorism: Attributes of Terrorist Events, or ITERATE. Developed by Edward Mickolus and the Central Intelligence Agency, the project has gathered and categorized data on over 100 variables that relate to political terrorism for the years 1968 to 1978; this data base is updated annually. (128) As a source of information for the decision-maker, ITERATE, according to Mickolus, has a number of uses that include "summarizing trends, comparing terrorist campaigns cross-nationally over time, and evaluating policy prescriptions for crisis management and incident negotiation support." (129)

Among the terrorism research projects undertaken by the Rand Corporation (130) has been the development of a chronology of terrorist events spanning the period 1968-74. (131) When compared with the ITERATE system, however, the Rand chronology appears limited. From the private security sector, Risk International, Inc., under the project direction of Charles A. Russell, has produced an incident data base that contains information on over 5,000 terrorist events. According to Russell, "incidents are broken down by date, time, country and city, target, nationality of target, group involved, number in group, weapons or explosives used, ransoms demanded or paid, hostages taken, disposition of hostages, other demands. Materials are filed by incident types." (132) Finally, perhaps the most ambitious current data system under development for use in crisis decision-making and contingency planning is under the auspices of the Cybernetics Technology Office (CTO) of the Defense Advanced Research Projects Agency (DARPA). The "Preliminary Design for the Terrorism Crisis Management Decision Aid System" includes the following categories: (1) terrorist group profiles; (2) country profiles; (3) incident files; (4) counterforce incident files; and (5) analytical programs for data retrieval, analysis, and graphic display.

In addition to providing the decision-maker with easily retrievable information on various aspects of political terrorism (of course this information is also of importance to the corporate sector, for such things as investment planning), such raw data lends itself to more sophisticated statistical and mathematical analysis. For instance, Waterman and Jenkins of the Rand Corporation have developed a heuristic model using a rule-based computer system to provide crisis managers with guidelines for dealing with unstructured and often unfamiliar situations. (133)

> The heuristic model is a model of a situation stated in terms of heuristics (rules of thumb) which describe the dynamics of the situation. It is particularly useful for problem domains that are not well formalized and for which no generally agreed upon axioms on theorems exist. The domain we have chosen for investigation - international terrorism - is just this type of domain. (134)

The model provides for the articulation of a series of steps that lie behind the intuitive judgments made by analysts in reaching a particular conclusion. The assumptions of the model are threefold: first, that terrorism can be analyzed in a formal manner; second, that a limited number of rules that prod thinking and formalize the domain will enhance analysis; and third, that a model of terrorist activity can be formulated as a rule-directed model to help crisis managers make decisions in ill-specified domains. In sum, the authors, in conjunction with other Rand analysts, have created an artificial intelligence model which would serve as an aid in the analysis of terrorist incidents. Using data fed into it regarding a current incident, the computer is able to derive conclusions about the terrorists' identity and probable behavior during the incident. The system forces the analyst to make explicit if unstated assumptions, and then demonstrates how these assumptions logically interact, pointing out inconsistencies. The system provides a straightforward way of proceeding toward a solution. The initial work by Waterman and Jenkins focused on the formalization of a domain for terrorist bombings. Future research using heuristic modeling is projected to investigate the introduction of probability measures for all rules, the analysis of other terrorist activities, and the development of agents that are capable of making predictions about future terrorist activities. (135) Whether this model has been employed by decision-makers in such situations is not certain.

The Waterman and Jenkins model is only one example of this type of research. Bennett and Saaty, to cite a second example, have devised a six-stage procedure to integrate hierarchical analysis with on-the-scene negotiating. According to the two authors, "In addition to the usefulness of heuristic models in improving the skills of analysts working with the problem of international terrorism, it appears that minicomputers with heuristic modeling systems built into them may be extremely useful in the management of crisis situations." (136)

As was noted above, the federal government has a strong interest in such applied research, evidenced in the DARPA Terrorism Crisis Management Decision Aid System. Agencies currently involved include the Arms Control and Disarmament Agency, the Special Operations and Research Staff of the FBI, the National Security Council and its Special Coordinating Committee, and the State Department's Office for Combating Terrorism. And according to Kupperman, this research is being conducted on an interagency basis, in addition to partially being "contracted out" to private research organizations such as Rand.

The above constitutes only a brief overview of one part of the counterterrorism research and development effort. For a more thorough examination of the basic and applied research literature, the reader is directed to the Mickolus, Heyman, and Schlotter article in this volume. With the exception of sensitive or classified research being conducted by or for the U.S. government, which must be excluded for obvious reasons, the authors identify and critically examine all major research themes, pointing out those areas where future work should be continued and identifying certain neglected resources that offer potentially valuable information for researchers and policymakers. In addition to this broad-gauged review of the R & D effort, the volume also contains an interesting study by Edward Heyman of the diffusion of transnational terrorism. Employing the techniques of spatial geography, Heyman examines how and why terrorism has spread throughout the international arena during the last decade. In his analysis, he (1) identifies the origins of the current wave of international terrorism, (2) introduces a conceptual framework and techniques for identifying and monitoring the diffusion process, (3) proposes reasons that account for this diffusion, and (4) discusses the elements of transnational terrorism that promote its rapid diffusion. The importance of such information for government policymakers who must respond to such developments is discussed in the conclusion, and recommendations are presented.

INTERNATIONAL CONVENTIONS AND COOPERATION

It has been in the area of international conventions and cooperation that the United States has been the least successful in responding to the terrorist threat, even though it has been quite active in pressing for international legislation. Although the increasing magnitude of terrorism has been recognized by the community of nations, the political dynamics of international terrorism have impeded a unified response. The international community is ideologically divided over the issue of terrorism. The primary reason for this split, according to Dugard and Moore, stems from the ambiguous status of wars of national liberation. (137) When they are characterized as wars of self-determination, the nonaligned majority of Third World nations not only identifies with these movements, but believes that stipulations contained in the Geneva Convention which forbid the taking of hostages or attacks against uninvolved civilians are not applicable in such cases. In effect, as Moore suggests, for the nonaligned Third World nations there exists a "congruence between self-determination and terrorism. (138) For these nations the terrorist is seen as a legitimate figure, carrying on a just struggle. Furthermore, states such as Libya, Iraq, and South Yemen go beyond moral support, and provide training, arms, money, and sanctuary to terrorist groups.

It has been this group of states that has rendered ineffective the attempts by the United Nations and other international bodies to establish enforceable international regulations against terror. The inability of the United Nations to formulate an international framework for the prevention and punishment of terrorism is consistent with its lack of success in controlling larger-scale conflicts. What follows is a brief review of the existing record.

Following the events at the Munich Olympics, the secretary general of the United Nations, Kurt Waldheim, asked the General Assembly to adopt measures to prevent international terrorism. In response to this request, the United States proposed to the General Assembly a draft of a convention for the prevention and punishment of certain acts of international terrorism. The draft was a skillful attempt to proscribe international antiterrorist activities while avoiding the issue of national liberation conflicts, but the nonaligned Third World majority managed to block the U.S. effort. This rejection illuminates the difficulty of achieving consensus on the issue of terrorism at the U.N. In this particular instance, the Ad Hoc Committee on Terrorism created by the General Assembly ended up deadlocked in debate over the definition of what constitutes terrorism. In 1973, the General Assembly did adopt a convention that would lead to the extradition or prosecution of individuals who attacked, kidnapped, or murdered diplomats or other internationally protected persons. While this was a step in the right direction, complete adherence to the convention has not occurred. In 1976, West Germany submitted a treaty to the General Assembly concerning the taking of hostages. It has run into the same sort of bottlenecks.

On the narrower issue of hijacking, international conventions have been initiated, but their effectiveness has been limited. At the Hague Conference in December 1970, a Convention for the Suppression of Unlawful Seizure of Aircraft was proposed that requires signatory states to extradite hijackers or prosecute them. Only 74 states signed the convention. Similarly, only 79 states signed the Montreal Convention of 1971, which requires the extradition or prosecution of persons who sabotage an aircraft. Finally, in 1973 the International Civil Aviation Organization (ICAO) held a conference in Rome at which the United States proposed a convention that included suspension of all international air navigation to and from any state that violated existing conventions. However, the international response to terrorism in the United Nations has proven to be ineffective as a result of the failure of several states to agree to specific measures.

More successful attempts at cooperation have occurred at the regional and bilateral levels. One of the more encouraging international developments occurred in 1973, when the United States and Cuba agreed to extradite hijackers promptly. While the 1973 agreement has formally expired, its provisions are still being observed. Regionally, the Organization of American States' Convention to Prevent and Punish the Acts of Terrorism formally commits OAS members to preventing and punishing acts of terrorism, especially kidnapping, assassination, and other assaults against foreign representatives. But the United States has not been successful in moving the OAS to adopt harsher anti-terrorist legislation. Also at the regional level, West Europe, despite U.S. encouragement, has only achieved mixed success in cooperating on the terrorism issue. In 1976, the ministers of the interior of the European Community and senior intelligence and police officers did establish a network of consultation for dealing with terrorist incidents and a system for the routine exchange of information. With this cooperation at the police and military levels, it was hoped that further cooperation could be achieved. Thus the 1977 Strasbourg Conference sought to adopt a convention that would, in effect, turn Europe into a truly hostile area for terrorists, by ensuring that terrorists could no longer evade the law by slipping across one of Europe's many borders. This did not occur because certain states sought to maintain the right to grant political asylum under certain conditions. The convention suffered a further weakening of its credibility as a result of the release of Muhammad Daoud by France. Finally, on July 17, 1978 the leaders of Britain, Canada, France, West Germany, Italy, Japan, and the United States, meeting in Bonn, reached an agreement to cut off commercial airline service to or from any country that harbors hijackers.

To summarize, the United States has not been very successful in moving the international community to establish enforceable measures to prevent or punish international terrorism. The response, in the United Nations and elsewhere, has been characterized by disparate efforts, many of them neither adopted nor implemented. Whether future measures will be adopted under United Nations auspices is debatable, given the absence of a consensus among its members on how great a threat is posed by terrorism. It would seem, in view of past experience, that the regional and bilateral levels hold more promise for cooperation.

CONCLUSION

This study has presented an overview of the major steps undertaken by U.S. policymakers and the law enforcement community, as well as within the private sector, to prevent or limit terrorist effectiveness. These policy responses have taken a variety of forms and, like their terrorist targets, have been innovative and in certain areas tactically effective. On the one hand, a great deal of stress has been placed on preventive security measures using new and sophisticated technologies, including video, photoelectric, ultrasonic, and infrared systems, vibration detectors, different types of sensors, and other forms of monitoring and surveillance equipment. These measures have been employed in the areas of executive protection, airport security, and the safeguarding of vital installations, the goal being prevention through the hardening of the target. Additionally, new technological improvements in weaponry and other tactically oriented equipment have been developed for specialized units. On the other hand, emphasis has also been placed on the use of psychological and other social science techniques and methodologies, as was evident in the examination of strategies for hostage-negotiations, which were based on behavioral concepts. The methodologies of the social sciences were also employed in the creation of data systems and predictive and heuristic models. Finally, stress has been placed on contingency planning, crisis management, and other organizational preparations to effectively respond to specific incidents. The response has thus been an extensive one. But as with those who employ terrorism, the successes have only been tactical. Neither side has achieved its long-range goals.

NOTES

(1) Abraham Guillen, The Philosophy of the Urban Guerrilla, trans. Donald C. Hodges (New York: Morrow, 1973), pp. 233, 250.

(2) Robert Kupperman and Darrell Trent, Terrorism - Threat, Reality, Response (Stanford, Calif.: Hoover Institution, 1979), p. 7.

(3) See Brian Jenkins, The Five Stages of Urban Guerrilla Warfare (Santa Monica, Calif.: Rand, 1974).

(4) Paul Shaw, Planning for Executive Protection (Gaithersburg, Md.: International Association of Chiefs of Police, 1976), p. 6.

(5) Bowman H. Miller and Charles A. Russell, "The Evolution of Revolutionary Warfare: From Mao to Marighella and Meinhof," in Kupperman and Trent, Terrorism, p. 187.

(6) Richard Clutterbuck, Living With Terrorism (New Rochelle, N.Y.: Arlington House, 1975), chs. 2-3. Also discussed in Congressional Committee Staff Study, Political Kidnappings, 1968-1973 (Washington, D.C.: Government Printing Office, 1973).

(7) Dilshad Najmuddin, "The Kidnapping of Diplomatic Personnel," The Chief of Police, February 1973, p. 18.

(8) Charles Wise and Stephen Sloan, "Countering Terrorism: The U.S. and Israeli Approach," Middle East Review, Spring 1977, pp. 55-59.

(9) Shaw, Planning, p. 11.

(10) Taken from a special report by Brian Jenkins titled "International Terrorism: Trends and Potentialities," prepared for inclusion with U.S. Senate, Committee on Governmental Affairs, "An Act to Combat International Terrorism,", 95th Cong., 2d sess., 1978, p. 123. Also see J.S. Kakalik and Sorel Wildhorn, Private Police in the United States: Finding and Recommendation (Washington, D.C.: Government Printing Office, 1972).

(11) U.S. House of Representatives, Committee on Internal Security, "Terrorism," pt. 1, 93d Cong., 2d sess., 1974. For a discussion of the

various Burns programs, see the statement and interview with Fred Rayne, director of the Burns International Investigation Bureau, pp. 3086-3113.

(12) Executive Protection Handbook (Miami, Fl.: Burns International).

(13) S.A. Davis, "Terrorism as a Security Management Problem," unpublished paper, p. 5.

(14) U.S. Department of Justice, Private Security Advisory Council to the Law Enforcement Assistance Administration, Prevention of Terrorist Crimes: Security Guidelines for Business, Industry, and Other Organizations (May 1976), p. 1.

(15) Davis, "Security Management Problems," pp. 3-4.

(16) U.S. Department of the Army, Personal Security Precautions Against Acts of Terrorism 1978, pp. I-1.

(17) Executive Protection Handbook, p. 1.

(18) Paul Fugua and Jerry Wilson, Terrorism: The Executive's Guide to Survival (Houston, Tex.: Gulf Publishing, 1978), p. 8.

(19) Shaw, Planning, pp. 11-23.

(20) For a useful inventory of these various security systems see Albert Mandelbaum, Fundamentals of Protective Systems: Planning, Evolution, Selection (Springfield, Ill.: Charles C. Thomas, 1975).

(21) An awareness of one's surroundings can be most helpful in detecting potential kidnappers. Usually the kidnapper will observe his/her target for some time in preparation for the actual seizure. Thus, an awareness of strangers or automobiles that reappear frequently near one's residency may tip off the executive that he/she is a likely target. See the Executive Protection Handbook; also Richard Clutterbuck, "Business: Fending off Attack," Atlas, January 1978, pp. 35-36.

(22) Brooks McClure, "Hostage Survival," Conflict, no. 1-2, (1978), pp. 21-48.

(23) During most of the 1960s the motivation was that of "fleeing from prosecution, attempting criminal extortion, or acting out of mental derangement." Robert Bell, "The U.S. Response to Terrorism Against International Civil Aviation," Orbis, Winter 1976, pp. 1328.

(24) W. William Minor, "Skyjacking Crime Control Models," The Journal of Criminal Law and Criminology, March 1975, p. 94.

(25) Ibid., pp. 94-95.

(26) For a discussion of this point see Charles Russell and Bowman Miller, "Profile of a Terrorist," Military Review, August 1977, pp. 21-34.

(27) Clutterback, Living With Terrorism, p. 140.

(28) For a useful discussion see John Dailey and Evan Pickrel, "Federal Aviation Administration's Behavioral Research Program for Defense Against Hijackings," Aviation, Space, and Environmental Medicine, April 1975, pp. 423-27.

(29) Ibid., p. 424.

(30) Michael Fenello, "Technical Prevention of Air Piracy," International Conciliation, November 1971, p. 31.

(31) Harry Murphy, Prevention of Aerial Piracy to the U.S., 1972-1978 (Gaithersburg, Md.: International Association of Chiefs of Police, 1979), p. 4.

(32) For a description of events leading to mandatory screening see Kenneth Moore, Airport, Aircraft, and Airline Security (Los Angeles: Security World Publishing, 1976).

(33) Originally these systems affected unprocessed photographic film carried in baggage. While some improvements have been made to the systems, they still may damage film if a series of checks are undergone during a trip. See Chris Eliot, "Security in the Air," Aerospace International, February-March 1978, p. 13.

(34) Murphy, Prevention of Aerial Piracy.

(35) For a further discussion see Eliot, "Security in the Air," p. 12-15. Also see "A Survey of Security Equipment for Airport Use," Interavia, no. 2 (1975), pp. 179-182.

(36) Discussed in Kupperman and Trent, Terrorism, pp. 86-7.

(37) For a more detailed discussion see Murphy, Prevention of Aerial Piracy, pp. 6-9, 16-22.

(38) Edward Mickolus, "Negotiation For Hostages: A Policy Dilemma," Orbis, Winter 1976, p. 1309.

(39) See Lewis Hoffacker, "The U.S. Government Response to Terrorism," Vital Speeches, February 15, 1975, pp. 266-68.

(40) Judith Miller, "Bargain With Terrorists?" New York Times Magazine, July 18, 1976, pp. 40-41.

(41) Ibid.

(42) For support of this argument see H.H.A. Cooper, Hostage Negotiations: Opinions and Alternatives (Gaithersburg, Md.: International Association of Chiefs of Police, 1977). Also see the recently published study by Murray Miron and Arnold Goldstein, Hostage (New York: Pergamon, 1979).

(43) Cooper, Hostage Negotiation, pp. 34-37.

(44) Francis A. Bolz, Jr., "Hostage Confrontation and Rescue," in Kupperman and Trent, Terrorism, pp. 395-96.

(45) Ibid., p. 400. This approach is essentially that developed by Dr. Harvey Schlossberg of the New York City Police Department's Psychological Services Department. See Harvey Schlossberg and Lucy Freeman, Psychologist with a Gun (New York: Coward, McCann, and Geoghehan, 1974).

(46) Conrad Hassel, "The Hostage Situation: Exploring the Motivation and the Cause," Police Chief, September 1975, p. 58. Also see John Cully, "Defusing Human Bombs - Hostage Negotiations," FBI Law Enforcement Bulletin, October 1974, pp. 10-14.

(47) Essentially this is the message from the National Advisory Committee Task Force on Disorders and Terrorism. U.S. Department of Justice, Law Enforcement Assistance Administration. See Report of the Task Force on Disorder and Terrorism, 1976.

(48) Bolz, "Hostage Confrontation," pp. 401-2.

(49) Miron and Goldstein, Hostage, pp. 93-94.

(50) Ibid., Appendix A, contains a description of the negotiation selection procedures.

(51) Francis Bolz, Detective Bureau Hostage Negotiating Team (New York: New York City Police Department).

(52) Bolz, "Hostage Confrontation," p. 402.

(53) The California Specialized Training Institute will provide a course outline to federal, state, and local law enforcement agencies.

(54) Brian Jenkins, Terrorism and Kidnapping (Santa Monica, Calif.: Rand, 1974); Should Corporations To Be Prevented From Paying Ransom (Santa Monica, Calif.: Rand, 1974).

(55) Brian Jenkins, Hostage Survival: Some Preliminary Observations (Santa Monica, Calif.: Rand, 1976); Brian Jenkins, Janera Johnson, and David Ronfeldt, Numbered Lives, (Santa Monica, Calif.: Rand, 1977).

(56) Ric Blacksten and Richard Engler, Hostage Studies (Arlington, VA.: Ketron, Inc., 1974)

(57) Stephen Sloan and Richard Kearney, "An Analysis of a Simulated Terrorist Incident," Police Chief, June 1977.

(58) Abraham Miller, "Negotiations for Hostages: Implications from the Police Experience," Terrorism: An International Journal, no. 2 (1978).

(59) Miron and Goldstein, Hostage.

(60) John Stratton, "The Terrorist Act of Hostage-Taking: A View of Violence and the Perpetrators," Journal of Police Science and Administration, no. 1 (1978), pp. 6-8.

(61) Mickolus, "Negotiation For Hostages," p. 1318.

(62) Miller, "Implications from the Police Experience," p. 129.

(63) Ibid., p. 142.

(64) For the most thorough discussion of this see Donald Cook, "Hostage Negotiations - A Model" (M.A. diss., Sam Houston State University, 1977). Also see Miron and Goldstein, Hostage.

(65) John Stratton, "The Terrorist Act of Hostage-Taking: Considerations for Law Enforcement," Journal of Police Science and Administration, no. 2 (1978), p. 124.

(66) John Cully, "Defusing Human Bombs - Hostage Negotiations," pp. 10-11.

(67) Bolz, "Hostage Confrontation and Rescue," p. 400.

(68) Miron and Goldstein, Hostage, p. 94.

(69) For a general discussion see Stratton, "The Terrorist Act of Hostage-Taking."

(70) David Tarr, "The Strategic Environment: U.S. National Security and the Nature of Law Intensity Conflict," (Paper delivered at the annual meeting of the Midwest Political Science Assoc., Chicago, April 19-21, 1979).

(71) For a brief account of the Cyprus affair, see Kupperman and Trent, Terrorism, p. 41.

(72) This act prohibits the use of the Army of Air Force for law enforcement within the United States, except when authorized by some other provision of the law. The president can waive this limitation.

(73) Abraham Miller, "SWAT (Special Weapons and Tactics) - The Tactical Link in Hostage Negotiations," in Terrorism and Business, Threat and Response, ed. Yonah Alexander and Robert Kilmarx (New York: Praeger, 1979).

(74) Douglas Allback, "Countering Special-Threat Situations," Military Police Law Enforcement Journal, Summer 1975, pp. 34-35. Also see Richard Swan, "Special Threat Situation Team Training," Military Police Law Enforcement Journal, Spring 1974, pp. 36-40.

(75) Miller, "SWAT," p. 197.

(76) Gerald Boyd, "Special Weapons and Tactics Teams: A Systems Approach," FBI Law Enforcement Bulletin, September 1977, pp. 23-24.

(77) Miller, "SWAT," pp. 201-3.

(78) Allback, "Special-Threat Situations," p. 36.

(79) Boyd, "Special Weapons," p. 25.

(80) For a comparison of U.S. and West German approaches, see W. Ronald Olin, "An Evaluation of the United States Counter-Terrorist Response," Police Chief, June 1979).

(81) "A New Breed of Commando," Time, October 31, 1977, p. 44.

(82) For a detailed discussion of each role see Allback, "Special-Threat Situations," pp. 36-37. Also see G.N. Beck, "SWAT - the Los Angeles Special Weapons and Tactical Teams," FBI Law Enforcement Bulletin, April 1972.

(83) John Wolf, SURGE - The Sustained Response Group (Gaithersburg, Md.: International Association of Chiefs of Police, 1977), pp. 11-12.

(84) Thomas Conrad, "Do-It-Yourself A-Bombs," Commonweal, July 1969; Alan Adelson, "Please Don't Steal the Atomic Bomb," Esquire, May 1969; and Robert Jones, "Nuclear Terror Peril Likely to Increase," Los Angeles Times, April 25, 1976.

(85) David Krieger, "Terrorists and Nuclear Technology," Bulletin of the Atomic Scientists, June 1975, p. 28.

(86) Mason Willrich and Theodore Taylor, Nuclear Theft: Risks and Safeguards (Cambridge, Mass.: Ballinger, 1974).

(87) Brian Jenkins, Terrorism and The Nuclear Theft: Risks and Safeguards (Cambridge, Mass.: Ballinger, 1974).

(88) "The Ultimate Fear: Atom Bomb in Terrorist Hands," Chicago Tribune, July 22, 1979, p. 1ff.

(89) Michael Flood, "Nuclear Sabotage," Bulletin of the Atomic Scientists, October 1975, pp. 31-33.

(90) David Rosenbaum, "Nuclear Terror," International Security, Winter 1977, pp. 141-42.

(91) "7,152 lbs. of Atom Bomb Materials Lost," Chicago Tribune, July 23, 1979.

(92) Krieger, "Terrorists and Nuclear Technology," p. 28.

(93) Augustus Norton, "Nuclear Terrorism and the Middle East," Military Review, April 1976, p. 4.

(94) Bruce Blair and Gary Brewer, "The Terrorist Threat to World Nuclear Programs," Journal of Conflict Resolution, September 1977, pp. 379-403.

(95) "The Ultimate Fear," p. 1ff.

(96) Colonel Qaddafi of Libya has publicly expressed his willingness to buy a nuclear device.

(97) Norton, "Nuclear Terrorism," p. 4.

(98) Ibid., pp. 4-5.

(99) For a discussion of this position, see Comptroller General of the United States, Improvements Needed in the Program for the Protection of Special Nuclear Material (Washington, D.C.: Government Printing Office, 1973).

(100) "The Ultimate Fear," p. 1ff.

(101) "James Bond Truck Fleet Moves Deadly Freight," Chicago Tribune, July 22, 1979, p. 16.

(102) W. Meyer, S.K. Loyalka, W.E. Nelson, and R.W. Williams, "The Homemade Nuclear Bomb Syndrome," Nuclear Safety, July-August 1977, pp. 428-29.

(103) Nuclear Fuel Cycle Program Staff, "Safety and Security of Nuclear Power Reactors to Acts of Sabotage," Nuclear Safety, November-December 1976, p. 666.

(104) Ibid., pp. 666-67.

(105) Meyer et al., p. 428.

(106) O.E. Jones, Advanced Physical Protection Systems for Nuclear Materials, ERDA Report SAND-75-5351 (Sandia Laboratories, NTIS, 1975); J.F. Ney, Protecting Plutonium: Physical Safeguards, ERDA Report SAND-75-6068 (Sandia Laboratories, NTIS, 1975).

(107) Norton, "Nuclear Terrorism," p. 5.

(108) "The Ultimate Fear," p. 1ff.

(109) Kupperman and Trent, Terrorism, p. 201.

(110) See Robert Mullen, "Mass Destruction and Terrorism," Journal of International Affairs, Spring-Summer 1978, pp. 63-90.

(111) For a description of man-portable weapons see James Digby, Precision-Guided Weapons, Adelphi Paper No. 118 (London: International Studies Institute, 1975).

(112) Kupperman and Trent, Terrorism, p. 128.

(113) U.S. Department of Justice, Task Force on Disorder.

(114) U.S. House of Representatives, "Terrorism," pt. 11, p. 3133.

(115) U.S. House of Representatives, Committee on Foreign Affairs, "International Terrorism, Hearings," 93d Cong., 2d sess., June 1974, pp. 13-14.

(116) U.S. House of Representatives, "Terrorism," pt. 11, p. 3134.

(117) Lewis Hoffacker, "The U.S. Government Response to Terrorism: A Global Approach," Department of State Bulletin, March 18, 1974, pp. 274-78.

(118) U.S. Senate, Committee on Governmental Affairs, Reorganization Plan No. 3 of 1978, Establishing a New Independent Agency, The Federal Emergency Management Agency, Report No. 95-1141, 95th Cong., 2d sess., August 23, 1978.

(119) Kupperman and Trent, Terrorist, p. 164.

(120) Ibid., p. 165.

(121) U.S. Senate, "An Act to Combat Terrorism," p. 27.

(122) In addition to the cabinet committee, the departments and
agencies involved include the Departments of State, Defense,
Energy, Commerce, and Justice, the Central Intelligence Agency,
Federal Aviation Administration, and Nuclear Regulatory Commission. For a discussion of their specific roles and scope of authority
see Ibid., pp. 26-41.

(123) J. Bowyer Bell, A Time of Terror (New York: Basic Books, 1978),
pp. 128-29.

(124) W. Ronald Olin, "An Evaluation of the United States Counter-
Terrorism Response Capability", Police Chief, June 1979, p. 36.

(125) U.S. Department of Justice, Task Force on Disorders, p. 216.

(126) Ibid., pp. 215-216.

(127) Kupperman and Trent, Terrorism, p. 121.

(128) Edward Mickolus, International Terrorism: Attributes of Terrorist Events Data (Ann Arbor: Inter-University Consortium for
Political and Social Research, University of Michigan, 1976).

(129) Mickolus, "Statistical Approaches to the Study of Terrorism," in
Terrorism: Interdisciplinary Perspective, ed. Yonah Alexander and
Seymour Maxwell Finger (New York: McGraw-Hill, 1977), p. 211.

(130) Rand has probably been the primary private research firm
contracted by the Defense Advanced Agency for the study of
terrorism. For the scope of the Rand program see Brian Jenkins,
Rand's Research on Terrorism (Santa Monica, Calif.: Rand, 1977).

(131) Brian Jenkins and Janera Johnson, International Terrorism: A
Chronology, 1968-1974 (Santa Monica, Calif.: Rand, 1975).

(132) Bowman H. Miller and Charles A. Russell, "The Evolution of
Revolutionary Warfare: From Mao to Marighella and Meinhof," in
Kupperman and Trent, p. 198. This terrorist events data file is
currently restricted in its use to Risk International, Inc.

(133) D.A. Waterman and Brian Jenkins, Heuristic Modeling Using Rule-
Based Computer Systems (Santa Monica, Calif.: Rand, 1977).

(134) Ibid., p. 1.

(135) Ibid., pp. 37-40.

(136) James P. Bennet and Thomas Saaty, "Terrorism: Patterns for
Negotiation - A Case Study Using Hierarchies and Holarchies," in
Kupperman and Trent, Terrorism, pp. 312-13.

(137) John Dugard, "Towards the Definition of International Terrorism",
American Journal of International Law, July 1973; John Moore,
"Toward Legal Restraints on International Terrorism," American
Journal of International Law, July 1973.

(138) Moore, Airport, p. 88.

3 Restrictions Encountered in Responding to Terrorist Sieges: An Analysis
Clive C. Aston

Hostage-taking to achieve political ends is certainly not a phenomenon new to Western Europe. (1) In 197 B.C. the Romans put down Idibilus' revolt in Further Spain and required the defeated tribes to give hostages as a guarantee of their future good conduct. Later, during Tyrone's rebellion in Ireland at the end of the 16th century and again in 1793 during the counterrevolution in Vendee, France, this tactic was employed with equal success. If a single important hostage could not be found, then the taking of multiple, less important hostages was deemed equally effective. For instance, the abduction of Richard the Lionhearted by Duke Leopold of Austria in 1193 secured him a vast ransom from England; Barbarossa took 300 hostages in order to obtain a favourable peace treaty with Milan in 1158. (2) In fact, the very word "kidnapper" is believed to have originated in the harbor towns in England around 1678, when organized gangs stole children and sold them to American traders whose country badly needed labor. (3)

However, it is only within the past decade that hostage-taking by nonstate actors for political ends has become widespread in Western Europe, at times seeming to reach almost epidemic proportions. Even though there were no political incidents in 1968 or 1969, the next eight years saw 966 people taken hostage in 33 sieges, 51 kidnappings, and seven kidnap/sieges. In the two years preceding the siege at the Munich Olympics, 35 people had already been seized, of whom five were murdered in cold blood. Yet it took the fiasco that Munich became, more than any other single incident in Western Europe, to focus most painfully government attention on the problems encountered in responding to a political hostage-taking. Even worse was the shocking realization that those charged with combating it were ill-informed, ill-equipped, and ill-trained.

This chapter sets out the findings of an operational analysis of terrorist sieges that have occurred in Western Europe during the past decade. The underlying assumption of this study revolves around the belief that an understanding of the problems encountered in responding to past incidents is a necessary prerequisite for drawing up accurate contingency plans for the future.   Such an analysis leads to the identification of five distinct clusters of operationally restrictive variables that must be considered and will inevitably limit a host governments' response options. The media and public opinion will not be mentioned here as they are not a variable but rather a constant non-inveighing factor.   Indeed, a Harris public opinion poll in the United States indicated that "frightened people seem inclined to accept, and may even demand that government take measures ordinarily regarded as repressive." (4)

NATURE OF THE SEIZURE

The first variable is the nature of the seizure, or how and why it occurred. While not all sieges come into being for the same reason, it is possible to distinguish two main forms; those the terrorists have not planned and those they have.

Unplanned

Here again it is possible to make a further distinction between four types of unplanned sieges.

1. Spontaneous

However unlikely it may seem, sieges can occur spontaneously, when passions or emotions have been raised to a fervent pitch for some reason. These sieges perhaps most closely resemble those conducted by a "frightened man on a binge." (5) Here, the terrorists are unlikely to have engaged in any preplanning or made any preparations for a lengthy siege or, for that matter, even given much thought to the consequences of their act.   Logically, they will be trapped into unfamiliar role behavior by a situation for which they are highly unlikely to be psychologically prepared, and may, therefore, act in the manner they feel they are supposed to or the way the media has shown others to have acted during similar situations. The only example of this was the Harkis siege at Toulouse Airport on August 7, 1975, in which the terrorists surrendered peacefully to the police after several hours and released their 30 hostages unharmed.

2. Kidnap/Siege and Attempted Kidnap/Siege

A kidnap/siege will occur when the responding authorities locate the hideout where the terrorists are hiding their kidnap victim and physically surround it as they would for a siege.   An attempted kidnap/siege will come into being when the terrorists are foiled in their kidnap attempt by, for example, the police responding too quickly for them to escape with their hostage, or by being delayed by the potential kidnap victim for a sufficient length of time to allow the police to arrive, as was the case with the attempted kidnap/siege by the Hrvatsko Revolucionario Bratstvo faction of the Ustashi at the Yugoslavian embassy in Stockholm on April 7, 1971. (6)

Here again the terrorists are forced into a situation for which they are unlikely to be psychologically prepared. They have now lost the initiative they normally possess during a kidnapping and have also lost their own freedom of movement and apparent invisibility. (7) As a consequence, they will most likely become frustrated and angry, and will probably exhibit increased aggression toward the police on the outside, who will be perceived as the source of their frustration, and potentially toward the hostages as well. Interestingly enough, this form of siege does appear to be more particularly violent. In fact, six of the seven incidents that can be subsumed under this category involved an exchange of fire between the police and the terrorists once the location had been surrounded. More significantly, on only two occasions have the terrorists surrendered peacefully. This represents a termination rate of five out of seven by assault versus six out of 33 for the other sieges. Moreover, four of the nine victims of this form of siege were executed in cold blood by the terrorists after they had been seized, versus six of the 892 victims of the other 33 sieges. (8)

3. Other Form of Attack Frustrated and Hostages Taken in an Escape Bid

When another form of attack is interrupted or frustrated by the police, the terrorists may take hostages in an escape bid. In many ways, this form of siege closely resembles those conducted by an "escaping felon." (9) Terrorists in these circumstances can also be described as "caught in an unplanned situation . . . confused, frightened, and . . . being forced to make snap decisions in a crisis without the opportunity to assess the situation realistically." (10) In all five examples of this which have occurred in Western Europe, the only demand was for safe conduct, which was granted twice.

4. Hostages Taken Incidentally to Prevent Them from Becoming a Hinderance to the Main Attack

It is perhaps incorrect to refer to this as a siege, since the police are unlikely to become involved until after the main attack is over. Nonetheless, the terrorists here will have planned their action in some detail but the hostages will represent an additional complication they may not have counted on and will play little if any part in their plans. The hostages were seized simply because they happened to be in the way and because the terrorists did not want them to hinder the main attack or warn the authorities. In none of the four cases where this has occurred have the terrorists presented any demands or attempted to use the hostages in any way. Examples of this occurred on November 26, 1973, when six members of the Euzkadi ta Azkatasuns (ETA) held over 100 guests hostage while they burned down the Biscay Yacht Club in Bilbao; on March 25, 1977, when five members of the Front pour la Liberation de la Corse (Front for the Liberation of Corsica) held four soldiers while they blew up a military post near Bastia; on July 2, 1978, when five members of the Squadre Proletarie di Combattemento (Fighting Proletarian Squads) held a magistrate while they blew up a law court in Florence; and on October 13, 1978, when five members of Les Militants pour la Defense d'Israel (Fighters for the Defense of Israel) held four occupants while they set fire to the Palestinian library in Paris.

Planned

Although rightly described as "the epitome of terrorist techniques," (11) this form does not account for the overwhelming proportion of all sieges. In fact, in only 23 of the 33 sieges and seven kidnap/sieges does the taking of hostages appear to have been planned ahead of time. Here again, though, two main variations can be discerned.

1. Other Form of Attack Successful and Hostages Taken in an Escape Bid

Here the terrorists will have conducted more preplanning than in any of the variations mentioned above. The primary aim of the attack is not the taking of hostages but rather, for instance, an assassination, as was the case with the assassination of Yusuf Sebai, the secretary general of the Afro-Asian People's Solidarity Conference, in Nicosia on February 18, 1978. Although it can generally be assumed the terrorists will have planned the incident well and been well briefed beforehand, this particular case, which is the only example of this form, was almost Chaplinesque at times, with the two terrorists leaving their guns within easy reach of the hostages and demanding safe conduct from an airport that was no longer in operation.

2. Sieges Aimed Solely at Taking Hostages

Here it can be assumed the terrorists will have worked out most of the modalities of their act beforehand, but there is a high degree of discrepancy in the professionalism involved. During some sieges, the terrorists have conducted themselves with almost military precision and discipline, standing guard or sentry duty while the others slept, and being fully prepared and equipped for the siege. In fact, during the Chopin Express siege, one of the terrorists told the police "I have got plenty of pills... I can stand it forever." (12) During other sieges, such as the Black December siege of the Indian High Commission in London on February 20, 1973, there appeared to have been only slightly more planning than for sieges that occurred spontaneously. With variations as great as this, it is almost impossible to draw any general conclusions about how terrorists will conduct themselves, other than that they often appear to be more organized, more professional, more calculating, and, at least initially, more adamant in their demands.

LOCATION OF THE SIEGE

It is an accepted principle of customary international law that executive jurisdiction, the jurisdiction within which a state has sole decision-making power, is primarily territorial. (13) As a result, the physical location of a siege can be said to determine jurisdiction and thereby identify the decision-making body with ultimate authority over questions of response. Although sieges do not always occur within the same sort of location, it is possible to differentiate three jurisdictional variates.

Wholly within the Jurisdiction of One State

If a siege occurs within the territory and, therefore, jurisdiction of one state, the ultimate authority for deciding how to respond will rest with that state. If it occurs on private property, the State will still retain jurisdiction but may be liable for redress through the local law system for any damage caused by its agents during the response. This exclusive authority stems from a fundamental principle of international law which lays down as a basic right that each state shall have absolute jurisdiction "over persons and things and over events occurring within its territory." (14) (There are two exceptions to this, which form the other two categories to be examined later in this section.)

Under the federated structure of some states, authority over certain matter devolves from the federal to the regional level. The most pertinent of these, after executive jurisdiction, is judicial jurisdiction, whereby the regional authorities are invested with the power and duty to investigate, arrest, and bring to justice all those suspected of contravening the criminal law of the state and region. Unless the offense is deemed to be of severity sufficient to constitute a federal matter, the federal authorities may not intervene unless so requested by the regional authorities or unless their intervention is expressly provided for under the criminal code. For example, in West Germany, the specialized antiterrorist Border Patrol Group 9 is notionally part of the Brenzschutz (Border Patrol), which is under federal control and may not, therefore, be deployed within a <u>Land</u> (state) unless so requested by that <u>Land</u>. In the same vein, a decision to release prisoners, for example, once they are committed to jail can only be taken by the minister of justice of the <u>Land</u> where they are incarcerated, as was the case with the release of five prisoners in exchange for Peter Lorenz who had been kidnapped by the Bewegung 2 Juni (June 2 Movement) on February 27, 1975.

In the past, this division of responsibility has caused friction and acrimony between the decision-makers at different levels, especially when the response has proven inept. In the aftermath of the Munich Olympics siege, for instance, Willy Brandt, West Germany's federal chancellor at the time, publicly criticized the Bavarian authorities for refusing to allow the Federal Criminal Office to participate in the planned assault at Furstenfeldbruck Airfield. (15)

A further potential source of friction results when the siege necessitates a response from more than one government agency, as is frequently the case. For example, the Federal Ministries of the Interior, Justice, Foreign Affairs, and Defense as well as their <u>Land</u> equivalents and numerous police agencies were all involved in the response to the Munich Olympics siege. Each of these possessed a separate chain of command and may have been unable or even have refused to act unless the appropriate order was received from the appropriate source.

Moreover, relevant information that may be on file with one agency is not always disseminated to other agencies who are also involved, because of interagency rivalry, or simply because it was not thought to be important at the time, or because the information flow had reached crisis proportions and it was overlooked.

In an effort to overcome these sources of friction, many nations have now formally created centralized antiterrorist crisis management teams to coordinate the response to a hostage incident.

Lastly, sieges that occur within a closed institutional location, for example within jails, not only present the potential problems mentioned above but add a further decision-making body. (16) The governor or director of the institution concerned, along with its staff, are responsible for maintaining order within the institution. It will be their decision whether outside assistance is required once a hostage incident occurs. Generally, if outside agencies are brought in, any plan of action will have to have the consent of the prison authorities before it can be implemented.

Within a Foreign Embassy or Consultate

Sieges that occur within a foreign embassy or consulate create additional problems for the host government. The question of jurisdiction over diplomatic premises is frequently expressed in terms of extraterritoriality, which "involves a pretense that acts and events occurring on the premises have occurred in a foreign country." (17) In recent years this has largely been superseded by a functional notion of inviolability based on the necessity "to insure the independence and convenience of official functions." (18) This was formally codified by the 1961 Vienna Convention on Diplomatic Relations, which came into force on April 24, 1964, and also serves as the basis for all bilateral treaties on diplomatic and consular representation.

Of paramount relevance in terms of the restrictions and obligations placed upon a host government is Article 22, which states:

1. The premises of the mission shall be inviolable. The agents of the receiving State shall not enter them, except with the permission of the head of the mission.

2. The receiving State is under a special duty to take all appropriate steps to protect the premises of the mission against any intrusion or damage and to prevent any disturbance of the peace of the mission or impairment of its dignity. (19)

Similarly, Article 31 of the 1963 Vienna Convention on Consular Relations, which came into force on March 19, 1967, states:

1. Consular premises shall be inviolable to the extent provided in this Article.

2. The authorities of the receiving State shall not enter that part of the consular premises which is used exclusively for the purpose of the work of the consular post except with the consent of the head of the consular post or of his designee or of the head of the diplomatic mission of the sending State. The consent of the head of the consular post may, however, be assumed in case of fire or other disaster requiring prompt protective action.

3. Subject to the provisions of paragraph 2 of this Article, the receiving State is under a special duty to take all appropriate steps to protect the consular premises against any intrusion or damage and to prevent any disturbance of the peace of the consular post or impairment of its dignity. (20)

Although section 2 provides the host government with an automatic authority to mount "prompt protective action," in Western Europe, permission has always been sought before an assault was undertaken.

Under both conventions, then, a host government is obliged to prevent a siege from occurring in a foreign embassy or consulate. If or, rather, when it does occur, a host government may not mount an assault against the premises nor take any decision affecting it without the agreement of the head of the mission or, as is more commonly the case in Western Europe, of the mission's Foreign Ministry. Agreement has not always been forthcoming, and friction has frequently developed as a result of differing opinions among the two states over how to respond, as was the case with the West German embassy siege in Stockholm in

April 1975, despite assertions to the contrary. (21)   Moreover, any damage to the mission must be compensated for by the host government, regardless of "however diligently the local police performed their duties in trying to prevent damage." (22)

It is worth mentioning that reciprocal agreement must be forthcoming if the foreign government should wish to deploy their own antiterrorist force for an assault against their mission. Indeed, it has been noted that "a direct, physical exercise of one State's power within the territory of another - such as sending officials on to foreign soil to make an arrest - is, unless permitted by the passive State, a manifest illegality of a very elementary kind." (23)   This permission has not always been forthcoming either, as was the case with the French Embassy siege in the Hague in September 1974, when Dutch authorities refused the French government permission to even disembark their antiterrorist squad from the aircraft after it landed at Schipol Airport. (24)

Within an International/Intergovernmental Organization

Sieges that occur within international or intergovernmental organizations present similar restrictions on a host government's response. Most notable is, again, inviolability.

Article 2, Section 3 of the General Convention on the Privileges and Immunities of the United Nations, which was adopted by the General Assembly on February 13, 1964, (25) states:

> The premises of the United Nations shall be inviolable. The property and assets of the United Nations, wherever located and by whomsoever held, shall be immune from search, requisition, confiscation, expropriation and any form of interference, whether by executive, administrative, judicial, or legislative action. (26)

This notion was also incorporated into the Interim Agreement on Privileges and Immunities of the United Nations concluded between the Secretary General and the Swiss Federal Council on the establishment of a United Nations headquarters in Switzerland. This convention came into force on January 1, 1948, and of particular relevance here is Article 2, section 2, which states, "The premises of the United Nations shall be inviolable. The property and assets of the United Nations in Switzerland shall be immune." (27)

Similarly, the Convention on the Privileges and Immunities of the Specialized Agencies, (28) which was approved by the General Assembly on November 21, 1947, (29) also refers to inviolability. Specifically, Article 3, section 5 states that "the premises of the specialized agencies are immune." (30)

Other conventions afford similar inviolability to the premises of many intergovernmental organizations. (31)   For instance, Article 3, section 4 of the Agreement Between the Republic of Austria and the

Organization of Petroleum Exporting Countries Regarding the Headquarters of the Organization of Petroleum Exporting Countries, which
came into force on December 30, 1965, notes:

> The headquarters seat shall be inviolable. No officer or official of
> the Republic of Austria, or other person exercising public authority
> within the Republic of Austria, shall enter the headquarters seat to
> perform any duties therein except with the consent of, and under
> conditions approved by, the Secretary General. The consent of the
> Secretary General may, however, be assumed in the case of fire or
> other disaster requiring prompt protective action. (32)

As can be seen from these conventions and agreements, a host
government is circumscribed in its decision-making latitude over how to
respond to a siege if it occurs within an international/intergovernmental
organization. Moreover, any decisions that affect the organization
must be undertaken in consultation with the appropriate body within it.

NATURE OF THE HOSTAGES

The act of taking a hostage is frequently condemned as "a violation of
the person and an infringement of the freedom and basic human rights
to which everybody is entitled under international law." (33)
Numerous conventions already exist which oblige a host government to
guarantee and protect certain human rights of all those within its
jurisdiction. Although the Universal Declaration of Human Rights does
not have the force of law, the same fundamental principles have been
transformed into treaty provisions that establish legal obligations on the
part of each ratifying state through the United Nations General
Assembly's adoption of the International Covenant on Civil and Political
Rights and its subsequent entry into force on March 23, 1976.
According to the covenant's Article 2,

1. Each State Party to the present Covenant undertakes to respect
   and to ensure to all individuals within its territory and subject to
   its jurisdiction the rights recognized in the present Covenant,
   without distinction of any kind, such as race, colour, sex,
   language, religion, political or other opinion, national or social
   origin, property, birth or other status.

2. Where not already provideᴄ for by existing legislative or other
   measures, each State Party to the present Covenant undertakes
   to take the necessary steps, in accordance with its constitutional
   processes and with the provisions of the present Covenant, to
   adopt such legislative or other measures as may be necessary to
   give effect to the rights recognized in the present Covenant.

3. Each State Party to the present Covenant undertakes:

(a) To ensure that any person whose rights or freedoms as herein recognized are violated shall have an effective remedy, notwithstanding that the violation has been committed by persons acting in an official capacity;

(b) To ensure that any person claiming such a remedy shall have his right thereto determined by competent judicial, administrative or legislative authorities, or by any other competent authority provided for by the legal system of the State, and to develop the possibilities of judicial remedy;

(c) To ensure that the competent authorities shall enforce such remedies when granted. (34)

The rights thereby guaranteed that are of primary relevance here are specified in Articles 6 and 9:

Article 6 (1)   Every human being has the inherent right to life. This right shall be protected by law.   No one shall be arbitrarily deprived of his life.

Article 9 (1)   Everyone has the right to liberty and security of person. (35)

Similarly, the Council of Europe Convention for the Protection of Human Rights and Fundamental Freedoms, which came into force on September 3, 1953, states:

Article 1   The High Contracting Parties shall secure to everyone within their jurisdiction the rights and freedoms defined in Section 1 of this Convention.

Article 2 (1)   Everyone's right to life shall be protected by law.   No one shall be deprived of his life intentionally save in the execution of a sentence of a court following his conviction of a crime for which this penalty is provided by law... .

Article 5 (1)   Everyone has the right to liberty and security of person. (36)

Other conventions already prohibit the taking of hostages in certain circumstances. The Article 3 common to the four Geneva Conventions of 1949, which all came into force on October 21, 1950, reads:

(1) Persons taking no active part in the hostilities, including members of armed forces who have laid down their arms and those placed hors de combat by sickness, wounds, detention, or any other cause, shall in all circumstances be treated humanely, without any adverse distinction founded on race, colour, religion or faith, sex, birth, wealth, or any other similar criteria.

To this end, the following acts are and shall remain prohibited at any time and in any place whatsoever with respect to the above mentioned persons:

(b) taking of hostages;... (37)

More specifically, Article 34 of the Geneva Convention Relative to the Protection of Civilian Persons in Time of War categorically states, "The taking of hostages is prohibited." (38)

Similarly, the seizure of passengers on board civilian aircraft is proscribed by the three antiskyjacking conventions. For example, Article 1 of the Hague Convention of 1970 for the Suppression of Unlawful Seizure of Aircraft, which came into force on October 14, 1971:

Any person who on board an aircraft in flight:

(a) unlawfully, by force or threat thereof, or by any other form of intimidation, seizes, or exercises control of, that aircraft, or attempts to perform any such act, or

(b) is an accomplice of a person who performs or attempts to perform any such act commits an offence. (39)

While neither the United Nations nor the League of Nations before it have been successful in establishing a general convention against terrorism, (40) two regional intergovernmental organizations have done so. (41) For example, the Council of Europe Convention on the Suppression of Terrorism, which came into force on August 4, 1978, does not prohibit the taking of hostages but does regard the act as a nonpolitical offence and thereby provides for the extradition of hostage-takers. Specifically, Article 1 states:

For the purposes of extradition between Contracting States, none of the following offences shall be regarded as a political offense or as an offence connected with a political offence or as an offence inspired by political motives:...

c. a serious offence involving an attack against the life, physical integrity or liberty of internationally protected persons, including diplomatic agents;

d. an offence involving kidnapping, the taking of a hostage or serious unlawful detention;...

f. an attempt to commit any of the foregoing offences or participation as an accomplice of a person who commits or attempts to commit such an offence. (42)

Although the final draft Convention Against the Taking of Hostages has not yet been adopted by the General Assembly, (43) various already accepted principles of international law can be seen to be applicable, but are dependent upon the nature of the hostages who have been seized. However, to suggest that hostages taken in sieges can be likened to the characters in Orwell's Animal Farm, in that "all animals are equal but some are more equal than others," (44) is perhaps misleading and probably empirically incorrect. (45) Nonetheless, it is true that some categories of potential hostages are "more equal than others" in terms of the protective obligations their presence imposes on a host government. For our purposes here, hostages have been divided into those who are citizens of the host government and those who are not, and then further subdivided into civilians, politicians/symbolic leaders, and, lastly, diplomatic staff.

Civilians of a Host Government

It can be stated as axiomatic that a state is under a fundamental duty to protect its citizens. Indeed, it has rightly been suggested that one of the most elementary goals actively sustained by societies in the pursuit of order is precisely this obligation "to ensure that life will be in some measure secure against violence resulting in death or bodily harm." (46)

A terrorist siege involving hostages whose only crime was that they happened to be in the wrong place at the wrong time will most acutely focus the citizenry's attention on whether the government is willing or capable of providing this protection. Moreover, "if the terrorist weapon can be shown to pay off against a particular government then that government and its political moderates will find their power and authority undermined." (47) Failure can lead to a loss of the people's confidence in the government, which may result in the withdrawal of support and thereby precipitate an early election. This potentially may bring about the downfall of the government in favour of another that is perceived as more committed to the maintenance of law and order. Interestingly enough, a government's failure, or what has been popularly perceived as a failure, to provide this protection has been taken up as a campaign issue by right-wing parties during elections in both West Germany and Austria.

Politicians/Symbolic Leaders of a Host Government

It has been suggested that a hostage is frequently a mere symbol as far as the hostage-taker is concerned. (48) Nowhere is this more the case than with politicians and other symbolic leaders, such as royalty, or leading figures in the commercial or industrial sectors, whose very occupation is representative of the "bourgeois-capitalist system" the terrorist usually wants to change or destroy. An attack against one of these individuals is essentially an attack against the system itself. From the terrorists' point of view, it is also more cost-effective to attack a symbol of the system or an individual who constitutes an integral part of the system than to engage in a larger-scale revolutionary war, for which they may not be structurally or logistically equipped.

A host government's obligations to protect its citizens naturally includes its politicians and various symbolic leaders. In fact, this obligation may be assumed to be of a greater importance or of a more pressing nature solely because of the symbolism involved. In England, for example, royalty and senior cabinet ministers are routinely guarded by armed members of New Scotland Yard's Criminal Investigation Department, regardless of any specific threat against them. Other politicians and, for that matter, any individual will normally be accorded the same level of protection should the need arise, for example if his or her name has been found on a terrorist group's list of potential targets.

Should this protection not be forthcoming after a specific threat, feelings of alienation will almost certainly develop in the individual and among his colleagues, which may result in the withdrawal of their support for the government. Furthermore, should the protection fail to thwart an attack, this may lead to the belief the host government is unable to protect itself and is being impotent against the terrorists. This may result in a minor propaganda victory for the terrorists at the very least, as terrorism is "par excellence, a weapon of psychological warfare." (49)

Civilians of a Foreign Government

International attempts at codifying a host government's obligations toward nationals of a foreign country have so far generally met with failure. (50) The most that can be said is that under customary international law, a host government is obliged to provide "a modicum of respect for the life, liberty, dignity and property of foreign nationals, such as may be expected in a civilized community, . . . unhindered access to the courts and reasonable means of redress in the case of manifest denial, delay or abuse of justice." (51) More important, the treatment an alien receives may be reciprocally meted out to nationals of the host state in the alien's country, as indeed occurred to West Germans in Egypt and Libya following the Bonn government's decision to impose travel and residence restrictions on Arabs after the Munich Olympics siege in 1972.

In Western Europe, this obligation was specifically written into the European Convention on Establishment, which came into force on February 23, 1965. Of particular relevance here is Article 4:

Nationals of any Contracting Party shall enjoy in the territory of any other Party treatment equal to that enjoyed by nationals of the latter Party in respect of the possession and exercise of private rights, whether personal rights or rights relating to property. (52)

If, for any reason, a foreign national is injured as a result of any activity beyond the control of the host government, the "State's duty is discharged if the alien is permitted redress through the municipal law system." (53)   Otherwise, "a State is amenable to a claim when it is directly inculpated, either because its officials failed in their duty to prevent the act from occurring, or because the actor was a State agent." (54)

Foreign Dignitaries

The protection a host government is obliged to provide for foreign dignitaries is codified under international law as well as under various national legislative decrees, such as the British Diplomatic Privileges Act of 1964. (55)   However, here the degree of protection is commensurate with the type of dignitary in question. As a result, it is possible to identify three categories that can be subsumed under this heading.

1. Diplomatic Personnel

Diplomatic personnel have been regarded as worthy of special protection at least since 423 BC. (56) However, it was not until the Treaty of Westphalia in 1648 that an attempt was made to systematically codify "the special duties of protection which the receiving state owed the representatives of the sending state." (57) In more recent times, this practice has been expressed in Article 29 of the Vienna Convention on Diplomatic Relations which states:

> The person of a diplomatic agent is inviolable. He shall not be liable to any form of arrest or detention. The receiving state shall treat him with due respect and shall take all appropriate steps to prevent any attack on his person, freedom or dignity. (58)

Similarly, a host government is obliged to protect consuls, as Article 40 of the Vienna Convention on Consular Relations states:

> The receiving State shall treat consular officers with due respect and shall take all appropriate steps to prevent any attack on their person, freedom or dignity. (59)

By 1971, the increase in the number of terrorist attacks against diplomatic personnel led the United Nations to study the issue and eventually to adopt the Convention on the Prevention and Punishment of Crimes Against Internationally Protected Persons, Including Diplomatic Agents, and its subsequent entry into force on February 20, 1977. Specifically, according to Article 1, section 1 (b),

> any representative or official of a state or any official or other agent of an international organization of an intergovernmental character who, at the time when and in the place where a crime

against him, his official premises, his private accommodation or his means of transport is committed, is entitled pursuant to international law to special protection from any attack on his person, freedom or dignity, as well as members of his family forming part of his household. (60)

2. A Foreign Head of State or Government

It has been noted that "if a state agrees to a private or official visit by a Head of State or Government, international law obliges the host state to protect his personal safety and dignity. (61) This practice was also codified under the Convention on the Prevention and Punishment of Crimes Against Internationally Protected Persons, Including Diplomatic Agents. Specifically, Article 1, section 1 (a) requires special protection for

a Head of State, including any member of a collegial body performing the functions of a Head of State under the constitution of the State concerned, a Head of Government or a Minister for Foreign Affairs, whenever such a person is in a foreign state as well as members of his family who accompany him. (62)

3. Personnel of International/Intergovernmental Organizations

The final category includes the secretary general and the secretariat of the various international/intergovernmental organizations. While the permanent representatives of the member countries to the United Nations are accorded the same privileges and immunities enjoyed by other diplomatic agents, (63) only the secretary general and all assistant secretaries general of the secretariat are similarly immune. (64) Other employees only enjoy exchange privileges and repatriation facilities in time of an international crisis, on the same level as diplomats of comparable rank. (65) Experts on missions for the United Nations are only "accorded such privileges and immunities as are necessary for the independent exercise of their mission." (66)

The executive head of the various specialized agencies is also accorded the privileges and immunities normally extended to diplomats. (67) The secretary general and deputy secretary general of the Council of Europe also enjoy the same privilege. (68) Similarly, the executive secretary "and such other permanent officials of similar rank as may be agreed between the Chairman of the Council of Deputies and the Governments of Member States" of NATO (69) and the secretary general, deputy secretary general, and chiefs of departments of OPEC (70) are also granted the privileges and immunities of a diplomat. However, the secretariat staffs of these organizations are only accorded very limited privileges, such as repatriation in times of international crisis.

A host government, then, is under a very special obligation to protect these individuals. Failure to do so could, at the very least, lead to international condemnation and censure. However, holding a government "'strictly accountable' . . . usually plays right into the terrorists' hands, particularly when one of the kidnapper's major purposes is to harm the relations between the countries in the hope of discrediting the government they are trying to overthrow." (71)

A further operationally restrictive variable that must be recognized here derives from the emerging field of study of hostage victimization. (72) Of initial importance may be the need to provide medical attention for those wounded during the seizure. It has been noted that this "initial weapons effect is basically a common one incapacitating the respiratory and/or the circulatory system." (73) However, after excluding those wounded during the main attack before hostages were taken, only seven of the 901 siege victims were wounded during their actual seizure.

Once the siege occurs, a hostage will initially be scared, psychologically disoriented, and probably in shock, with all these effects exacerbated by the presence of violence in one form or another. If the hostage survives his initial capture, and only nine people have been killed during the initial seizure, his natural physiological processes will take over and he will start trying to cope with the stress of the situation. Interestingly enough, it has been observed "that the psychological stress response is an adaptive mechanism that helps the body avoid breakdowns in function, while at the same time . . . the stress response itself can lead to breakdowns and disease. (74) One is here reminded of the 105 children taken hostage at the Bovensmilde Elementary School by South Moluccans on May 23, 1977 who all developed gastroenteritis during their first week of captivity.

Perhaps the most important and still least understood reaction is the bond of identification that develops between the hostages and the terrorists. This process of transference of loyalties or, as it has become known, the Stockholm syndrome - after an incident during a criminally motivated bank siege at the Kreditbanken at Norrmalmstorg in central Stockholm on August 23, 1973, during which one of the hostages apparently had intimate relations with the would-be bank robber and later refused to testify against him - does not develop immediately but appears to be well entrenched by the third day of captivity. Most if not all hostages have later admitted to having some positive feelings toward their captors (75) and, indeed, it has been defined as "that unholy alliance between captor and captive, involving fear, distrust or anger towards the authorities on the outside. (76) The degree of identification is dependent on "(1) the length of time the hostage and captors are confined; (2) the quality of the interaction - were the hostages well treated?; (3) the existence of predetermined racial or ethnic hostilities between the hostage and captor; (4) the predisposition on the part of some hostages to seek out and relate to their captors." (77) This process has now led to the formulation of a fundamental axiom of hostage negotiations: the "longer the hostage situation lasts, the less likelihood the victims will be killed." (78) However, another product of the Stockholm syndrome is that "law enforcement must know that it can never rely upon the victim for help or even to help himself." (79)

NATURE OF THE TERRORISTS

Research on the nature of terrorist groups and on the behavioral dynamics of different groups under different circumstances is still far from complete. From what factual data we do have (80) it becomes possible and indeed mandatory to dispel some of the patently absurd generalizations about terrorists that still unfortunately abound.

To begin with, early assumptions that terrorists exhibited "successive regressions to paranoid schizophrenic reactions which were accompanied by inpourings of crude, murderous/suicidal introjected paternal impulses." (81) have never been universally proven. Nor has the notion that, somehow, terrorists represent a new phenotype. (82) It is also highly unlikely that terrorists are any "more or less . . . a whole group of psychopaths" (83) than were the Special Operations Executive Agents who operated in occupied Western Europe during World War II, although they too were termed terrorists. (84) Even recently, at a major international conference on international terrorism, one speaker is reported not only to have stated that a "typical terrorist" does exist but even to have described her creation as an "introspective, moody, egocentric, exhibitionistic would-be-artist without talent and with an urge to be a martyr." (85)

Other, more qualified specialists are reported to have serious doubts about whether a "terrorist personality" even exists, (86) and the only profile of terrorists yet published ignores this notion entirely. (87) Even if a psychopathic terrorist personality is found to exist, "there is little evidence to support the popular beliefs, either that mentally ill offenders are necessarily dangerous, or that all dangerous offenders are mentally ill." (88) Naive oversimplifications and gross generalizations about the personality of terrorists overlook the highly significant reinforcing effect of various cultural, environmental, and structural factors that may lead an individual to engage in terrorism. Suppositions that make that mistake can easily lead to the creation of a self-fulfilling fallacy. In fact, it would be as utterly impossible for any two terrorists to be precisely the same in personality as it would be for any two individuals.

Moreover, it must be remembered that "terrorist" is all too often used as a pejorative term. Even Menachem Begin concedes that during his leadership of the Irgun Zvai Leumi, "our enemies called us terrorists." (89)

Therefore, until such time as more research can be conducted on this topic, it seems more appropriate, and indeed a safer proposition, to remain content with the basic recognition that terrorists are, after all, still human. Indeed, it has been speculated that "human frailty is, perhaps, the only constant they all share." (90) As such, there would be no reason to suppose their behavior will not be governed by the same fundamental principles and processes that apply to all human inter- actions. If a notion such as that a terrorists' "cause . . . is the sine qua non of his actions; except for his belief in the cause, he would be in all respects rational" (91) can be accepted as paradigmatic, then other findings from, for instance, group dynamics should be equally valid. (92) For example, it can be assumed that the mere possession of a firearm or other type of weapon in conjunction with a threat to use it against one of the hostages will, at minimum, result in an increased latent potential for violence. This is especially pertinent if one of the terrorists begins to feel a need to prove himself to others in his group, probably in an effort to increase his status and improve his hierarchical position. This was undoubtedly the case with the leader of the group of South Moluccans who seized the Beilen train on December 2, 1975 and who was later wounded when his weapon accidentally discharged.

It can be stated as axiomatic that not all terrorist groups aspire to the same goals, nor are they driven by the same primary motives and cannot therefore be assumed to engage in hostage-taking for the same reasons nor, for that matter, be counted upon to respond in the same ways. In fact, it has been suggested that these differences "may be due to the group's ideology, the availability of targets, regional cultures of violence, societal norms, group strength in terms of firepower, logistics, and personnel, public support for the group (real and perceived), security systems of the potential targets, and the preferences of the group's leaders." (93) Some groups, such as the Japanese Rengo Sekigum (United Red Army) exhibit a greater proclivity toward violence and are presumably more likely to kill their hostages if demands are not met. This appears to be the assumption the French government worked under during the Japanese Red Army siege of the French embassy in the Hague on September 13, 1974, when it agreed to enter into negotiations with the terrorists only after it learned who they were and that other members of the same group had previously been responsible for the killing of 25 Puerto Rican pilgrims at Lod Airport in Israel on May 30, 1972. Other groups, such as the various student groups that have seized hostages, have never killed one of their hostages.

Different groups have different norms and standards of behavior which can be assumed to function as a model or guide for future behavior, especially during similar operations, and will almost certainly be adhered to by the various members of the group if they wish to retain their membership in it. For example, if a group or a faction within that group has engaged in hostage-taking before, their previous behavior and conduct, for instance releasing women and children or sick hostages, is more likely to be replicated by other members of the same faction in the future once that particular norm has been established. For this reason, accurate files on past incidents and up-to-date intelligence on any changes in leadership or apparent behavior patterns are an operational necessity.

It can also be assumed that claims of membership in a particular terrorist group imply a willingness to live up to group expectations of behavior and, more significantly, that the need to be seen as a member of a particular group is more overpowering and primary than the fear of retaliation or punishment because of membership. Freud's observation about group identification under conditions of external danger seems highly applicable to terrorist groups as well.

For the moment it [the group] replaces the whole of human society, which is the wielder of authority, whose punishments the individual fears, and for whose sake he has submitted to so many inhibitions. It is clearly perilous for him to put himself in opposition to it, and it will be safer to follow the example of those around him and perhaps even "hunt with the pack." In obedience to the new authority he may put his former "conscience" out of action, and so surrender to the attraction of the increased pleasure that is clearly obtained from the removal of inhibitions. (94)

A further Freudian theory of group behavior that appears to be equally applicable are the group's transference reactions towards their leader, who fulfills the function of a parent surrogate. It has been noted that members of the group who are directly exposed to external danger "become extraordinarily sensitive to his [the leader's] demands, continually attempting to do and say things that will please him, reacting with bitter disappointment at any apparent slights, and becoming depressed or aggrieved whenever they are not in communication with him." (95) One example of this need to impress and gain the approval of the leader occurred during the OPEC siege, when Gabriele Kroecker-Tiedeman boasted to Carlos, the leader, "I've killed two." (96)

Terrorist groups can be classified according to various criteria, such as ideology, tactical and strategic goals, structural and organizational size, or sociological composition. (97) However, three specific indices are sufficient for our purposes here: political orientation, strategic goals, and theatre of operations. Some groups, such as the Harkis or the Action pour la Renaissance de la Corse (ARC), are either not overly politicized or have an unclear, even confused political orientation and are not amenable to any form of categorization other than "nationalist-separatist." The Ambonese, on the other hand, have evolved into a Marxist group, following their initial political uncertainty, and now refer to themselves as South Moluccans, reflecting their claim for the return of the entire South Moluccan archipelago from Indonesia, and should, therefore, be termed an "exile minority." Conversely, the Irish Republican Army-Provisional Wing (IRA-Provo) seemed to adopt a left-wing stance only when it became apparent that their American sources of arms were drying up. Moreover, due to the constant fractionalizing and splintering that goes on within terrorist groups, for practical considerations or in imitation of Beau Geste groups are frequently formed and then renamed after one or two forays. It should not, however, be assumed that all terrorist groups are necessarily left-wing. The Ustashi, for example, was originally formed under the direct sponsorship of the Italian Fascists in the early 1930s and still retains much of its early right-wing orientation. (98)

Despite the increasing linkages between terrorist groups and the occasional revolutionary conferences they hold, (99) there is no evidence to suggest that all terrorist groups share a common long-term goal. Admittedly, a superordinate goal has bound diverse groups together for a specific action, such as the Japanese Red Army attack on Lod Airport in the name of the Palestinian revolution, but this is the exception rather than the rule. Even the Palestinian Liberation Organization (PLO), which perceives itself as the sole legitimate representative and virtual government in exile of the Palestinian people, does not always enjoy a commonality of purpose, and has experienced frequent outbursts of acrimony between its constituent factions, if not outright belligerency. Nor is there any reason to believe that a worldwide coalition of terrorists, a "Terror International," exists or is even feasible. Some groups, such as the Japanese Red Army, espouse world revolution whereas others, such as the Italian Brigate Rosse (Red Brigades), are bent on destroying a host government but appear to offer no structural substitute. Operating on an entirely different level are groups such as the ARC, who solely want independence for what they consider to be their land while, others, such as the Harkis, desire no more than equality with the indigenous population. Furthermore, some groups appear to exist solely for the purpose of combating their rivals, such as the Jewish Defense League versus the Palestinians, or the Ulster Defense Association versus the IRA.

The name chosen by the terrorists for their group is often heavily imbued with symbolism and is frequently a commemoration of some past achievement or defeat. For example, one of the smallest and most secretive of the South Moluccan factions is the Action Group January 18, which was named after the date of the first meeting between the South Moluccans and the Vietnamese Liberation Front. Conversely, Black September and Black June were named after the months when devastating offensives had been mounted against Palestinian strongholds in Jordan in 1970 by the Jordanian Army and in Lebanon in 1976 by the Syrian Army, respectively. Groups with names such as these can be expected to intensify their activities on those particularly symbolic dates in order to restore their prestige and revitalize their self-esteem. Similarly, a certain date may be chosen for an operation that commemorates some occurrence in the group's past, especially if it represents a defeat for which they must now exact revenge, as was the case with the Saudi Arabian embassy siege in Paris by Black September exactly one year after their defeat at Furstenfeldbruck Airfield. Abu Daoud, the organizer of the raid, was held to be responsible for it and his release from a Jordanian jail was demanded in the Paris siege.

It has been suggested that "kidnappings are more likely in countries where the terrorists are operating on home terrain and have an underground organization" and that "barricade and hostage incidents are more likely when the terrorists are operating abroad or in countries where they lack the capability for sustaining underground opera-tions." (100) Although this may be a matter of expediency more than anything else, the experience of Western Europe does appear to bear this out. Of the 21 hostage incidents that can be attributed to groups operating abroad, 16 were sieges and five were kidnappings. Similarly, the South Moluccans, who generally have not integrated into Dutch society and do not possess any real underground network outside of their own communities, have only conducted sieges. However, there are some notable exceptions to this rule. The Palestinians, for example, possess an undeniable organizational ability and an effective, albeit generally unknown, underground capability in Western Europe, but have never engaged in kidnapping outside of Lebanon. The Rote Armee Fraktion (Red Army Faction), on the other hand, has now apparently abandoned sieges in favor of kidnappings following their abortive attack on the West German embassy in Stockholm in 1975. Furthermore, with the possible exception of the South Moluccans, terrorist groups operating in Western Europe have employed hostage-taking as only one of many tactics, including bombings and assassinations, and many groups now appear to have almost foresaken political hostage-taking in favor of these. For example, the ETA recently began to employ the IRA-Provo tactic of "kneecapping" their kidnap victims instead of demanding a ransom, as was the case with the kidnapping of Ignacio Iturzaeta on September 13, 1978.

GOVERNMENTAL POLICY

The final variable to be considered is governmental policy, and specifically how policy can limit response options.

Various authors have argued that a government of the type found in Western Europe must formulate its counterterrorist policies in accordance with several basic rules or principles if public trust and confidence are to be retained. In fact, terrorism has been called "the indirect strategy that wins or loses only in terms of how you respond to it." (101)

One such principle is "firmness and the determination to uphold constitutional authority and the rule of law." (102) Decisions on policy and its implementation must remain the sole purview of those democratically elected to fulfill that function, and not be shared with special departments invested with unlimited powers and no public accountability. The constitution itself must not be temporarily abrogated for a selected few, as was the case in West Germany during the first week of October 1977, when, following the kidnapping of Hans-Martin Schleyer, the president of the Employers' and Industrial Association, special legislation was drafted and passed within three days denying the fundamental right of access to a lawyer to roughly 90 imprisoned terrorists. Moreover, any policy finally adopted must be within the law. In some countries this has necessitated a change in the legal code; again, this has occurred in West Germany, where, at the time of the Munich Olympics, the police were forbidden by law to "shoot to kill." At the same time, laws must not be changed to the extent that they become repressive. This, it has been argued, may be precisely the response the terrorists are hoping for, as one of their objectives may be "to provoke a government to ill-judged measures of repression that will alienate public opinion." (103) Finally, the response must be authorized by those in elected positions of power as part of an overall strategy and not conducted by individuals solely motivated by revenge, as occurred in Northern Ireland in the kidnapping of a Roman Catholic priest, Father Hugh Murphy, in Ulster on June 18, 1978 by a Royal Ulster Constabulary sergeant and constable in revenge for the kidnap and subsequent murder of a fellow RUC officer, Constable William Turbitt, the day before. (On December 14, 1979, the two officers were arrested and charged for this incident.)

A second fundamental principle for a Western European government to adhere to is the necessity of being "seen to act in order to restore confidence." (104) This, of course, does not diminish the importance of intelligence gathering nor preclude hostage-negotiation in favor of an assault. Rather it refers to the requirement that a "government must be seen to be doing all in its power to defend the life and limb of citizens." (105) This is most readily accomplished by the simple process of physically responding to a siege and surrounding the building, setting up police cordons, and putting up roadblocks. Interestingly enough, this requirement necessarily implies that a government must respond to a terrorist siege even though it has been suggested that one alternative response could be "no contact, whereby the entire situation is ignored." (106)

Finally, it has been "offered as a fundamental premise that all counterterrorist measures ought to constitute in themselves a civilized response to an uncivilized action." (107) Whether the Israeli government's Mivtzan Elohim assassination squads, formed to avenge the 11 Israeli athletes killed by Black September at the Munich Olympics, constitute a civilized response is, of course, dependent on the observer's value orientation toward Israel. In this particular case, however, the outcome apears to have been counterproductive, especially after the arrest and conviction of one of the squads for killing the wrong man in Lillehammer, Norway on July 21, 1973 and the international condemnation and friction that followed. It also appears to have initiated a new wave of Palestinian terrorism directed against Israel and particularly against the "softer" targets of Israelis living abroad, with retaliatory assassinations, such as that of Colonel Yosef Alon, the air attache at the Israeli embassy in Washington, D.C. on July 1, 1973, and a wave of letter bombs sent to Israeli diplomats throughout the world. Nonetheless, this illustrates how far one government has been willing to go in response to a siege and serves as a reminder that terrorism "almost inevitably begets counterterrorism and sets in motion a downward spiral towards intensified competition of all concerned in the refinements of barbarism." (108)

Every policy that is finally adopted will have evolved from a number of factors - the individual government's previous experience, the desire to be seen as supporting some specific regional or international goal such as political order, the necessity of balancing long-term goals against the exigencies of the moment, the perceptions and personalities of the key decision-makers involved and their desire to increase their status and self-esteem, an appreciation of the public's demands and an estimation of what measures they will accept and tolerate, as well as a basic recognition of the three general principles outlined above. The policy itself can be placed on a continuum ranging from a no-concession stance, as has always been the case in Turkey, to a more flexible approach, as is the case in the Netherlands, to outright capitulation, as was initially the case in Austria but has since been altered due to international pressure.

The no-concessions policy is based on the belief that the best deterrent against future operations is to never give in to demands, no matter what the cost in terms of hostages' lives. For example, Sir Robert Mark, the former commissioner of the London Metropolitan Police who directed the response to the Balcombe Street siege, commented,

> Though we were deeply concerned about the fate of the two hostages I did not consider for a moment that they were not expendable. I felt heartfelt sympathy for Mr. and Mrs. Matthews [the two hostages] but felt that human life was of little importance when balanced against the principle that violence must not be allowed to succeed. (109)

The more flexible approach treats every incident as unique and is based on the belief that an ad hoc response is more appropriate. Nevertheless, there are certain boundaries to such ad hoc procedures. Colonel Ulrich Wegener of the West German Border Patrol Group 9 antiterrorist squad, for example, said that: "the moment the hijackers throw the first dead hostage from the plane . . . we are faced with the necessity to act. From that moment on, force is the only answer." (110)

Outright capitulation to demands may succeed in saving the lives of the hostages but may also serve to invite future operations against the same government. One of the Palestinian skyjackers of a British Airways VC-10 in March 1974 later confirmed that Holland had been chosen as a landing place solely because his superiors had told him the Dutch authorities were more tolerant and sentences were relatively light there. (111)

There is, however, no firm evidence in Western Europe to suggest that one form of policy has a greater deterrent value than another. In Turkey, for example, although acts of terrorism such as the taking of hostages have always been punishable by hanging, kidnappings and sieges still occur. Austria, although rapidly capitulating at first, has not become a regular target for terrorists since. It must be remembered that a deterrent is only effective if the terrorists are willing to allow themselves to be deterred and to date this does not appear to be the case.

On a more immediate, tactical level are the contingency plans by which a government lays down what, for example, can and cannot be negotiated, or at least what can be negotiated in return for the release of the hostages. These contingency plans, in turn, must be devised in accordance with that particular government's policy and capabilities. In Italy and Spain, for example, the payment of a ransom is illegal and any contingency plan must take this into account. Similarly, a contingency plan must realistically be based on a government's capabilities. As assault, for example, should not be contemplated unless trained personnel are available to conduct it, as the ineptitude of the Furstenfeldbruck Airfield assault proved. The government's policy on the sanctity of a hostage's life must also be taken into consideration. For instance, the principles governing the response of the Cologne Criminal Police to a hostage incident state: "The protection of the lives and physical well-being of the hostages and innocent bystanders has absolute priority over the apprehension of offenders or the safeguarding of property. (112) Indeed, a major conference on hostage-taking in 1976 concluded:

> In purely operational terms, advance contingency planning was seen to be critical and the following elements were seen to be essential in any initial response plan: clarity of command, availability of specialists, establishment of communications, establishing secure location (containment), control of firepower, option to negotiate, option to deploy special weapons, media briefings, accurate infor-mation gathering. (113)

Furthermore, contingency plans must be drawn up in advance under stress-free conditions, since there will be little time, and certainly not the right atmosphere, to engage in any effective, organized planning that takes into account the probable social impact that will result during the actual siege. It was also concluded that governments should keep promises made during negotiations with the terrorists, as "bad faith bargaining was seen to be a harmful tactic, not only because it diminishes public trust in the State, but also because of its possible effect on subsequent incidents, either precipitating additional, retalia-tory incidents or causing future offenders to employ measures (e.g. retention of women, children or sick hostages . . .) to ensure meeting of demands and fulfillment of promises." (114)

CONCLUSION

The main attribute of this form of typology is it provides a common conceptual framework for a crosscase analysis of the various opera-tional restrictions imposed upon a host government. Once the restrictions and modalities of an incident are understood, a govern-ment's response to it can be planned accordingly. The schema presented above is intentionally devoid of any provision for an analysis of the effectiveness and deterrent value of different forms of response. This needs to be done solely on a case-by-case basis, as it may otherwise constitute a misleading exercise. The response is the result of specific factors germane to each siege which, statistically at least, will never be exactly duplicated because of temporal and spatial variants. It must be remembered that each time a siege occurs, its outcome will also function as a new modifier to the future plans and intended behavior of the primary actors involved. While it is simply not known if or to what extent this learning process aids hostages in coping more appropriately with the trauma of being seized a second time, it is well known that a government will base future contingency plans on an evaluation of its success or failure in handling past incidents.

Finally, an analysis of the professionalism of some groups in the planning and execution of their sieges would tend to indicate this learning from past experiences is not an exclusive process. For example, the two Palestinians who seized four hostages on the Chopin Express train at Marchegg, Austria in 1973 had been foiled 20 days earlier when an Austrian border guard found their appearance and manner suspicious and turned them back. They were forced to modify their plans as a consequence and were successful on the next attempt. Nor, indeed, should it be assumed that terrorists are incapable of modifying their plans and behavior according to the often very detailed and readily available academic articles and conference papers on various aspects of a government's contingency plan, such as hostage-negotiation, if they so desired. This possibility was clearly intimated as fact by "Carlos" during the OPEC siege when he told Riyadh al-azzawi, the Iraqi charge d'affaires who acted as a mediator, "Tell Kreisky . . . that I know all the tricks." (115)

NOTES

(1) Western Europe is here defined as the 20 member-countries of the Council of Europe: Austria, Belgium, Cyprus, Denmark, France, the Federal Republic of Germany, Greece, Iceland, the Republic of Ireland, Italy, Luxembourg, Malta, the Netherlands, Norway, Portugal, Spain, Sweden, Switzerland, Turkey, and the United Kingdom of Great Britain.

(2) Wolf Middendorf, "Geiselnahme und Kidnapping," Kriminalistik 26, no. 12 (December 1972): 553.

(3) Ibid., p. 559.

(4) Cited in Brian Jenkins, "Testimony Before the Senate Government Affairs Committee," January 27, 1978, p. 6.

(5) This is the first of three categories of hostage-takers presented in "Hostages - a Viewpoint," RCMP Gazette 38, no. 10 (1977): 1.

(6) There are other factions within the Ustashi besides the Hrvatsko Revolucionario Bratstvo. See Stephen Clissold, "Croat Separatism: Nationalism, Dissidence, and Terrorism," Conflict Study No. 103 (London: Institute for the Study of Conflict, January 1979), p. 15.

(7) That terrorists hold the initiative during a kidnapping has been noted as a fundamental advantage of this form of hostage-taking. See Richard Clutterbuck, Kidnap and Ransom: The Response (London: Faber and Faber, 1978), p. 66; also Brian Jenkins, Janera Johnson, and David Ronfeldt, Numbered Lives (Santa Monica, Calif.: Rand, 1977), p. 9.

(8) A further nine people were killed during the initial seizure and another 11 during the assault which terminated the incident.

(9) This is the second of four categories of hostage-takers presented in "Hostage-Incident Response," Training Key no. 234 of the International Association of Chiefs of Police, reprinted in RCMP Gazette 38, no. 10 (1977): 12.

(10) Ibid.

(11) Frank Ochberg, "The Victim of Terrorism - Psychiatric Considerations," in Dimensions of Victimization in the Context of Terroristic Acts, ed. Ronald D. Crelinsten (Montreal: Universite de Montreal monograph, September 1977), p. 31.

(12) Cited in Guardian, September 29, 1973.

(13) See for example D.W. Greig, International Law (London: Butterworths, 1976), p. 210. Equally accepted is the protective principle of objective jurisdiction. This has been expressed by P. O'Connell International Law, 2nd ed. (London: Stevens and Sons, 1970), p. 827:

> Acts done outside a jurisdiction, but intended to produce and producing detrimental effects within it, justify a state in punishing the cause of the harm as if he had been present at the effect, if the state should succeed in getting him within its power.

However, in this section we are solely concerned with the restrictions placed on a host government in responding to a siege by the physical location and not with questions of which state has the authority to impose penal sanctions on the hostage-takers.

(14) Greig, International Law, p. 210.

(15) The Daily Telegraph, October 8, 1972. It is interesting to note that in May 1975, "the Lander agreed to the Federal Criminal Office exercising central control over police measures against terrorist violence." (Frank Gregory, "Protect and Violence: The Police Response," Conflict Study No. 75 (London: Institute for the Study of Conflict, September, 1976), p. 12.

(16) For a more detailed examination of the problems encountered in responding to sieges within jails, see James P. Needham, Neutralization of Prison Hostage Situations - A Model, AD/A-030 306 (Washington, D.C.: U.S. Department of Commerce, National Technical Information Service, August 1976).

(17) O'Connell, International Law, p. 903.

(18) Cherif Bassiouni and Ved P. Nanda, eds., A Treatise on International Criminal Law, 2 vols. (Springfield, Ill.: Charles C. Thomas, 1970) 2: 98. See also Ian Brownlie, Principles of Public International Law (Oxford: Clarendon Press, 1973), pp. 339-41.

(19) United Nations, Treaty Series (hereafter UNTS) 500, no. 7310; 96.

(20) UNTS, 596, no. 8638; 261.

(21) Guardian, April 24, 1975, and Financial Times, April 26, 1975.

(22) Greig, International Law, p. 580.

(23) R.Y. Jennings, "The Limits of State Jurisdiction," 32 Nordisk Tidsskrift for International Ret, 212, cited in Sami Shubber, Jurisdiction Over Crimes on Board Aircraft (The Hague: Martinus Nijhoff, 1973), p. 54, n. 23.

(24) International Herald Tribune, July 8, 1976.

(25) This convention is not universally in force, but only in those countries that have deposited their instruments of accession or subsequent ratification with the secretary general of the United Nations. For a complete list of countries where it is in force, see Multilateral Treaties in respect of which the Secretary-General performs Depository Functions: List of Signatures, Ratifications, Accessions, etc. as at 31 December 1978, ST/LEG.D/12, pp. 35-39.

(26) UNTS, 1, no. 4; 15.

(27) UNTS, 1, no. 8; 167. The United Nations Headquarters Agreement with the United States goes a step further and provides that officials of the U.S. shall not enter the headquarters building without the consent of the Secretary General (UNTS, 11, no. 147; 11, Article 3, s. 9 a). The ILO Headquarters Agreement with Switzerland is similar (UNTS 15, no. 103; 377, Article 7).

(28) The Specialized Agencies include the International Labour Organization, Food and Agriculture Organization, United Nations Educational, Scientific, and Cultural Organization, International Monetary Fund, International Bank for Reconstruction and Development, and the World Health Organization.

(29) This convention is not universally in force, but only in those countries which have indicated a specialized agency in their instruments of accession or subsequent ratification deposited with the secretary general of the United Nations. For a complete list of

countries where it is in force, see Multilateral Treaties, pp. 40-50.

(30) UNTS, 33, no. 521; 261.   See also ILO in UNTS, 33, no. 103, Articles 4 and 7; WHO in UNTS 26, no. 155; 331, Articles 4 and 7; WMO in UNTS 211, no. 524; 277, Article 7; ICAO in UNTS 96, no. 1335; 155, s. 4 (i).

(31) OEEC in European Yearbook, 1955, p. 245, Article 3; Council of Europe in UNTS 250, no. 3515; 12, Article 4; NATO in UNTS 200, no. 2691; 3, Article 6.   The Protocols to the ECSC, EEC, and the Euratom Conventions refer to "buildings and premises."

(32) Agreement Between the Republic of Austria and the Organization of Petroleum Exporting Countries Regarding the Headquarters of the Organization of Petroleum Exporting Countries (Vienna: OPEC, 1965).   Interestingly enough, it was this very issue of inviolability that finally persuaded OPEC to settle on Austria as the location for its headquarters rather than Switzerland.   Switzerland was the first choice but its government was unwilling to extend the same privilege.

(33) Statement by the Chilean representative, Mr. Arnello, during the discussion on the Draft Convention Against the Taking of Hostages at the 57th Meeting of the 6th committee on November 29, 1976, Official Records of the General Assembly, Thirty-First Session, A/.C.6/31/SR.57, para. 66.   For a highly moralistic condemnation of terrorism and hostage-taking, see Bernard Avishai, "Terrorism," New York Review of Books, March 8, 1979.

(34) Official Records of the General Assembly, Thirty-first Session, Annexes, agenda item 123, document A/31/391.

(35) Ibid.

(36) UNTS, 213, no. 2889; 221.

(37) The Geneva Convention for the Amelioration of the Condition of the Wounded and Sick in Armed Forces in the Field, in UNTS, 75, no. 970:   31; the Geneva Convention for the Amelioration of the Condition of the Wounded, Sick and Shipwrecked Members of Armed Forces at Sea in UNTS 75, no. 971:   85; the Geneva Convention Relative to the Treatment of Prisoners of War in UNTS, 75, no. 972: 135; and the Geneva Convention Relative to the Protection of Civilian Persons in Time of War in UNTS, 75, no. 973:   287.

(38) UNTS, 75, no. 973; 287.

(39) United States Treaties and Other International Agreements (hereafter USTOIA), 22, p. 2 (1971), no. TIAS 7192, p. 1644.   See also the Tokyo Convention of 1963 on Offences and Certain Other Acts Committed on Board Aircraft (in force on December 4, 1969), UNTS 704, no. 10106; 219, Article 1 and also the Montreal Convention of 1971 for the Suppression of Unlawful Acts Against the Safety of Civilian Aviation (in force on January 26, 1973), USTOIA, 24, p. 1 (1973), no. TIAS 7570, p. 568, Article 1.

(40) Since its formation on December 18, 1972, the U.N. Ad Hoc Committee on International Terrorism has been unable to even agree on a definition of its subject matter, let alone propose a draft convention. (See, for example, the Report of the Ad Hoc Committee on International Terrorism, Official Records of the General Assembly, Thirty-second Session, Supplement No. 37 (A/32/37). The equivalent committee of the League of Nations, however, did succeed in adopting a Draft Convention for Prevention and Punishment of Terrorism on January 15, 1936, but this was only ratified by India and never entered into force. (For the text of this Draft Convention, see Manley O. Hudson, International Legislation (Washington: Carnegie Endowment for International Peace, 1941), 7, no. 499: 862.

(41) To date, only the Council of Europe and the Organization of American States have adopted general conventions against terrorism. For the text of the 1971 OAS Convention to Prevent and Punish the Acts of Terrorism Taking the Form of Crimes Against Persons and Related Extortion that are of International Significance, see USTOIA (1971), no. 8413, especially Articles 1 and 2.

(42) European Treaty Series, no. 90, p. 2.

(43) With its 35th meeting on February 16, 1979, the Ad Hoc Committee on the Drafting of an International Convention Against the Taking of Hostages concluded its work and recommended that the General Assembly adopt the draft convention. For the text of this convention, see Official Records of the General Assembly, Thirty-fourth Session, Supplement No. 39 (A/34/39, pp. 22-29.

(44) George Orwell, Animal Farm (London: Penguin Books, 1975), p. 104.

(45) However, this is precisely the case with kidnap victims, in that some are indeed perceived to be more worthy of kidnapping than others. See for example Clutterbuck, Kidnap and Ransom; Sir William Hayter, The Politics of Kidnapping (London: Interplay, 1971); W.D. Mangham, "Kidnapping for Political Ends," in the Seaford House Papers, 1971 (Royal College of Defence Studies, 1972), pp. 1-23; and Edler Baumann, The Diplomatic Kidnappings (The Hague: Martinus Nijhoff, 1973).

(46) Hedley Bull, The Anarchical Society: A Study of Order in World Politics (London: Macmillan, 1977), p. 4-5.

(47) Paul Wilkinson, "Terrorism versus Liberal Democracy: The Problems of Response," Conflict Study No. 67 (London: Institute for the Study of Conlict, January 1976), p. 11. See also Paul Wilkinson, Terrorism and the Liberal State (London: Macmillan, 1977), pp. 80-92. Menachem Begin recalled, in this regard, "Even if the attack does not succeed, it makes a dent . . ., and that dent widens into a crack which is extended with every succeeding attack." The Revolt (London: W.H. Allen, 1979), p. 52.

(48) Harvey Schlossberg, cited in "Patient Sieges: Dealing with Hostage-Takers," Assets Protection, no. 3 (1975), p. 22.

(49) Wilkinson, Liberal State, p. 81.

(50) An exception to this general failure was the Havana Convention on the Status of Aliens of 1928; see League of Nations Treaty Series 132, no. 3045; 301, especially Article 5. For a more detailed examination of this issue, see Jordan J. Paust, ""Nonprotected" Persons or Things," in Legal Aspects of International Terrorism, ed. Alona E. Evans and John F. Murphy (Lexington, Mass.: Lexington Books, 1978), pp. 341-97.

(51) Georg Schwarzenberger, A Manual of International Law (Milton, Oxford: Professional Books, 1976), p. 84. See also Hans Kelsen, Principles of International Law, rev. and ed. Robert W. Tucker (New York: Holt, Rinehart and Winston, 1966), p. 366; and Shigeru Oda, "The Individual in International Law," in Manual of Public International Law, ed. Max Sorenson (New York: St. Martin's Press, 1968), p. 485.

(52) European Treaty Series, no. 19, p. 115.

(53) O'Connell, International Law, 2; 941.

(54) Ibid., p. 943.

(55) In fact, this particular act transforms the Vienna Conventions into internal law by scheduling them. See C.F. Amerasinghe, State Responsibility for Injuries to Aliens (Oxford: Clarendon Press, 1967), chs. 5-8.

(56) James Murphy, "The Role of International Law in the Prevention of Terrorist Kidnapping of Diplomatic Personnel," in International Terrorism and Political Crimes, ed. M. Cherif Bassiouni (Springfield, Ill.: Charles C. Thomas, 1975), p. 286. For a more detailed examination of diplomatic kidnappings, see Baumann, Diplomatic Kidnappings and John F. Murphy, "Protected Persons and Diplomatic Facilities," in Evans and Murphy, Legal Aspects, pp. 277-339.

(57) Murphy in Bassiouni, International Terrorism, p. 287.

(58) UNTS, 75, no. 7310.

(59) UNTS, 75, no. 8638.

(60) U.N. Document A/RES/3166, reprinted in International Legal Materials 8, no. 1, (January, 1974): 41-49. For a more detailed examination of this convention, see Louis M. Bloomfield and Gerald F. FitzGerald Crimes Against Internationally Protected Persons: Prevention and Punishment (New York: Praeger, 1976), especially chs. 4 and 5.

(61) Francis Deak, "Organs of States in their External Relations: Immunities and Privileges of State Organs and of the State," in Sorensen, Manual, p. 387.

(62) International Legal Materials.

(63) UNTS, 75, no, 4, Article 4, s. 9 (g).

(64) Ibid., Article 5, s. 19.

(65) Ibid, Article 5, s. 18 (e and f).

(66) Ibid., Article 6, s.22.

(67) UNTS, 75, no. 521, s. 21.

(68) UNTS, 75, no. 3515, Article 16.

(69) UNTS, 75, no. 2691, Article 20.

(70) OPEC Agreement, Article 20 (a and b).

(71) Murphy in Bassiouni, International Terrorism, p. 296.

(72) For a more detailed examination of this subject, see for example, Crelinsten, Dimensions of Victimization.

(73) Martin E. Silverstein, "Medical Rescue as an Antiterrorist Measure: A Strategist's "Cookbook," in Research Strategies for the Study of International Terrorism, ed. Ronald D. Crelinsten (Montreal: Universite de Montreal monograph, September 1977), p. 96.

(74) Walton T. Roth, "Psychosomatic Implications of Confinement by Terrorists," in Crelinsten, Dimensions of Victimization, p. 48.

(75) See, for example, Ochberg, Victim of Terrorism" in Crelinsten, Dimensions of Victimization, p. 27; and Brian Jenkins, Hostage Survival: Some Preliminary Observations (Santa Monica: Rand, April 1976), p. 6. For an interesting description by an exhostage, see Geoffrey Jackson, People's Prison (Newton Abbot: Readers Union, 1974), pp. 59-72.

(76) Ochberg, "Victim of Terrorism," p. 27.

(77) Abraham Miller, "Hostage Negotiations and the Concept of Transference," in Terrorism: Theory and Practice, ed. Yonah Alexander, David Carlton, and Paul Wilkinson (Boulder, Colo.: Westview, 1979), p. 144. See also Ochberg, "Victim of Terrorism," p. 28.

(78) Patrick Mullany, "Panelist's Report," in Hostage-Taking: Problems of Prevention and Control ed. Ronald D. Crelinsten and Danielle Laberge-Altmejd (Montreal: Universite de Montreal monograph, October 1976), p. 139.

(79) H.H.A. Cooper, testimony before the United States Senate, Criminal Laws and Procedures Subcommittee, July 21, 1977, in Political Terrorism: Volume 2, 1974-1978, Lester A. Sobel (Oxford: Clio Press, 1978), p. 19. See also Miller, "Hostage Negotiations," p. 144-45.

(80) See, among many examples, Gustave Morf, Terror in Quebec:

Studies of the FLQ (Toronto: Clarke, Irwin, 1970); Gideon Fishman, "Criminological Aspects of International Terrorism: The Dynamics of the Palestinian Movement," in Crime and Delinquency: Dimensions of Deviance, ed. Marc Riedel and Terence P. Thornberry (New York: Praeger, 1974); John B. Wolf, "Organization and Management Practices of Urban Terrorist Groups," in Terrorism 1, no. 2 (1978); and Charles A. Russell and Bowman H. Miller, "Profile of a Terrorist," in Terrorism 1, no. 1 (1977).

(81) David G. Hubbard, The Skyjacker: His Flights of Fantasy (London: Collier MacMillan, 1973), p. 21.

(82) D.V. Segre and J.H. Adler, "The Ecology of Terrorism," in Encounter 40, no. 2 (1973): 17-24.

(83) Maurice Cullinane, "Panelist's Report," in Hostage-Taking p. 225. See also "The Terrorist Organizational Profile: A Psychological Evaluation," SOARS, FBI Academy, unpublished, n.d., pp. 2-17.

(84) On October 18, 1942, Hitler issued his infamous "commando order," which stated that henceforth all saboteurs were to be executed as terrorists. See M.R.D. Foot, SOE in France (London: Her Majesty's Stationery Office, 1976), pp. 186-87.

(85) Jillian Becker, cited at the West Berlin International Scientific Conference on Terrorism, November 14-18, 1978, in World of Medicine 23, no. 1 (1979): 44.

(86) See, for example, Wilfried Rasch, head of the West Berlin Free University's Institute of Forsenic Psychiiatry, cited in ibid.

(87) Russell and Miller, "Profile of a Terrorist."

(88) T.G. Tennet, "The Dangerous Offender," in British Journal of Hospital Medicine, September 1971, 271.

(89) Begin, The Revolt, p. 59. In fact, the press censorship in South Africa and, formerly, in Zimbabwe-Rhodesia stipulates that all those engaged in fighting against the government must be referred to as "terrorists."

(90) Cooper cited in Sobel, "Political Terrorism, pp. 18-19.

(91) Conrad V. Hassel, "The Hostage Situation: Exploring the Motivation and the Cause," Police Chief, September 1975, p. 55.

(92) In fact, it has been argued "that organization for criminal behaviour is shaped by the same system problems and concerns as organization for any other form of behaviour." A.K. Cohen, "The Concept of Criminal Organization," British Journal of Criminology 17, no. 2 (1977): 105.

(93) Edward F. Mickolus, "Negotiating for Hostages: A Policy Dilemma," Orbis 19, no. 4 (1976): 1318.

(94) Sigmund Freud, Group Psychology and the Analysis of the Ego (London: Hogarth, 1922), p. 85.

(95) Irving L. Janis, "Group Identification Under Conditions of External Danger," in Group Dynamics, ed. Dorwin Cartwright and Alvin Zander (New York: Harper and Row, 1968), p. 82.

(96) Cited in Sunday Telegraph, February 8, 1976.

(97) For useful typologies of terrorist groups, see Brian Crozier's testimony in U.S. Senate, Judiciary Committee, Administration of the Internal Security Act, 93d Cong., 2d sess., pt. 4, May 14, 1975, "International Terrorism," pp. 182-83; Paul Wilkinson, Political Terrorism (London: Macmillan, 1974), p. 32-44; and Richard Shultz, "Conceptualizing Political Terrorism: A Typology," Journal of International Affairs 32, no. 1 (1978): 9-10.

(98) Clissold, "Croat Separatism: Nationalism, Dissidence, and Terrorism," pp. 3-4.

(99) For example, on December 27-29, 1974, a conference of right-wing terrorist groups was held in Lyons to discuss plans to overthrow the existing political order in Western Europe. Groups from Belgium, Czechoslavakia, Denmark, France, Italy, the Netherlands, Spain, Switzerland, Sweden, West Germany, and Yugoslavia attended and agreed to create a new transnational organization called the New European Order. But to date this group appears to be inactive.

(100) Jenkins et al., Numbered Lives, p. 1.

(101) David Fromkin, "The Strategy of Terrorism," in Foreign Affairs 53, no. 4 (1975): 697.

(102) Wilkinson, Liberal State, p. 123.

(103) Andrew J. Pierre, "The Politics of International Terrorism," in Orbis 19, no. 4 (1976): 1255. See also Mickolus, "Negotiating for Hostages," p. 1323; I.M.H. Smart, "The Power of Terror," in Contemporary Terrorism: Selected Readings, ed. John D. Elliot and Leslie K. Gibson (Gaithersburg, Md.: International Association of Chiefs of Police, 1978), p. 28; and Brian Crozier, A Theory of Conflict (London: Hamish Hamilton, 1974), p. 143.

(104) New Dimensions of Security in Europe, ISC Special Report (London: Institute for the Study of Conflict, May 1975), p. 45.

(105) Wilkinson, Liberal State, p. 124.

(106) "Session Synthesis," in Hostage-Taking, p. 118.

(107) Anthony Cooper, "Panelist's Report," in ibid., p. 101.

(108) Georg Schwarzenberger, "Hijackers, Guerreros and Mercenaries," Current Legal Problems 24 (1971): 261.

(109) "The Memoirs of Sir Robert Mark: Part 3, Face to Face with Terror in the Streets," in Sunday Times, October 1, 1978.

(110) Cited in Sunday Times, October 23, 1977.

(111) Cited in Financial Times, December 23, 1975.

(112) Wolf Middendorf, "New Developments in the Taking of Hostages and Kidnapping," Polizeiblatt 31, no. 11 (1974): 5.

(113) "Session Synthesis," in Hostage-Taking, p. 119.

(114) "Final Synthesis: Analysis and conclusions," in ibid., pp. 269-70. See also the warning to this effect by Black September following the Furstenfeldbruck Airfield assault in Summary of World Broadcasts, September 9, 1972, ME/-4088/A/6-7.

(115) Cited in Sunday Observer Review, February 15, 1976.

Responding to the Victims of Terrorism: Psychological and Policy Implications
Abraham H. Miller

The psychiatrist Otto Rank once wrote "For the time being I gave up writing . . . there is already too much truth in the world . . . an overproduction which apparently cannot be consumed." (1)   Rank's reflections might be highly appropriate in considering the current state of intellectual affairs in the substantive areas of terrorism. In some of these areas there has not only been far and away too much descriptive writing, but much of it has the appearance of being hesitant about proceeding to the next logical step of intellectual development. There has been an outpouring of scintillating description, case studies, and historical narratives. Such entry items in a new and developing field are most appropriate.   They are a necessary first step in any quest toward creating the conceptual apparatus required for the evolution of scholarly inquiry.   Indeed some of the initial undertakings were exceptionally laudatory, holding forth not only the promise of new insights but even glimmers of theoretical formulations and intellectual concerns with relating generalizable knowledge to policy matters. If such expectations were not unwarrantedly adduced from the quality of material that initially broke ground in this field, then there is reason for the current state of affairs to be tainted with disappointment. Description and case analysis pile on top of description and case analysis, and legalistic platitudes on top of legalistic platitudes. Legal experts bemoaning the lack of legal safeguards continually hold forth that human decency as translated into international legal policy will yet save us from the indiscriminate horror of terrorism. In a not altogether dissimilar vein, one scholar enamored with vignettes and description has argued over a broad corpus of engaging material that terrorism as a subject matter is immune from social science inquiry. (2) At all levels of scholarly analysis, concerns with linking policymaking agenda items to generalizable knowledge culled from intellectual inquiry appear to be beyond the interest or capabilities of scholars and decision-makers.
    In order to take some hesitant steps in that direction, I address this

issue not so much with new knowledge but rather with a variety of established insights, tentative observation, and troublesome questions that I have brought together in an effort to look at some policy concerns related to victims of terrorism. My purpose is to take some existing knowledge, from a variety of perspectives, and relate that material to issues of victimization, especially victims of hostage and barricade situations, for the bulk of my firsthand experience is with such people. I believe that a fair reading of the attitudes of the mass public and even of important decision-makers would show very little understanding of the consequences of victimization, especially the long-term consequences of having been a victim. Moreover, it is my position that victims of terrorism deserve special consideration because they are frequently made victims in order to serve as surrogates for the state. Some nation-states, Israel and the Netherlands most notably, have shown a profound understanding and appreciation of this fact. The United States has not, but there are indications that this orientation is changing and, hopefully, work such as this will contribute to that change.

THE VICTIM AND THE PROBLEMS
OF SURVIVING

The first problem any victim confronts is surviving the episode. That is often a short-term problem. The second and more persistent problem is surviving the guilt that ensues after the episode. Survivor's guilt is so prevalent among those who live through catastrophe that the phenomenon is almost axiomatic in psychological studies of disaster. Survivor's guilt has often been seen as resulting from the chance or luck aspects of surviving, leaving the survivor with the nagging question, "Why me?" "Why did I survive when friends, relatives, and loved ones all around me perished?" From this perspective, it was understandable that survivors of floods, earthquakes, wars, and the Holocaust would manifest deep and continual feelings of guilt. Our knowledge of the prevalence of survivor's guilt was heightened recently by a study undertaken by David Cohen of a group of shipwrecked sailors. Prior to Cohen's work, one of the major explanations of survivor's guilt derived from the indiscriminate aspects of surviving. One survived because of chance, because of unforeseen and unplanned circumstances over which the survivor had virtually no control. The survivors in Cohen's study, however, had escaped death because of their own skills and resources. They had mastered the sea, and they had lost only one of their party. Yet their subsequent experiences demonstrated that they were far more adroit at mastering the sea than mastering the psychological affliction of having survived. (3)

In our culture, survivor's guilt is somewhat exacerbated by an almost inherent tendency to blame the victim. Victims are plagued by the question of what they could have done to avoid being victimized. In some cases, this attitude is a search by others for contributory negligence to avoid confronting their own vulnerability. It is a way of saying, "It couldn't happen to me. I would not have been there. I would have gotten out." (4)

The alleged culpability of the victim is most prominently seen in rape cases. Even with greater understanding of rape as a crime that is involved less with the fulfillment of sexual drives than with the expression of power and dominance needs, public perceptions and public attitudes toward victims change slowly. The lack of sympathy toward the victim, moreover, has become part of the liberal ideology toward rape - an ideology that has been primarily concerned with the belief that the rapists tend to be black and the victims tend to be white. To provide a benign interpretation for this perception, liberals have cast rape in broad sociological terms that have provided a great deal of compassion for the victimizer and terribly little for the victim.

The problems of the victims of terrorism are complicated because they often become victims because of what they represent symbolically rather than who they are. Even in cases where a specific victim is targeted, the victim's symbolic role is often vital. Witness the kidnapping of Aldo Moro by the Italian Red Brigades. Moro was not just Aldo Moro but the five-time head of the Italian government, an obvious political symbol. The terrorists seemed to have less of a quarrel with Moro himself than with what he represented. The hostages at the American embassy in Tehran were in all likelihood largely unknown as individuals to their captors.

Even lesser citizens, those who are not government office holders, can be elevated to the precarious and unenviable status of being surrogate victims for the state. Martin Villa, the Spanish minister of the interior, has said of the current wave of terrorism in his country that it is basically an attempt to gain access to political channels through violence that is more symbolic than effective. Professor Baljit Singh (5) has described terrorism as a means of using symbolic violence to gain access to the public agenda. Of course, there is Brian Jenkins' often-quoted statement, "Terrorism is theatre." (6) And the more absurd the scenario the more likely the hapless victims will be little more than convenient targets. One immediately thinks of the unfortunate Puerto Rican pilgrims who were gunned down by the Japanese Red Army in Israel's Lod Airport in an effort to turn world opinion toward the cause of a Palestinian homeland.

The brutal Palestinian Liberation Organization operation executed by Japanese terrorists at Lod Airport illustrates that the more absurd the scenario the more likely the victims will be surrogate targets for the state. It is thus reasonable to inquire whether the state, being unable to provide for the safety of these people, incurs any special obligation for their plight?

The obligation of the state, as a first step toward policy considerations, may perhaps be better understood if the full impact of victimization is better understood. In this merger of social science data and policy concern, we begin to see the direction that some of the work in terrorism should be taking. This is not to argue that an understanding of the nature of victimization automatically mandates certain policy choices. What it does suggest is that such knowledge would be an important factor in the multiplicity of factors that enter such decision-making considerations. Indeed, there will be some situations where not even all the ingredients that should go into the process of decision-making are known, but at some point the importance of scholarly knowledge as an ingredient in the policy process must make itself felt. And this is true even where all the ingredients are not known and even when the scholarly data is studded with caveats. Ultimately, decision-making from rudimentary knowledge has got to be better than decision-making in an intellectual vacuum.

The experiences of the victims of terrorism are as diverse as are the modes of terrorist operations. It is beyond the limits of this paper to discuss the effects and implications of all such situations. Rather, I want to look specifically at the consequences of being subjected to extreme stress as a result of being held hostage. I have spent some time interviewing hostages and it appears that there are commonalities between their short-term experiences and that of other individuals who have been subjected to intense stress over a relatively long-term period. This observation provides a corpus of literature to set up as a backdrop for the hostage experience. Aside from the policy considerations noted, there is an additional factor that ensues in the aftermath of the hostage situation. Until very recently, there has been little if any sympathy for the problems that hostages face after their release from captivity. To no small degree some of these problems would, in part, be alleviated if relatives, friends, and the public at large had a better understanding of what being a hostage means as a psychological experience.

Many American hostages have been people affiliated in some way with the U.S. diplomatic corps. Studies commissioned by the U.S. Department of State have aired the complaint by some of these victims that having been a hostage is roughly equivalent to having been exposed to bubonic plague. Coworkers remain aloof, almost as if the victim's very presence is a reminder of everyone's vulnerability and the government's impotence to do anything for them. The careers of one-time hostages are said to plateau out, and not-so-subtle nuances from coworkers and superiors lead many to believe that early retirement is in the best interest of the service and, of course, the country. (The Department of State has gone on record firmly denying these allegations.)

Beyond the attitudes and reactions of coworkers and loved ones, victims carry their own baggage of guilt. Victims generally feel that there was something they should have done to defend themselves. These feelings are often in response to the overwhelming feelings of helplessness, powerlessness to control one's life, and loss of dignity that accompany being a captive. Hostages at the B'nai B'rith Building during the Hanafi Muslim siege in Washington, D.C. (March 1977) generally expressed their initial reactions in a fashion that underscored this theme: "At first I felt that I had to do something, but then I realized that might make things worse." (7) Similar statements were made to me by captives held at Entebbe. Although the intellectual recognition is there that in reality there was little they could do, the guilt of not having done anything is not alleviated by intellectually recognizing what was or was not a feasible response.

THE CONFOUNDING INFLUENCES OF TRANSFERENCE

The one special problem of hostages that is most unfathomable to the general public and the one which, at least in terms of relations to the general public, causes the most grief for the hostages is the experience of transference. In its simplest terms, transference is an intimate bonding that occurs between captive and captor. Such bonding is sometimes reciprocated, although certainly not always. It is even the existence of this type of bonding that forms the basis for some of the reliance on negotiation as a means of bringing a hostage situation to denouement.

We do not observe this intimate bonding in every hostage situation, and it is not likely to occur when there are predetermined racial or ethnic hostilities between captive and captor. Israeli officials, for example, inform me that there has not been one instance of transference between an Israeli hostage and an Arab captor. Nor is transference as likely to occur when some of the hostages have been abused. (8) This is not to say that transference does not occur under such circumstances, merely that it is far and away less likely to happen.

There are of course the observations of inmates of Nazi concentration camps who identified with their guards, some to the point of wearing SS insignia on prison uniforms, an offense punishable by summary execution. Although such examples exist, transference is more likely to occur in those situations where predetermined animosities and negative experiences do not occur.

The implications of the effects of transference for the hostage are important. Some idea of the range of activity that can be accounted for by transference is discernable from some of the psychological definitions of the phenomenon.

In speaking of the transference between followers and their leader, Ernest Becker notes,

> Leaders need followers as much as they are needed by them: the leader projects onto his followers his own inability to stand alone, his fear of isolation. We must say that if there were not natural leaders possessing charisma, men would have to invent them, just as leaders must create followers if there were none available. If we accent the natural symbiotic side of the problem of transference we come into the broadest understanding of it. (9)

Transference emerges not simply out of the symbiotic merging of needs, but out of the dependency as well. In hostage situations there is the common fate and it looms large in providing an impetus for the development of transference. If the captors receive what they want the hostages will go free. That the captors are bartering with the hostages' lives is an aspect of reality that is readily lost. In the sense of common fate we see the creation of transference out of symbiosis. But the captive is dependent on the captor. The hostage eats, sleeps, and tends to personal needs on a schedule determined by the captor. He becomes child-like in his dependence, and like a child he responds to the omnipotence of the parental surrogate. The psychologist Alfred Adler suggests that the child seeks to merge with the omnipotence of the parent out of cowardice, not out of desire. In contrast to Freud, Adler cautions that the fact that transference leads to complete subjection does not demonstrate its erotic character but shows that it is a problem of courage. Following Otto Rank, Adler sees the quest for immortality and not sex as the primary explanation of human passion.

Erich Fromm looked on transference through yet another variation of the theme of impotence. Fromm dealt with man's projection of his own human qualities of love, intelligence, and courage on another human being in order to overcome his own inner emptiness and impotence. In doing this, he feels strong, wise, courageous, and secure. To lose the object means the danger of losing himself. To Fromm the idolatric worship of an object based on the individual's alienation is the central aspect of transference. (10)

The process of transference was first noticed as a result of a bank robbery in Stockholm. The aborted robbery was transformed into a barricade-hostage situation. During the course of the episode, a young woman hostage allegedly initiated sexual relations with her captor. Her actions were in response to neither fear nor coercion but resulted from an intimacy that developed from a sharing of a common fate in a situation of mutual crisis and the projected dependence of the woman captive on her captor. The relationship persisted after the bank robber's incarceration.

FBI agents note that had observers been attuned to the problem of transference earlier, the phenomenon would have been called the Shade Gap syndrome, not the Stockholm syndrome. Their reference is to a kidnapping that took place in Shade Gap, Pennsylvania in 1960. When law enforcement officials came upon the kidnapper in a wooded area, he was walking hurriedly to escape pursuit and encirclement. A considerable distance behind him was the kidnap victim, straining to keep up. Yet the victim had only to turn 180 degrees to walk off to freedom.

If we look even superficially at the concept of transference, the behavior of Patricia C. Hearst becomes not incredible but quite explicable and even predictable. Her behavior was different only in degree from what is commonly observed. It is also true that her experience in terms of the severity of deprivation was also extreme, and her susceptibility was probably further reinforced by her age and inexperience.

The susceptibility of an individual to transference is best understood by the little-known and seldom revealed fact that hostage negotiators trained in the subtleties and nuances of building transference in a captor often undergo the experience themselves. One seasoned negotiator told me that in one experience he got so emotionally close to the captor that he later found it difficult to testify against him. Before going to court, the negotiator had to approach the subject and circumlocutorily asked his permission to testify.

The transference phenomenon sometimes persists after the hostages' release and is responsible for some of the continued difficulties that hostages face. In Dr. Frank Ochberg's interviews with Dutch journalist Gerard Vaders, who had been held hostage by South Moluccan terrorists, the victim was observed to have maintained positive feelings toward the kindlier of his South Moluccan captors and incurred the wrath of a portion of the Dutch community with his positive statements about his captors. (11) Similarly, one couple who had been captives at Entebbe were forced to move from their home in a predominantly Jewish neighborhood because of positive sentiments they conveyed to the press about their Arab and German captors.

A public better educated in the nature of transference would be less alarmed by such statements and would not be so readily manipulated by the media.

SOCIETAL ATTITUDES AND
THE VICTIM

Frank G. Carrington, (12) who has studied the implications of being a victim, has documented the emphasis this society has placed on the concern for offenders as opposed to victims. In recent years the legal system has extolled the rights of the accused, but similar concern for the rights of the victim have been slow in coming. Perhaps we are inclined to avoid identifying with the victim because such identification only exposes us to a confrontation with our own vulnerability to random attack.

As a society we have begun, albeit slowly, to recognize the plight of the victim. Several states have passed legislation to compensate victims of certain crimes and to compensate "good Samaritans" who have been injured when coming to the aid of a victim. There have been bills before the state and federal legislatures to provide public insurance for victims. Some judges are demanding restitution as part of the criminal's sentence, and restitution is now becoming a consideration for parole. Along these lines, it is interesting to note that a recent American Broadcasting Company series on crime has chosen to focus not on the criminal offender but on the victim.

Such concern for the victim would greatly assist those who suffer the mental anguish and stress of being held hostage. The stress and anguish as well as the long-term psychological consequences of captivity do not end with the hostages' release. They continue long after the immediate episode is brought to conclusion. Hostages often face public condemnation because the hostages are less critical of their captors than the public would like them to be. A greater public understanding of the impact of the crisis on the hostage would be an act of kindness that would make the hostages' entrance back into society less difficult. From this perspective, I would argue that much of the hostility toward Patricia Hearst, the victim and then compatriot of the Symbionese Liberation Army, was misplaced. It is all too easy to condemn her as the stereotypic spoiled little rich girl and zealously cry out against the buying of her freedom. The tragedy of the public condemnation of Patricia Hearst was not simply the additional burden she had to bear but the fact that little was done to provide the necessary education to the public which would have made life more bearable for the next survivor of a hostage situation. The experience of watching with anguish and anxiety the fate of the 50-some hostages at the American embassy in Tehran, at least began to bring some strong recognition of the need for training people to withstand the stress of being held hostage. Indeed, one of the greatest difficulties confronting any hostage is the ambiguity of the situation. As we will note below, the reduction of uncertainty can go a long way toward alleviating the stress of captivity. It is from such experiences and their interpretation through the theoretical framework of social science that we begin to accumulate the kind of knowledge that is vital for our policy response repertoire in dealing with contemporary terrorism.

THE COMPONENTS OF POLICYMAKING

As nature certainly abhors a vacuum, so policymaking should abhor ignorance. Our ability to prepare our embassy staffs, businessmen, and military personnel to deal with potential captivity will depend to some extent on our willingness to commit the resources and energy to establish a cumulative literature on the process and experience of having been a hostage. To date, this has not been done. Some idea of the value of such a project to a programmatic response to the hostage problem can be seen from the implications drawn of the existing psychological literature on captivity and stress for preparing individuals to deal with captivity. Obviously, not all such situations are alike in their severity or implications for the psychological processes. Nonetheless, they provide some indication of what we do know about the nature of human captivity and its ensuing problems.

A wide variety of the literature on concentration camps, for example, provides information on the desire and persistence of human beings to survive in order to testify. The need to share and articulate the experience can be a major factor in inmate survival. One survivor of Treblinka put it this way: "I found it almost difficult to stay alive, but I had to live, to give the world the story of this depravity, this bestial depravity." (13) Terence Des Pres (14) who has written about surviving, argues that the need to testify is an adjustment to the severity of a protracted crisis. Des Pres feels so strongly about this point that he takes issue with the commonly articulated notion of psychiatrist Robert Jay Lifton that concern with the dead is neurotic and arises only after guilt has set in. (15) Instead, Des Pres sees it as a coping mechanism.

Despite the striking differences between Des Pres and Lifton's subjects and individuals who have encountered the typically shorter and much less severe hostage situations, some remarkable behavioral similarities do appear to occur. The need to testify appears to be one. Witness the similarity of the description of this need as expressed by one survivor of Auschwitz and by one of the ill-fated captives on the Dutch train taken by South Moluccan terrorists. As the Auschwitz captive noted, "By taking on the role of an 'observer,' I could at least for a few moments detach myself from what was going on in Auschwitz and was therefore better able to hold together the threads of sanity." (16) Dr. Ochberg's respondent, Gerard Vaders, noted similarly,

> From the beginning it was different for me. I recognized the situation. The moment the Moluccans came in, I felt back in the war. I was thinking, "Keep your head cool. Face the crisis!" I knew there would soon be choices. Time to take risks. For instance, it was risky to sit there taking notes. That destroys your anonymity. I made the choice and took notes. (17)

Not unlike the Auschwitz survivor, Vaders coped with the situation by detaching himself, making himself an observer, bearing witness and preparing himself to testify. Vaders is a journalist, so the role was relatively easy for him to slip into. However, we probably are missing a great deal if we see this behavior only as a retreat to a comfortable and familiar role, and do not consider that this may well be a functional coping mechanism in hostage situations or other situations involving captivity. It would also be interesting to ponder and explore the role of testifying after the release from captivity. The need to testify during the actual experience of captivity is a means of coping. The need to testify after captivity may well be a means of coping with the effects of having survived.

One of the most insightful descriptions, if not analysis, of a hijacking was written by Dr. Richard Brockman, a psychiatric resident, and was appropriately titled "Notes While Being Held Hostage." (18) Brockman's testimony may be just as meaningful in coping with the aftereffects of captivity as the poignant testimony of Ann Akhmatov's Requiem is eloquent about the need to bear witness during captivity itself:

> During the terrible years of Yezhovschina, I spent seventeen months in the prison queues in Leningrad. One day someone recognized me.

Then a woman with lips blue with cold who was standing behind me, and of course had never heard my name, came out of the numbness which affected us all and whispered in my ear (we all spoke in whispers there):

"Can you describe this?"

I said, "I can."

Then something resembling a smile slipped over what had once been her face. (19)

PSYCHOLOGICAL KNOWLEDGE AND
VICTIM ASSISTANCE

Our understanding of the psychological processes at work during and after captivity can not only assist us in our responses to captives and our ability to render them assistance, but can be equally important in preparing those who risk being taken hostage to deal with captivity. As a matter of policy, the United States Information Agency runs a series of seminars for government personnel and business executives who might end up as hostages. Sir Geoffrey Jackson, the former British ambassador to Uruguay who was taken captive by the Tupamaros, psychologically prepared himself for the experience of captivity.

In the aftermath of the second South Moluccan episode, the Dutch government prepared a specially outfitted train similar to the one in which the victims were held and offered its use as a mechanism for preparing victims to reenter society. Hostages from the B'nai B'rith Building seized by Hanafi Muslims were provided with psychological therapy by the George Washington University Medical School. The hostages were described as eager to find relief, receptive to help, and responsive to suggestions they received. The crisis itself provided an impetus for many to reevaluate other aspects of their lives and the therapy sessions proved useful in assisting this. Scotland Yard has included hostages in its training seminars, perhaps an outlet for the testimony needs of the hostages. Dr. Frank Ochberg, formerly of the National Institute of Mental Health, has brought together hostages and professional students of terrorism for exchanges of experiences. Israel has lionized its hostage victims.

Such responses show a much-needed sympathy for the plight of actual and potential hostages. One of the worst aspects of being taken captive is the ambiguity and uncertainty of the experience both during and afterwards. Sir Geoffrey Jackson uniquely mastered that situation by anticipating it and by preparing a program of behavior for his wife in the event of his captivity. This provided him with a continual bonding to her and knowledge of where she was and what she was doing during the initial phase of his captivity. For her part, she returned to England and went through the agreed-upon ritual, and even left behind Sir Geoffrey's shaving kit and two sets of clothing, one for winter and one for summer. As she said to me, "It was a way of saying that I was confident that he was coming back to me. The only question was when." (20)

TOWARD A POLICY STATEMENT

As long as terrorism persists as a political means, kidnapping and hostage-taking will be part of the modus operandi of terrorists groups. It is clearly impossible to safeguard even the most likely victims from attack. In fact, certain forms of protection, as Sir Geoffrey Jackson insightfully concluded, only escalate the amount of force that will be used in the seizure of the victim and increase the likelihood that a kidnapping attempt will turn into an assassination. Deterrence and safeguards are important considerations, but so too is a reasonable utilization of psychological knowledge to prepare potential victims for living through captivity and its aftermath.

This paper has attempted to demonstrate some of the psychological mechanisms that are relevant to hostages' ability to cope with the totality of the experience of captivity. It has also discussed the symbolic role that hostages play as surrogates for their governments and what this writer at least sees as the obligation governments possess as a result of that role. It suggests that the United States as a nation consider following the lead taken by the Israelis, the Dutch, and the British in being responsive to the psychological needs of the hostages, and that the public at large be made aware of the impact of transference on hostages so that there is less public hostility towards hostages for what they are likely to say when they regain their freedom.

At this writing, the ultimate fate of the American hostages in Iran remains unknown, although one assumes that at some juncture the Iranians, not unlike the fugitive interrupted in the course of a robbery, will discover that the hostages are less an asset than a liability, and they will be turned free in exchange for some symbolic affirmation. Should this happen the hostages will require our understanding, support, and, more than likely, a dose of professional psychological guidance in reentering society.

Guidance is an interactive process, for there is a great deal to be learned from hostages about the mechanisms that enable one to functionally or dysfunctionally deal with continuous stress. It is highly desirable that such information be properly catalogued, perhaps even put into machine-readable formats, updated with each new episode, and distinctly incorporated into a program for preparing hostages to live through captivity and survive the aftermath. It is a policy that is programmatically vital and morally necessary.

NOTES

(1) Quoted in Jessie Taft, Otto Rank (New York: Julian Press, 1958), p. 175.

(2) For a discussion of this issue see Abraham H. Miller, "On Terrorism," Public Administration Review, July/August 1977, pp. 429-34.

(3) David Cohen, British Journal of Psychiatry 131, no. 1.

(4) Martin Villa, presentation to the Ditchley Foundation Conference on Terrorism, Ditchley Castle, Oxfordshire, England, November 1978.

(5) Baljit Singh, remarks to the 1977 Annual Meeting of the International Studies Association, St. Louis, Missouri, March 16, 1977.

(6) Brian Jenkins, remarks to the Fourth International Seminar on Terrorism, Evian, France, June 1977.

(7) Mary Belz et al., "Is There a Treatment for Terror," Psychology Today, October 1977, pp. 54-56; 108-12.

(8) For an in-depth discussion of this issue see Abraham H. Miller, Terrorism and Hostage Negotiations (Boulder, Colo.: Westview, 1979), ch. 3.

(9) Ernest Becker, The Denial of Death (New York: Free Press, 1973), p. 139.

(10) Ibid., p. 143.

(11) Frank Ochberg, "The Victim of Terrorism: Psychiatric Considerations," Terrorism: An International Journal 1 (1978):147-68.

(12) Frank G. Carrington, The Victims (New Rochelle, N.Y.: Arlington House, 1975).

(13) Jacob Glatstein et al., eds., Anthology of Holocaust Literature (New York: Atheneum, 1973), p. 180.

(14) Terrence Des Pres, The Survivor (New York: Oxford University Press, 1976), pp. 38-41.

(15) Robert Jay Lifton, Death in Life: Survivors of Hiroshima (New York: Random House, 1967).

(16) Alfred Kantor, quoted in Des Pres, Survivor, p. 46.

(17) Gerard Vaders, quoted in Ochberg, "Victim of Terrorism," p. 149.

(18) Richard Brockman, "Notes While Being Held Hostage," Atlantic, December 1976, pp. 68-75.

(19) Ann Akhmatov, quoted in Des Pres, Survivor, p. 28.

(20) Personal interview with Sir Geoffrey and Lady Evelyn Jackson, November 1978, Ditchley Castle, Oxfordshire, England.

5 Executive Protection: The View from the Private Security Sector

Harry Pizer

While no security system or plan is infallible, and while good fortune is one of those necessary intangibles that enhance even the most sophisticated and thorough security programs, the view from the private security field is that the vulnerability of corporate executives to terrorist assaults can be significantly reduced through proper security preparation. The term "executive security" is very broad and can be compared to the basic premises of law enforcement. The twin goals are to prevent and deter and/or detect and apprehend criminals. Every major corporation in today's world has a security department. The size of such departments can range from those that are as large and complex as a small police bureau to one-person operations. Regardless of the size of the security department, its responsibilities are the same - to protect corporate assets and company personnel against a wide range of potential threats. Among the most disruptive and dangerous of these threats to corporate assets, and particularly corporate personnel, is that of the politically charged terrorist group. In the pages to follow the nature of this threat will be examined and general comments concerning private security preparations for corporate executives will be presented. However, this will serve only as an introduction to a more detailed examination of the problems the private security manager faces if the corporate executive protection plan breaks down and a kidnapping occurs. What will be presented are simple but effective management response guidelines that private security managers can employ and adapt to their own specific circumstances. While these guidelines are not to be considered the only procedures for dealing with such crises, they do provide the corporate security manager with an outline of the immediate issues he must address in resolving such situations.

THE NATURE OF THE THREAT - HOW CAN WE RESPOND?

The phase of executive security that has recently been the most discussed and written about by nonprofessionals is the intriguing area of political terrorism. Although terrorism is a subject often discussed by corporate executives, it is the responsibility of the corporate security officer to devise the "hows and whys" of preventing or responding to an after-the-fact terrorist incident. However, before we turn our attention to these concerns, I would like to briefly examine the nature of the terrorist threat through the eyes of a private security professional.

From our perspective, the seriousness of the threat is succinctly delineated in a 1974 article in the Economist entitled "Terrorism: The Companies in the Guerrillas' Sights." According to the author, "Today, private corporations and prominent businessmen are as much the target for political terrorism as governments, and tend to be more vulnerable." (1)   The vulnerability and attractiveness of such targets was clearly recognized by the guerrilla terrorist theoretician Carlos Marighella, in his "Mini-Manual of the Urban Guerrilla." (2) This work, which is a tactical and organizational textbook for the urban guerrilla terrorist, "has become one of the principal books for every man who, as a consequence of the inevitable battle against the bourgeoisie and imperialism takes the road of armed rebellion." (3) With respect to the corporate executive, the "Mini-Manual" specifies in detail the techniques to be used by the urban guerrilla in exploiting these very vulnerable targets. According to Marighella, "The kidnapping of North American residents or visitors constitutes a form of protest against the penetration and domination of the United States in our country . . . North American firms and properties in the country, for their part must become such frequent targets of sabotage that the volume of actions directed against them surpasses the total of all other actions against vital enemy points." (4) The frequent implementation of these tactics by different terrorist groups is clearly portrayed in the statistics on kidnapping presented in the first chapter of this book.

While it is apparent that the corporate executive is quite vulnerable to such terrorist seizures, the private security professional does not view such circumstances as hopeless. However, while the probability of such seizures can be significantly lowered, it will require adherence to the following measures: analysis of terrorist tactics and organization, analysis of necessary security measures, and development of an executive protection program.

To begin with, much can be learned from the analysis of previous terrorist kidnappings, much that can be very useful to the private security manager. For instance, an examination of the circumstances leading up to the kidnapping of corporate officials indicates that approximately half of the seizures occurred while they were in their autos riding to or from work, while another 30 percent occurred immediately outside the executive's home or office. To deter such situations, it has been suggested that corporate executive be accompanied by one or more bodyguards.   However, many of the executives who have been kidnapped were accompanied by either boydguards or armed escorts.   In most instances the terrorists who conducted the seizure knew the executive's daily routine and the size of his bodyguard or armed escort force.   This information allowed the terrorists to prepare for the seizure, and to employ enough forces to overpower and either kill or wound the executive's security forces.   Thus from the analysis of such circumstances we have been able to devise procedures for the executive to avoid making the job easy for the terrorist. These procedures include frequent changes in travel routes and daily routines. We also recommend special training for either the executive or his chauffeur in offensive-defensive driving techniques.   Finally, the corporate executive should be put through an awareness training program that prepares him to identify potentially threatening situations.   Such awareness can significantly lower the executive's vulnerability.

While this is only one aspect of the overall security plan, it does get at something that is a "must" if the plan is to be effective. Our point is simply this: in order for the executive protection plan to work, the executive must have faith in the plan, he must be constantly cognizant of the possible dangers to him, and he must be completely cooperative with corporate security personnel, adhering to the security plan they develop.   There are definite limitations to even the most sophisticated alarm and monitoring systems, lock and high-impact entrance facilities, and other special equipment and technical security systems. The degree of protection depends not simply on technical security equipment.   The overall plan must include the close cooperation of the executive being protected.   And beyond the executive, his or her spouse and family members should be included in security preparation.   When the executive's spouse and/or family realize that the chances of survival are greatly enhanced by rigid adherence to an executive protection program, the family members can constantly remind the executive of the responsibility to the family, and consequently they will demand adherence to the steps outlined in the protection program. Of course the spouse and family members also should be educated in security awareness procedures, so that they are able to spot unusual circumstances around their residence. In fact, from studying former hostages and their families we have found that they realized after the seizure occurred that they had warnings of surveillance by the terrorists which they had ignored or hadn't taken seriously. Security awareness training for the family, as well as for the executive, can alert them to the actual procedures followed by terrorists in preparation for a kidnapping. According to one security expert, the most frequently employed procedures utilized "by terrorists to observe an intended victim include the following: 'lovers' sitting for long periods in a parked car or on a nearby park bench, a car 'breakdown'providing an excuse to borrow tools or to use the telephone, a vendor's stand situated at a good vantage point near home or office, a 'telephone repairman' to tap the victim's line, anonymous calls asking for the victim or testing to see who is home at certain hours, 'road repairmen' observing movements over a long period without arousing suspicion." (5)

Before an executive protection program-antiterrorism plan is formulated and implemented, there are several factors that the private security professional must take into consideration. As in any strategy, one begins with an assessment of the enemy. Your response will be based on your opponents' intentions, motivations, and capabilities. The security officer and his top management should never underestimate terrorist groups or forget they are intelligent, ruthless, and inspired. Although we label these groups terrorists, they consider themselves patriots, and many of their members stand ready to die for their cause. The record indicates that because of educational background and class, these individuals tend to be very innovative and extremely capable. These are all factors the security officer must give serious consideration.

So in developing the executive protection plan, the private security manager must address a number of issues, many of which will be unique to his situation. Nevertheless, there are a number of security guides and handbooks that can greatly assist the security professional. These guideline procedures will resolve many of the initial questions and problems. However, the more difficult questions can only be answered from within your own organization, based on corporate policies, corporate structure, and from those individuals who fall under the umbrella of executive protection. It can range from a highly sophisticated, militaristic-type program to the very simple policy of being constantly alert. The degree of protection will depend on the individual and on the organization involved. Certain corporations have become highly symbolic targets for terrorists, and obviously such factors must be taken into consideration. Each program should provide no less than a basic primer to all corporate personnel on executive and facility protection. Any plan designed to prevent or deter the kidnapping of an executive and one that the executive can also feel comfortable with is an optimum plan. One of the major problems with any program is the problem of keeping the executive on his regimen. For it is when he wants to get away from his protective umbrella, when he becomes bored with the routine set out in the program, or when he begins to believe the danger no longer exists is when he becomes vulnerable. Finally, each executive protection program should have a detailed contingency plan for dealing with the breakdown of security procedures and the kidnapping of a corporate representative.

REACTIONS TO A KIDNAPPING:
SECURITY MANAGEMENT GUIDELINES

Before I turn my attention to specific procedures the professional security manager should consider in responding to the seizure of one of his firm's executives, I would like to review specific rules for hostages that should be included in the security education program conducted for the corporation's executive officials. An executive protection program should not be considered complete without behavioral instructions for executives to follow if they are kidnapped. These general rules are deduced from the actual experiences of former hostages. While the personality and resolve of each hostage will ultimately determine how he or she copes with the tension and stress of such situations, there nevertheless are procedures derived from previous hostage experiences that potential future hostages can profit from. In the event an executive is held individually or as part of a group of hostages, his or her actions could be very important for personal survival. Without going into the psychological reasons for the suggested behavioral practices, the following hostage "Do's and Don'ts" (also listed in Appendix A) should be discussed with corporate officials during the corporation's security education program.

To begin with, one should obviously avoid any clashes with the captors. One should be extremely courteous and polite to the terrorists, obeying their orders on command. Avoid complaining or acting belligerent and noncooperative toward the hostage-takers. Do not refuse any favors offered by the terrorists. This includes offers of food, beverages, tobacco, and so on. Avoid gestures or motions that the terrorist will find challenging or offensive. Never deliberately turn your back on the terrorists, particularly not the terrorist leader. Generally, it is not advisable to debate with the captors, especially on political issues. You may have to listen to political lectures from the terrorists. Do so in a friendly, interested manner. At the very most, only mildly interject your own views, while lending a sympathetic ear. Be cautious in making suggestions concerning the demands being made for your release. Your suggestions could backfire, and the consequences could be quite harsh for you. Still, there have been instances where the suggestions of a hostage has helped resolve the situation. For instance, Barbara Hutchinson, a U.S. embassy public affairs officer in Santo Domingo talked her captors out of demanding an exhorbitant ransom she knew her government would not pay. In another incident a hostage rewrote the terrorist demands, eliminating those he knew would never be accepted. (6) While such successful cases exist, it is my recommendation that the hostage move very gingerly when considering such recommendations.

Since the period of captivity may extend for some time, the hostage should calm down and settle into the situation. Attempt to get to know your captors as fellow human beings. Do not hesitate to answer questions about yourself, except if your position, post, or purpose of travel poses an additional problem for you. Try to be helpful and involve yourself in day-to-day chores, if your captors permit this. Develop ways to pass long periods of confinement. Finally, do not despair, for negotiations and rescue plans will be underway to secure your release. In fact, you should remain alert for signs/signals from outside rescue efforts. To summarize, there are steps the hostage can follow to make the captor-captive relations more bearable. Patience, courage, temper control, and calm are all necessary survival procedures that the hostage must develop if he or she is to survive the ordeal.

In addition to preparing the corporate executive to cope with such situations, the private security advisor must develop contingency plans for responding in the event of an actual kidnapping. To begin with, a fixed management response team should be developed and maintained. It should be composed of a chairman or plan coordinator, members of the corporation's professional security staff, and three or four other executives capable of making corporate decisions and of assigning to other executives various functions discussed below and listed in Appendix B.

In responding to such situations, there are a number of critical issues that the security managers and corporate officials must be concerned with. The following discussion addresses these issues and presents a generalized but effective set of management response guidelines that are applicable to specific situations (these guidelines are also listed in Appendix B).

Immediately following an actual seizure the plan coordinator and management team evaluate and analyze the incident to determine who is involved, what their demands are, and other pertinent information. Once the incident is verified, key executives in the corporation and law enforcement agencies should be notified. Within the United States the latter means the FBI. However, if the kidnapping takes place outside the United States the situation can become quite complicated. There are countries that prohibit, by law, payment of ransom and there are foreign law enforcement agencies that give a higher priority to the apprehension of the terrorist than to the safe return of his victim. While this "no ransom" policy is generally not applied to employees of private corporations, the management response team must abide by local laws and customs. Of course, local law enforcement officials have a great deal they can contribute to such situations. Therefore, it is highly recommended that the management team, in conjunction with local U.S. embassy officials, work closely with host government law enforcement personnel in dealing with such kidnap/ransom situations. Thus lines of communication with company representatives at the place of occurrence and with all other involved agencies and parties should be quickly operationalized.

If not already contained in the contingency plans, special accommodations should be established to provide the management response team with a command center that contains all necessary special equipment (telephones, tape recorders, etc.), supplies, and staff with which to conduct negotiations. Plans and working parameters for negotiations, as well as a negotiating team, should also be immediately established. Once these procedural and organizational matters are completed, tentative plans for payment of the ransom demanded by the terrorist must be made and release procedures must be settled. Procedures for communicating with the terrorists, choice of a chief negotiator, and the role of local law enforcement agencies are just a few of the problems facing the management response team. Of course, given these problems and the organizational and procedural processes that must be quickly set in motion to respond to the seizure of corporate executives, the need for contingency planning would appear to be undeniable.

CONCLUSION

I began by stating that the task of corporate executive protection is a most difficult one, and that the only road to success is through the development of a thoroughly designed and executed plan to protect the executive and the corporate headquarters. What I have attempted to provide are insights and general guidelines that pertain to this planning process. While these are not to be construed as hard and fast rules, they do reflect the kinds of steps we in the private security field have undertaken to lower the vulnerability of the corporate executive. How successful these developments have been in preventing executive kidnapping is uncertain. However, without the efforts that have been undertaken in the private security sector, I have little doubt that the number of politically motivated kidnappings would be significantly higher.

NOTES

(1) "Terrorism: The Companies in the Guerrillas' Sights," Economist June 1974.

(2) Contained in Jay Mallin, ed. Terror and the Urban Guerrilla: A Study of Tactics and Documents (Coral Gables, Fla.: University of Miami Press, 1971).

(3) Ibid.

(4) Ibid.

(5) Brooks McClure, "Hostage Survival," Conflict, no. 1-2 (1978).

(6) Ibid.

APPENDIX A

Do's and Don'ts of Captor-Captive Relations

1. Do be extremely courteous and polite to the terrorist.

2. Do not debate, argue, or discuss political issues with the terrorists or among the hostages.

3. Do talk in a normal voice. Avoid whispering when talking to other hostages or raising your voice when talking to a terrorist.

4. Do not complain or act belligerent or noncooperative when dealing with the terrorist or other hostages.

5. Do not deliberately turn your back to a terrorist, particularly not to the terrorist leader.

6. Do not refuse any favors offered by the terrorists. This includes offers of food, beverages, tobacco, etc.

7. Do be calm at all times and prepare yourself for the possibility of an extended period of captivity.

8. Do be cautious in making a suggestion to the terrorist, especially concerning their handling of the ransom process.

9. Do remember that negotiations and rescue plans are in progress for your benefit.

10. Do be alert for signals/signs from outside rescue efforts.

11. Do obey all terrorist orders and commands.

12. Do not worry about your family. They have been notified and are being kept up to date as to your situation and are being cared for.

13. Do not hesitate to answer questions about yourself except if your position, past, or purpose of travel poses an additional threat to you.

14. Do be helpful and offer to share in doing the day-to-day chores.

APPENDIX B

Security Management Response
Guidelines

A. Notice of Incident

Immediately following a reported incident or threat, the plan coordinator and the management team will evaluate and analyze the incident to determine either:

(1) that the kidnapping has actually occurred

(2) that the threat to kill, injure, or abduct is genuine

B. Notifications

Immediately after verification of the incident or threat the following notifications will be made:

(1) Corporate

Key executives and others on a "need to know" basis

(2) Law Enforcement Agencies

(A) Within the U.S.A.
FBI
Local law enforcement

(B) Outside the U.S.A.
FBI
INTERPOL - Washington, D.C.
Department of State - U.S.A.
Local U.S. embassy
Highest-ranking law enforcement agency of country of occurrence
State Department (or equivalent) of country of occurrence
Federal Aviation Administration

C. Corporate Action

(1) Establish lines of communication with company representatives at place of occurrence and with all other involved agencies/parties as necessary

(2) Instructions to senior company employee

(a) determine what policy/laws prevail

(b) determine what national or local agencies will be involved

(c) determine expected degree of cooperation

(d) assign representative to assist family: physical protection, medical or spiritual assistance, plans for removal to safe area or from country, act as spokesman, etc.

(e) decide how to handle news media

(3) Form negotiating team, institute plans and working parameters (team of four or five people)

(a) establish each individual role: group leader, prime negotiator, liaison with government/law enforcement, telephone monitors, etc.

(b) set up security measures at corporate and at negotiating office

(c) establish code for communications

(d) establish method to determine if subject is alive and well

(e) make tentative plansfor payment and receiving subject

(f) miscellaneous matters

D. Supplies and Equipment

If required, the local company office may have to provide hotel accommodations, apartment or house with telephones, cars with trustworthy drivers, tape recorders, etc.

E. Anticipated Problems

(1) In certain countries, it is prohibited to negotiate with kidnappers or terrorists - neutral territory must be found

(2) Law enforcement/foreign government often are more interested in apprehending the perpetrator than in rescuing subjects of attack.

(3) Certain insurance representatives prefer to save as much insurance money as possible, endangering subject.

(4) Families of subject attempt to interfere with negotiating team and refuse to leave the country

(5) Company must resist all outside pressures and maintain control of situation at all times

(6) News media tends to hinder negotiations

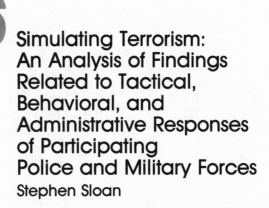

6

Simulating Terrorism: An Analysis of Findings Related to Tactical, Behavioral, and Administrative Responses of Participating Police and Military Forces
Stephen Sloan

While the repertoire of terrorist tactics has become increasingly complex, the seizure of hostages still remains a major means by which militants in all parts of the political spectrum can dramatize their causes, hold authorities at bay, and engage in an exceedingly profitable form of criminal extortion. Although the successful operations conducted by the Israeli commandos and the West German Border Patrol Group 9 were brilliant military accomplishments, there is a tendency to forget that the attacks were always on the razor's edge of failure. Furthermore, the availability of such highly trained units is limited, and a wide variety of political constraints make their deployment an exceptional alternative in the battle against terrorist hostage-taking.

Since the tragedy at Munich, the state of the art in antiterrorist techniques has improved dramatically. In the tactical arena, a wide variety of new weapons and associated hardware is now available to police and military units, and there has been a diffusion of counter-measures among foreign police and military forces. The proliferation of special weapons and tactical units among even smaller departments shows the growing recognition of the terrorist threat within the law enforcement community. This record of development has also carried over to the behavioral sciences. The systematic development of hostage-negotiation techniques represents an awareness by responding authorities that even the most tactically sophisticated approaches are severely limited when the major concern of officials is the safe release of the hostages. As in the case of the development of specialized tactical units in the United States, there has been an attempt to disseminate negotiation skills to all levels of the law enforcement community. (1) Finally, the sophisticated strategies of contemporary terrorism have forced authorities to refine their administrative skills in the face of an invidious threat to the civic order. The call for an integrative approach in both the public and private sectors has led to the evolution of crisis management techniques for bureaucrats and executives.

While the state of the art and the dissemination of information has

115

been impressive, the level of preparedness of the units charged with responding to an incident has been uneven. The degree of tactical and negotiation skills and management capabilities varies in civilian forces from the high levels of motivation and training of units among certain departments to a minimum of preparedness among many smaller jurisdictions. The levels of preparation within the military have been more standardized, but even here performance varies. Furthermore, each service often works on its own series of assumptions as it attempts to define its mission in the "war on terrorism."

This diversity has serious implications for the ability of law enforcement agencies to counter the challenges posed by the threat of terrorism.

THE EXPANSION OF TERRORISTS' TARGETS

While there is great diversity among the responding units that must meet the threat, there are common patterns in terrorists' operations that require that police and military forces at all levels achieve at least a minimum level of skills to effectively respond to incidents. It can be assumed that particularly among sophisticated terrorist groups there is a constant concern with effective risk assessment. It would, therefore, be logical to suggest that whenever possible these groups will seek the softest targets possible. Consequently, it can be anticipated that as certain highly sensitive or symbolic personnel and facilities are subject to tighter security, the terrorists will seek new targets of opportunity. When this factor is coupled with the terrorists' often-proclaimed view that there are no innocent victims or noncombatants, it can be anticipated that the range of targets will expand and diversify as the terrorists probe for weaker links within an increasingly security-conscious political order. This will be enhanced by the fact that there are a wide variety of sensitive targets with great symbolic importance in less populated and less secured locales. For instance, the dispersion of nuclear energy plants to less populated areas for ecological reasons, as well as the movement of corporate headquarters from urban centers to suburbia, extends the terrorists' geographical field of operations. In addition, the expansion in general aviation and the growth of local airports that have the capacity to handle executive jets give the would-be skyjacker a greatly expanded series of potential targets. It is for these reasons that a higher standard of training and subsequent performance must be encouraged for all types of departments. This is not to suggest that all law enforcement agencies should or can have the same level of performance that is required in large urban centers or jurisdictions where there are particularly sensitive targets. However, this consideration makes it essential that smaller departments receive a level of training that prepares them to develop an effective response strategy, thus enabling them to engage in vital holding actions until more specialized support units are called in from the Federal Bureau of

Investigation, the highway patrol, state tactical units, or the tactical teams of larger metropolitan departments. The need to achieve a degree of minimum effectiveness also applies to the military, even though there is less disparity because of the thrust toward standardized training. A small reserve unit with its usual complement of weapons might be a very attractive target for a terrorist group precisely because it would be more vulnerable than a large regular installation.

TRAINING FOR POTENTIAL INCIDENTS:
STRENGTHS AND DEFECTS

The uneven levels of preparedness, particularly among civilian forces, are partially the result of the diversity that characterizes the training among police departments and sheriff's offices to prepare for the criminally motivated and/or politically inspired hostage taking incident. As a general rule, the most realistic training has been conducted among military police units. This is to be expected, given the fact that part of their mission is to protect military installations from assaults by either conventional forces or guerilla groups. Furthermore, these units are consequently subject to training exercises that include full-scale military operations. In contrast, the level of training in response to incidents is understandably less even among large urban departments, since it is not a major responsibility of any civilian force to engage even in quasi-military operations with the exception of relatively rare situations involving large-scale civic disturbances, and even here military support can be obtained from the National Guard. Moreover, civilian forces lack the time, funding, personnel, or equipment to engage in military-type operations which, as a matter of public policy, go beyond the duties of the police. Nevertheless, the level of training in paramilitary operations is impressive among certain departments, most notably the Los Angeles and New York police departments. The development of more adequate training for smaller units has also been encouraged through the courses offered by the FBI at Quantico, Virginia. However, the level of training is often cursory since most departments, even if they have acquired a large variety of weapons and related hardware, have neither the resources nor the time, much less the interest, to engage in continuous and highly demanding field exercises. Moreover, the cost for a smaller department could be prohibitive. The occasional training program in which the local tactical team "plays at" engaging in a hostage-taking exercise every few months is the rule and not the exception, and does little to adequately prepare forces to meet a real incident.

Even highly realistic exercises - particularly within the military - have problems associated with the fact that these are "in-house" training programs. As a result, those who take on the role of terrorists are often drawn from the same unit that must respond to the attack. The individuals consequently may professionally "speak the same language" and share the same values as the personnel on the other side of the barricade. Furthermore, they will be working together long after the exercise is completed. Such common attributes cannot be carried over to actual terrorist groups who do not live by the rules of the civic order they are attacking, much less share the same assumptions of the law enforcement community that they are dedicated to destroying. Secondly, the level of training, even among civilian forces, tends to emphasize procedural techniques and tactical responses to hostage-taking incidents. The dynamics of hostage-terrorist interaction, the tensions created by media coverage, and the broader issues of the involvement of key civilian policymakers are usually not built into the exercises or evaluated, since the programs are narrowly defined to only train the police. It was in part for these reasons that an open-ended simulation technique was developed to assist police and military units in obtaining effective training.

THE SIMULATIONS TECHNIQUE

It is not the purpose of this article to discuss in detail the simulation technique that was developed by the author over the years. It should also be stressed that the use of simulation as a means of providing effective training is certainly not unique to the following study. Nevertheless, the lessons learned from the different exercises, which are incorporated into the forthcoming book Simulating Terrorism, can assist those who must be prepared to effectively respond to an actual incident. (2)

The simulation technique initially involved the development of a scenario and subsequent operations order by those individuals who played the role of terrorists. The scenario was primarily based on an analysis of patterns that emerged from an examination of past incidents, a threat assessment based on the intelligence evaluation of the locale where the exercise was conducted, and the research agenda of the author. (3) The latter involved building certain types of threats and demands into the scenario in order to evaluate the responses of the police or military forces involved.

With the exception of a liaison officer from the participating unit, none of the members of the responding forces were aware of the type of exercise in which they would be involved. Other than being told that they would be in a drill and given a safety briefing, the participants had no knowledge that a terrorist simulation would be conducted in which a number of them would take their normal roles as members of the reponding police forces while others would be taken hostage.

Throughout the simulations, there was no formal script. The ultimate outcome, whether it was a resort to force, successful negotiations, or stalemate, was solely dependent on the manner in which the police, the terrorists, the hostages, and other concerned parties interacted. In essence, the simulations were in the tradition of improvisational theater, where the actors' feelings and subsequent performance depend on how they interact with the environment in which they find themselves. Furthermore, while an outer time limit was placed on the duration of the exercises, the participants did not know this. For them, as in the case of an actual incident, the strife event could end in five minutes, five hours, or, theoretically five days.

Since 1976, the author has organized and conducted ten simulations with civilian and police units that are essentially representative of the forces that would have to respond to a terrorist hostage-taking. These simulations involved the following organizations: the 51st Security Squadron, Osan, Korea (twice); the Special Operations Team and other units of the Tulsa Police Department; the Port of Portland Police and associated units, including security personnel from the Oregon Air National Guard; the Minot, North Dakota Police and a state special weapons and tactical unit in conjunction with personnel drawn from the 91st Security Squadron at Minot Air Force Base; the Armed Offenders Squad and personnel drawn from the Hostage Negotiation Course of the New Zealand Police, held at the Police College in Trentham; a simulated skyjacking aboard the mock-up of an aircraft cabin that has been incorporated into the training program of flight attendants of Braniff International Airlines; units of the Seventh Special Forces Group (Airborne), First Special Forces (Canal Zone); the Norman, Oklahoma Police Department; and the University of Oklahoma Police Department. In addition, the author did a follow-up study of the effectiveness of the simulations technique by returning to Portland to evaluate the performance of the local force in responding to an actual skyjacking on August 22, 1979. (4)

While each of these simulations had unique aspects, certain common patterns that emerged have implications for the training and response abilities of representative police and military units. Although it might be suggested that the patterns might differ in the case of an actual incident, it should be stressed that the simulations were exceedingly realistic and the types of mistakes that occurred would not only happen in an actual hostage-taking but would probably be amplified.

The ensuing observations are essentially based on an analysis of the respective simulations. However, additional findings resulting from discussions with security personnel and material related to the organization and administration of law enforcement agencies have also been incorporated. These patterns are subject to debate, and it is hoped that they can be employed to encourage discussion among concerned personnel.

PATTERNS OF BEHAVIOR

Certain patterns of behavior raise serious questions concerning the tactical response, levels of negotiative skills, and administrative capabilities that go beyond the experience of the civilian and military forces who participated in the simulations. A good simulation, like good theater, often is more than an imitation of life, enabling both the audience and the actors to gain insight into their individual and collective behavior. It is, therefore, hoped that the following impressions follow that tradition.

The "It Can't Happen Here" Syndrome

At the inception of a number of the simulations there was often an attitude of disbelief on the part of the first officers who responded to the call or who were first contacted by the terrorists. This disbelief in part may have reflected the cautious view that the purported assault was a hoax. The reluctance to accept the reality of the situation also indicated that the responding officers needed more information in order to clarify the situation as a prerequisite for developing an effective response. It should of course also be noted that in certain instances the lack of belief was based on the fact that the participants were involved in a simulation, not an actual event. However, this factor lessened in all of the exercises as time passed and the responding forces were forced to get into their roles.

Perhaps most significant was the consideration that the lack of willingness to accept the situation might be the result of the fact that the responding personnel and the organizations they represented could not believe that such an event could happen in their jurisdiction, affirming the view that "terrorism is what happens to other people." The assumption that "it can't happen here" was particularly prevalent in smaller departments, in jurisdictions where there was little reason to believe that a politically motivated terrorist hostage-taking incident would take place. In contrast, a willingness to accept such an eventuality was more apparent in larger departments, where, given the nature of available targets, there was a greater sensitivity to the potential for terrorist incidents. Thus in the case of a simulation involving the seizure of an oil refinery in Tulsa, the responding officers were more willing to accept the likelihood of the event and get into their roles since by necessity the police department was particularly sensitive to the possibilities of high-technology terrorism. The same willingness to accept the reality of the event was evident at Portland International Airport; local police there constantly lived with the possibility of a skyjacking, bombing, and other "dramatic" incidents of criminality at the airport. Furthermore, the police had experienced actual incidents, and, therefore the "It can't happen here" syndrome was largely negated.

It would seem that the perception of a potential threat would have a direct relationship to the willingness of the responding authorities to rapidly accept that a crisis was developing. The more local a department, the more rural the jurisdiction, the more probable an expression of disbelief. It can, therefore, be suggested that in the development of effective threat assessment for all departments a realistic analysis of potential incidents be disseminated to the members of the department so that threats are neither overstated nor minimized. It is vital that the law enforcement community at all levels recognize that there are no safe havens from potential attack, only varying degrees of vulnerability.

There was more willingness to accept that an incident was occurring among participating military units, for several reasons. First, given the mission of the security forces, they must be constantly prepared to counter an armed assault from regular forces, guerrilla units, or terrorists on the installations they protect. This level of sensitivity was particularly apparent in locales where the possibility of armed conflict was always real. The Air Security Squadron in Korea, for example, had little difficulty in accepting the development of a potential incident since they lived with that possibility every day. This sensitivity was also apparent among military units that were charged with protecting key domestic installations. Thus air security units guarding nuclear weapons and other vital installations must work on the assumption that there is a high possibility of an attack on the installation they are assigned to. As a result, there was no room for the luxury of a slow reaction time. Second, as a rule, the military forces were far more sensitive to the importance of effective intelligence and, consequently, were more concerned with developing adequate threat assessments. In carrying out their responsibility to prevent or effectively respond to covert or overt operations, the military units placed more emphasis on the need for security consciousness.

The probable result of this unwillingness, particularly on the part of various civilian police forces, to accept the fact that an incident could occur in their jurisdiction is that valuable time will be wasted in developing an effective response to the crisis. The simulations served to indicate that local departments might find it difficult to accept the fact that they were confronted with more than ordinary forms of criminal action. This lack of acceptance could also delay local units' decision to call other agencies that could assist them in meeting a terrorist threat.

Administrative Shock and Early Immobilism

The expressions of disbelief that at times slowed reaction time often acted as barriers to the development of effective administrative measures at the outset of the simulations. These early delays and disorganization were particularly found among civilian police departments who as a matter of course had not developed contingency plans for terrorist incidents, in contrast to military units, who by necessity had to be prepared for full-scale assaults by hostile forces. However, irrespective of the level of preparedness and the existence of contingency plans, the initial responses on the part of all the forces that were involved in the simulations were characterized by various degrees of initial disorganization and confusion. The inability of the responding units to develop an effective early response was the result of physical, technical, and behavioral consideration that were often apparent at the inception of an incident.

Physically - particularly when an on-site command post had to be established - there were constant difficulties in acquiring a facility that would be large enough to accommodate the personnel that would be involved at the start of the crisis. This lack of room, the resultant high noise levels, and the discomfort caused by smoking in a confined area promoted an atmosphere of disorder that acted as a barrier to the development of effective administration. The problem was compounded by the fact that at the start of all of the exercises there were far too many unnecessary personnel in the command post. This lessened with the delegation of responsibility as the exercise continued, but contributed to the initial confused atmosphere.

The early inability to develop an effective administrative response was further hampered by technical problems in all of the exercises related to malfunctions or improper use of communications equipment. Delays in developing effective communication as a prerequisite for command and control were in some instances the result of the fact that there were no available phones or jacks in the designated command post. This problem would often be aggravated even when radios were available, since in a number of the exercises the equipment malfunctioned because of weak batteries and other breakdowns. The technical failures also carried over to such crucial equipment as the recording devices used to monitor conversations between the negotiation team and the terrorists. It was obvious that the need to constantly test and maintain equipment was often ignored, particularly in reference to devices that were not in use for routine duties. These breakdowns often raised other questions about the lack of preparedness of the responding forces. Particularly when telephones were the major means of communication and breakdowns were being experienced it became obvious that no contingency plans had been made with the local telephone company to provide for the requirements of the local forces.

The confusion related to mechanical breakdowns was intensified by the behavior of those who were utilizing the radios. In all of the simulations, there was a proclivity on the part of the responding officers to overcommunicate - to use their radios when it was unnecessary. Furthermore, the existence of limited channels led to confusion about developing a command net and secondary channels. This problem was not as blatant among the respective military units since their personnel were more fully trained in the requirements for radio discipline and procedure. Nevertheless, too many officers cluttered the airways by engaging in unnecessary transmissions simply because they had radios and wanted to be "part of the action."

As a result of these physical factors, it was often difficult for the senior officer present to obtain necessary information and initiate an early response, much less take full control of the situation. Even when there were contingency plans which called for clear lines of authority - as in the case of the base commander on military installations - that authority was difficult to exercise given the physical setting and mechanical malfunctions that placed added pressures on those who were responsible for dealing with the incident. These pressures were particularly acute when specialized units such as the bomb squad and other departments or agencies became involved in the command post, aggravating the problems associated with establishing a coordinated response and further heightening the confusion that marked the early administrative measures taken during the crisis. This lack of command and control among different units was lessened when they had a history of working together. Thus, for example, the coordination between the airport police and the airport fire department in the Portland exercise was most impressive; these units had constantly been subject to joint training exercises. The exercises confirmed the view that guidelines break down under the pressure of events, and illustrated the need for continuous training to avoid the immobilism that was often present at the start of the simulations.

An Action Orientation: An
Impediment to Effective Negotiation

Throughout all of the simulations a major objective was to provide the most realistic setting where designated negotiators could learn to refine their skills. While the level of prior training among the negotiators differed, certain common patterns emerged that suggest that the values held by the negotiation teams and their organizations could hamper the development of effective negotiation techniques and practices during a hostage-taking.

In all of the simulations there was one overriding pattern that characterized the departments and individuals who were responding to the crisis: they were all action oriented. The basic mission of the various forces was to tactically respond to a crisis and, in the case of military units in particular, to actually seize the initiative and go on the offensive. Therefore, there was always the problem of reconciling the desire to employ a tactical series of measures with the equally important task of engaging in effective negotiation.

Engaging in a negotiation process was a concept particularly alien to the military units involved in the exercises, since military forces were not trained to engage in discussion with hostile units. But the action orientation could also be observed among the police forces, since officers were not used to engaging in discussion with individuals undertaking the commission of a crime. It was therefore not surprising that the attitudes of the organization carried over to their personnel. A police officer and his military counterpart are trained to assert authority and give orders, and yet it was often those very people who were assigned the responsibility of negotiating with the "criminals" or the "enemies." Moreover, it was natural for these individuals and their superiors to think that negotiation was a sign of weakness on the part of authority. The temptation to resort to the more comfortable but often more dangerous tactical alternative was always present. This does not mean to suggest that in the exercises a number of negotiators did not perform well, nor does it imply that individuals who are not in law enforcement should ordinarily take on the negotiator's role. But it does raise questions concerning the ability to train people in a function that goes against the grain of the way they perceive the scope of their position.

In a number of the simulated incidents, the difficulties associated with taking on a negotiation function surfaced at the outset. From the beginning there was often reluctance on the part of the negotiator and his superiors to even initiate communication with the hostage-taker. Indeed, in one instance vital time in establishing communication was lost when the commanding officer insisted on the introduction of a field telephone into the barricaded area, in itself a negotiable item. Even when communication was initiated there was a tendency on the part of the designated negotiator to simply rely on procedural questions concerning the number of hostages and the type of demands, without attempting to really listen or to understand the motivation that would impel a person to take the drastic action of seizing hostages. In more than one instance, this unwillingness to listen to and, consequently, to begin to understand the "terrorist" was carried to such an extreme that the negotiators often demanded that certain actions be taken. In most instances it took time before the negotiation teams began to recognize that they had to develop some minimum level of trust and rapport with the hostage-taker.

This inability to establish the necessary relationships for the conduct of effective negotiation was often intensified by the negotiators' tendency to rigidly follow the dictum "Do not give anything away unless you receive something in return." Thus such symbolic gestures as moving tactical units back from the perimeter - a move that would have no impact on the effectiveness of the responding units but could serve as a sign of good faith and promote negotiations - were disregarded. Conflicts over trivial requests became a test of wills between the negotiators, their commanders, and the terrorists, which often promoted early polarization that negated effective resolution of the conflict without the resort to arms. While such inflexibility on small issues was usually rationalized as a delaying tactic to wear down the hostage-taker, it frequently was an empty battle of wills in which nobody won and the hostages lost.

The difficulty of developing an effective negotiation process was intensified by the relationship between the negotiators and their commanders and their physical placement within the command post. The relationship between the negotiator and the commander of an operation is fraught with potential difficulties. On one hand, the ultimate decision-making must be in the hands of the senior officer, yet the negotiator cannot be simply viewed as a conduit through which decisions are conveyed to the hostage-taker. He or she must be given a degree of initiative to establish rapport with the terrorists. Furthermore, a good negotiator's advice should weigh heavily in the decision-making process. The negotiator is therefore an individual who may not bear the ultimate responsibility of deciding a course of action, but who - by his actions - may greatly influence the outcome of a siege. The negotiator is a person caught in the middle.

The tensions faced by a negotiator in the simulations were often intensified by the placement of the negotiation team in reference to the commanding officer. In too many instances the commander sat with or behind the team. This placement often raised the question of whether the primary negotiator was most concerned with effectively providing a basis for resolution of the conflict with the hostage-takers or was essentially preoccupied with meeting what he perceived to be the expectations of his superior. In order to reduce the tension created by this situation, it may be advisable for the negotiator to not be in the direct proximity of his commander. However, if the separation is too great problems in communication can result. Thus in one exercise the negotiation team was located outside of the central command post, and valuable time as well as the risk of misinterpretation resulted because of the need to convey messages from the team to the base commander.

The difficulties of developing an effective negotiation posture were further complicated in the exercises by a frequent lack of coordination between the hostage-negotiation team and the tactical unit. At times they appeared to work at cross purposes; the negotiators sought to resolve the issue pacifically, while the tactical units stressed armed intervention. While this cannot be validated, one could also suggest that the perception by the men on the tactical team of the negotiators and vice versa often led to distrust. The negotiators may have been perceived by the tactical unit as having the tendency to be soft on the perpetrators, while the negotiators may have viewed their counterparts as being too willing to seek a solution through the resort to arms.

This lack of integration led to disaster in some of the exercises. In a simulation involving tactically sophisticated personnel, the captain in charge of the assault team seized the initiative and launched an attack while his senior commander appeared to be effectively engaging its negotiations. The abortive assault led to the wounding and death of the hostages, the responding unit, and the terrorists.

It can be suggested that while it might not be advisable to cross-train negotiation and tactical team members because of the expense involved and their different assignments, it is important to have them work as members of an integrated team in which each group learns to appreciate the unique problems the other must confront. The Tulsa Special Operations Division effectively bridged this gap by making the negotiators and tactical team members part of the same organization. (5)

It is exceedingly difficult to suggest from the simulations what type of individual should be recruited to become a negotiator. Neither age, rank, nor experience - individual or collective - provided a basis for predicting the performance of the negotiators. Yet certain characteristics that emerged from the simulations appear to be important in defining individuals who can effectively take on the responsibilities of negotiating. Whether these skills can to some degree be taught in a course is beyond the scope of this paper. What can be said, however, is that irrespective of the level of training, it takes a person who has the capacity to listen, who can be sensitive to the feelings of others, who can relate to different points of view without losing objectivity, who is difficult to provoke, and who has extraordinary patience to become a good negotiator. Two additional requirements should be added - an ability not to take oneself too seriously and a capacity to maintain a sense of humor even in the most trying circumstances.

Since the author does not specialize in the analysis of tactical techniques, observations in reference to the performance of the SWAT teams will by necessity be limited. At the outset, it should be noted that the standards, training, and subsequent performance varied greatly in all of the exercises. In general, as was noted before, the military forces were of higher quality than their civilian counterparts. However, this very fact created an ironic situation. It was often precisely because the military units were more schooled in the tactical response that they were often tempted to employ it, thus losing sight of the ultimate strategic goal of securing the release of the hostages. At times the civilian forces, recognizing their limitations, would prefer the route of negotiation. But at the same time it was obvious in all of the exercises that a civilian force unskilled in tactical operations posed a potentially serious danger to themselves, bystanders, and the hostages if they attempted to employ a military solution. The assumption that once an individual puts on a flack vest, wears a helmet, and carries an automatic weapon he is transformed into an effective tactical expert can lead to tragedy when ill-trained units "play" at being capable of engaging in field operations.

Settling in for the Siege

In all the simulations, after the initial disorganization, which usually lasted about an hour, a routine was established within the designated command post. The levels of effectiveness in managing the incident varied, but certain patterns emerged involving the realization that the crisis might become protracted.

With the arrival of the most senior commander, a more systematic delegation of responsibility took place, and a number of unnecessary personnel were either relieved or assigned to other duties. Consequently, the noise level and the discomforts resulting from overcrowding and smoking lessened. This change in itself helped to promote an environment that reduced the disorganization that characterized the early phases of the respective exercises. Nevertheless, certain physical factors which at the inception of the crisis were not viewed as important, created unnecesary discomfort as the siege wore on. For example the absence of chairs and working areas, which were ignored during the initial excitement, became bothersome fatigue factors as the hours passed.

The development of a routine was not solely the result of design; in part it reflected the development of a rhythm as people "settled in for the duration." It was particularly during this period that the negotiators felt increasingly comfortable in their new roles and began to act with greater confidence. The establishment of a rhythm within the command post and among the negotiators greatly facilitated the reduction of the anxiety that characterized the early stages of the siege. (6)

BEHAVIOR AT THE OTHER SIDE OF THE GUN

It is not the intent of this article to discuss in detail the reaction of the hostages in the simulations or the behavior of the terrorists, but to indicate patterns that were to have implications for the effectiveness of the responding forces.

At the inception of all the exercises, the terrorists, with varying degrees of success, were able to seize and hold the initiative. Yet, as in the case of an actual crisis, this was the time when the hostages were in the gravest danger. Since the terrorists were unsure of the outcome of their assault, any overt act on the part of the hostages could lead to disaster. Given this uncertainty and the great stress that the terrorists were feeling at this stage, any overt act by the responding forces would also have probably ended in bloodshed. The consequent need by both hostages and police to avoid provocative actions during this very dangerous period cannot be underestimated. It is during this period that it may be advisable for responding units to be careful to engage in only a very controlled display of symbolic force, since any provocative act could lead to a fatality. Thus, the elements of a high-visibility operation that are common at the outset of a siege, such as the arrival of unnecessary patrol cars and too many armed personnel, should be reduced.

As in the command post, the passage of time replaced the initial shock and disorientation of the hostages and the uncertainty of the terrorists by the development of a routine. While none of the participants in the exercises experienced in full measure the behavior that characterizes the so-called Stockholm syndrome, (7) a number of the captives made the natural attempt to establish some rapport with their captors in an attempt to be viewed as more than a dehumanized target. It is also interesting to see that in all the simulations there were individuals who attempted to take a hard line with the terrorists. These individuals, as a rule, were singled out for additional verbal abuse and physical discomfort and, not unexpectedly, were often the first to be killed when the frustration became intense. Perhaps the most common and aggravating emotion experienced by the hostages after the initial shock and disorientation was a feeling that they were being cut off and ignored by the outside world. Even when a great deal was being done to secure their release, most of the hostages felt isolated since control of communication and knowledge of the outside world was in the hands of their captors.   Based on these experiences, it is essential that the responding authorities do everything in their power to undercut the disastrous effects a sense of psychological isolation creates among hostages.   By negotiation and action, the word must be passed that the police and military units are doing everything possible to secure the safe release of the captives.

In addition to recognizing the pressures of isolation, the police must also not forget that their major concern is the plight of the victims. While this seems obvious, in virtually all of the simulations there was often a tendency on the part of commanders and staffs to be primarily concerned with the interaction between the negotiators and the terrorists.   Somehow the hostages became nameless pawns in a potentially deadly game, who often receded into the background of their prisons.

ENDING THE SIEGE: THE REASSERTION OF TENSION AND UNCERTAINTY

As the hostage-taking continued, the rhythm that was established often resulted in a grudging realization by the police and military forces that the crisis would not be resolved quickly.   The initial excitement and period of frantic activity was often replaced by a sense of increased boredom, and the resulting fatigue and frustration lessened the effectiveness of the forces in responding to the crisis.   But when it became clear that decisive action was to be taken because of either a breakthrough in negotiations or the decision to use tactical options, the tension and uncertainty that pervaded the command posts at the start of the incident returned.   This pressurized period was also experienced among the hostages and terrorists, who were confronted with the fact that the routine that may have been established was about to end.

It was precisely at this point in many of the exercises that a desire to either speed up the negotiation process or quickly prepare for a tactical assault emerged.   This process placed either option in jeopardy, since it was exactly during this crucial time that there was even more reason to maintain a routine and continue to lessen tension.   The potential for miscalculation based on hastily devised tactics could, and did, negate the positive developments that had resulted from hours of hard work.   There was often a sense of release on the part of the commander, his staff, and personnel in the field that at least now action would be taken.   But this sense of release not only neutralized the effects of incremental discussion and planning, but also often led to a disastrous tactical assault. It is vital that the responding forces go slow and keep a routine even when they think they are near resolving the crisis, either by force or negotiation.

EXTERNAL INTERFERENCE AND THE
QUESTION OF POLICE/MEDIA RELATIONS

In all of the simulations with the exception of the first exercise, which was conducted in an enclosed police shooting range, minor problems related to perimeter control did occur. However, in all but that one exercise concerns about a possible overreaction by members of the public who might witness part of the seizure proved unfounded. In two instances buses containing the armed "terrorists" and their captives were able to use public roads with barely any response from passing motorists. In the Portland case, 26 hostages were seized at the side of the main terminal, placed on a bus, and driven on a major thoroughfare to the area where they were held. In the Tulsa simulation, the terrorist bus not only used major roads during the rush hour, but also passed police headquarters. While the reasons for the lack of reaction have not been documented, it can be suggested that the indifference was partially the result of the natural tendency to ignore what we choose not to perceive. The disbelief that characterized the initial reaction of the police - the "it can't happen here" syndrome - carried over to the public.

Nevertheless, experiences in the early simulations did raise potential problems of securing the area in the event of an actual incident. For example, in the Norman simulation communication among the responding units was picked up by the local ambulance service, which initially had not heard over the net that a drill was in progress. As a result of such experiences, there has been growing concern that in the conduct of all simulations a frequently reiterated message be broadcast explaining that a drill is in progress. However, even with this precaution there is always a possibility that that portion of the message could be garbled. Perhaps even more disturbing is the fact that radio scanners are increasingly being bought by the general public which will heighten the difficulties created by civilians running to the scene of the incident. Thus it can be suggested that there be an increased emphasis on minimizing communication among units and employing surveillance channels as one means of discouraging the arrival of uninvited guests who may not only complicate an operation but put themselves in a dangerous position.

One of the major concerns in all of the simulations was a particular type of external involvement - the complex questions and problems associated with the role of the media in covering a terrorist incident. (8) Consequently, in all of the simulations individuals played the role of members of the media, and whenever possible actual representatives of the print and electronic press covered the story. To provide the most effective test possible, the reporters could not act as observers; if they wished to obtain effective coverage they had to aggressively report on what transpired. The results of media behavior during the simulations tended to highlight and duplicate the type of tensions that characterize police/press relations during an actual incident.

Even if the responding television stations or newspaper had guidelines, they were essentially not followed during the course of the simulations. The same ineffectiveness would also apply if the responding police also developed their own suggested procedures. The maintenance of standards was primarily based on the individual behavior of the reporters, the decisions of their editors, and the response of the on-scene police officers and their commanders. The code of behavior - written or unwritten - was in a sense only as strong as the willingness of a stringer not to attempt to get an exclusive or the ability of a patrolman to assist the reporter.

Adversary relationships developed, and in one extreme instance involved the seizure of individuals who were playing the role of reporters by members of a special weapons and tactical team, who wrestled the "reporters" to the ground, handcuffed them, and placed them under arrest. In another instance, the reporters for a large paper were angered when they were not permitted to enter the command post; for over an hour they were forced to wait in an airplane hangar until they obtained permission to interview personnel. Perhaps the most glaring incident involved the crew of a local television station, who effectively violated the perimeter established by the police and covered the story in front of the forward command post, and in the line of fire.

On the basis of all these exercises, it was clear that there are no simple guidelines that can reduce the possibilities for conflict between the media and the police. However, it was evident that if the local police, particularly the press relations officer, was respected by media representatives and if the police commander displayed sensitivity to the reporters' requirements to cover the story, this degree of mutual respect lessened the tensions that existed during the simulations. The exercises, therefore, provided one way by which the police and the press could more clearly recognize the problems that would arise in the event of a hostage-taking.

THE SIMULATION TECHNIQUE AND POLICY QUESTIONS

The simulations raised a number of policy questions that will be addressed in the concluding section as part of a broad analysis of the alternatives faced by authorities in responding to terrorism. To begin with, a few observations based on the exercises are in order.

First, despite the equipping of civilian forces with automatic weapons and related equipment, the pace of training remains uneven. In addition to serious questions related to the level of arms that a police force should have, it must be emphasized that a poorly trained but highly armed unit may be more dangerous to the hostages, the general public, and itself than a police department primarily equipped with pistols, shotguns, and more conventional weapons of law enforcement. The temptation to rely on hardware without the complementary essential training is particularly apparent among smaller departments who have acquired equipment because it was available through state and federal funding but who lack the time, resources, or inclination to develop full-scale training programs. The temptation to simply have the equipment as a status symbol cannot be dismissed as a factor. It is therefore important that these departments acquire only that type of weaponry that will enable them to engage in a holding operation, and be expected to train for that contingency.

The unevenness that characterized the tactical skills of the various departments also carried over to the training and subsequent performance of hostage-negotiation teams. While there have been a number of useful short courses to assist in training negotiators, serious questions remain concerning the mode of selection. While smaller forces cannot afford to have their own psychological staffs to engage in a protracted screening process, it is essential that consultants be brought in to assist them in recruiting the right types of personalities for a potentially arduous assignment. Until this happens, there will continue to be the temptation to select people on the basis of their availability and other factors not related to their capacities to become effective members of a negotiating team. During selection and subsequent training, it is vital that negotiators - like their tactical counterparts - be subjected to the most realistic exercises in order to prepare them for actual incidents. The mere possession of an untested series of techniques, as in the case of the acquisition of weapons without adequate evaluation, can be counterproductive, creating a false and potentially dangerous feeling of adequate preparedness.

In developing an effective response capability, it is important that an integrative approach be employed that allows the tactical and negotiations personnel to work together as closely as possible. In this manner the two groups can avoid the danger of working at cross purposes.

This need for coordination is also vital at all levels within a department. The utilization of realistic exercises to provide a basis of training and evaluation of an antiterrorist response program within the limits of budgetry and related constraints cannot be ignored. Furthermore, since acts of terrorist hostage-taking are almost without exception multijurisdictional from the inception of a crisis, there is an essential requirement that joint operations exercises be held with other units when possible. These exercises should not only include the members of the responding units, but senior civilian policymakers and elected officials who might have to one day resolve incidents in which miscalculations could prove fatal. In addition, the security officers and executives who are responsible for protecting their corporations from incidents and who would be involved in reacting to a crisis should also be involved in training. Given the sensitivity of a wide variety of potentially attractive private targets, the need for interaction between the public and corporate sector cannot be ignored.

Finally, while the inherent aspect of an adversary relationship will continue to exist between the media and the law enforcement agencies, the print and electronic press should at times also be invited to participate in training programs. In this way a level of mutual respect might develop, along with the development of suggested procedures that will not simply break down once they are translated from paper into reality in an actual crisis.

While the use of the simulation technique by itself cannot totally prepare authorities to meet the continuing threat of terrorism, it does provide one means by which measures related to tactics and strategies, techniques of administration, and broader issues related to public policy can be evaluated in an atmosphere that will produce the types of stress that exist in an actual crisis.

NOTES

(1) The author attended one of these courses: June 13 to 15, 1977, he participated in the Hostage Negotiation School conducted by the Federal Bureau of Investigation at the Robert R. Lester Training Center in Oklahoma City.

(2) To be published by the University of Oklahoma Press. The book will provide a detailed analysis of the simulations and suggest alternatives that can be employed by police and military forces in responding to a terrorist incident. Broader issues related to the development and execution of public policies to meet the continuing threat will also be discussed.

(3) For an examination of patterns that emerged from an examination of past incidents, see Stephen Sloan and Richard Kearney, "Non-Territorial Terrorism: An Empirical Approach to Policy Formation," Conflict 1, nos. 1 and 2 (1978): 131-44. For a concise analysis of the basic techniques of the simulation and the research objectives, see Stephen Sloan, "Simulating Terrorism; From Operational Techniques to Questions of Policy," International Studies Notes 5, issue 4: 1-8.

(4) A number of the findings were incorporated into an unpublished report by John E. "Jack" Cunningham and Stephen Sloan, titled "Simulation Versus Reality: Common Patterns in a Hostage-Taking Exercise and an Actual Skyjacking." Mr. Cunningham is chief of the Port of Portland Police Department.

(5) The debate over whether negotiators and tactical team members should be recruited separately and belong to different organizations or should form an integrated team is concisely discussed in Abraham H. Miller, "SWAT (Special Weapons and Tactics) - The Tactical Link to Hostage Negotiation," Political Terrorism and Business, ed. Yonah Alexander and Robert A. Kilmarx (New York: Praeger, 1979), pp. 195-211.

(6) The importance of establishing a rhythm in a siege situation is

cogently brought home by Dr. Dick Mulder, who was involved in responding to the hostage-takings by the South Moluccans in the Netherlands. See the transcript of his speech before the 25th General Assembly Meeting of the International Press Institute, March 10-12, 1976.

(7) The "strange feelings of camaraderie, closeness, empathy, friendship, even love [that] often develops between hostages and captives, between victim and victimizer," Frederick J. Hacker, Crusaders, Criminals, Crazies, Terror and Terrorism in Our Time (New York: W.W. Norton, 1976), p. 107.

(8) For a discussion of the complex issues raised by media/press relations, see Yonah Alexander, editor-in-chief, "Terrorism and the Media, A Special Issue," Terrorism, an International Journal 1, nos. 1 and 2 (1979). Michael T. McEwen and Stephen Sloan are special consulting editors. This issue contains the transcripts of two police/press meetings, one in Oklahoma City in 1976 and the other in New York City in 1977.

7 Subnational Threats to Civil Nuclear Facilities and Safeguards Institutions

Robert K. Mullen

Much has been said, at least in a general way, about the potential attractiveness of fuel cycle facilities for various subnational threat activities. For example, it has been suggested that reactors may be targets for sabotage; that nuclear material storage sites, fuel reprocessing facilities, and fuel enrichment facilities may draw the attention of subnational groups wishing to acquire special nuclear material through theft or diversion; and that special nuclear materials in transport may be particularly attractive targets for some subnational groups. (1)

The relative attractiveness of fuel cycle facilities to threats from terrorist or other subnational groups are in fact functions of the attributes, objectives, resources, capabilities, and access characteristics of such groups; the natures of the contained sensitive material or technology, and the demand for it (both licit and illicit); the quality of in-place physical security; the quality of material control and accounting safeguards; and other factors of a largely technological nature. These issues are examined in the following discussion.

RELATIVE ATTRACTIVENESS OF FUEL CYCLE FACILITIES

Reactors

Power reactors have been considered potentially attractive sabotage targets both because of the large radioactive inventories in their cores and spent fuel storage pools, and because of their symbolic value. A relatively minor act of sabotage that caused a reactor to go off line could in some instances highlight the vulnerability of power reactors to service interruptions. The fact that all central power stations, whether fossil fuel, or nuclear, are vulnerable to interruption through similar acts of sabotage may be irrelevant to the saboteur's aims, which may be to embarrass the government, or to create the impression that nuclear power plants are unsafe or unreliable.

Significant acts of reactor sabotage, that is, actions that could result in offsite releases of radiation, range from sabotage of the liquid or gaseous effluent holdup tanks to sabotage of the reactor core or spent fuel storage pool. The attractiveness of power reactors to saboteurs with such intentions is a matter of debate. A major point of contention is whether a subnational group would endanger the health and safety of the general population through an act that could result in the release of large amounts of radiation. It is frequently held that such acts would be avoided by subnational groups with domestic political aspirations, since in general such groups wish to maintain the goodwill or at least passive acceptance of the general population. (2) Exposing a segment of that population to a large release of radio-activity could annul goodwill, eliminate passivity, and result in undesirable countermeasures.

Irrespective of these considerations, sabotage attempts mounted outside the reactor exclusion area possess a range of potential capabilities for releasing radioactivity, depending upon the specific target within the power reactor complex and the mode of attack.

There are, for example, a range of weapons, some of them man-portable, that can penetrate the secondary reactor containment (the exterior concrete shell). Shoulder-fired antitank missiles utilizing shaped charge warheads have that capability. Such an attack could not, however, damage the reactor core. Although shaped charge projectiles could create a penetration of a few centimeters in diameter in this concrete containment, they would dissipate virtually all their energy in the process. Any secondary missiles that might be created during the penetration would be ballistically inefficient and possess random trajectories relative to the primary event. They would be incapable of penetrating the reactor core primary containment, but might cause some damage to electrical systems, valves, or other equipment within the reactor building. Collateral damage would likely be minimal, however, and in no case could a release of radiation be precipitated directly by such an attack.

There are, however, a few conventional munitions that could penetrate the secondary concrete containment and then damage the reactor core or core control systems to such a degree as to possibly lead to a radiation release. One type of munition that has that capability is the television-guided hard structure aerial bomb. It can penetrate several meters of concrete and deliver a significant quantity of high explosive to the interior of a building where, through appropriate fusing, it may subsequently be detonated. It is difficult to conceive, however, of subnational or mixed subnational-national groups mounting such a threat. In contrast to the shoulder-fired man-portable missile launcher (for which there is a precedent of subnational use, albeit against soft targets such as aircraft and fuel storage tanks), the raising of a threat employing hard structure munitions requires the mobilization of highly sophisticated military equipment and manpower. For a number of reasons, such a threat is considered to be virtually nonexistent except, perhaps, during war - a condition outside the scope of this paper.

The attractiveness of power reactors to subnational groups as sources of fissile material would appear to be marginal. Light and heavy water moderated reactors (LWRs and HWRs) and gas-cooled and advanced gas-cooled reactors (GCRs and AGRs) employ fuel that is enriched in fissile uranium to a maximum of about 4 percent (6 percent for some AGR designs). Chemical conversion to the hexafluoride gas, isotopic enrichment, conversion to oxide or nitrite, and finally conversion to uranium metal would be required to process fresh, unirradiated fuel to weapons-usable form (about 90 percent fissile uranium). While not an overwhelming task for a national group (safeguards measures aside), it would appear to be a daunting task for a subnational group either within or without a government.

The light water breeder reactor (LWBR), employing fuel that is enriched in fissile uranium to about 13 percent, seems to be little more attractive for the same reasons.

The high temperature gas-cooled reactor (HTGR), the pebble-bed or thorium high temperature reactor (THTR), and the liquid metal fast breeder reactor (LMFBR) either use uranium enriched to weapons grade, or plutonium. Each of these reactor types would appear superficially to be more attractive to potential subnational adversaries than would those described previously, at least as concerns the theft of fresh fuel.

The HTGR and THTR employ similar fuel: high enriched uranium and thorium carbides. (3) It should be noted, however, that the high enriched uranium is in the form of small spheres, and in fresh fuel is diluted 1:4 with thorium spheres. These uranium and thorium carbide spheres are coated with silicon carbide and pyrolytic carbon. Recovering the high enriched uranium from this fuel is a rather difficult proposition, requiring that the pyrolytic carbon be burned off, the remaining silicon carbide removed with highly specialized and hardened crushers or grinders, and the uranium chemically separated from the thorium.

For purposes of this discussion, fuel for the LMFBR is assumed to be a blend of plutonium and unenriched (or depleted) uranium as the oxides. Plutonium would constitute 10 to 20 percent of the heavy metal, and would in theory be directly utilizable in a nuclear weapon, although several hundred kilograms of the blended fuel would be required. Recovering the plutonium from unirradiated LMFBR fuel requires a fuel processing facility. This may not present significant difficulties to a subnational group, even if that group were required to construct such a facility. (4)

The bare sphere critical mass for plutonium oxide ranges from 35 to 90 kilograms (kg). (5) Reflected, that mass may be reduced to about 12 to 15 kg. (6) Since there are about 50 grams of plutonium in each LMFBR fuel pin, approximately 250 to 300 fuel pins would have to be processed to recover 12 to 15 kg. of plutonium. A subnational group bent on acquiring from unirradiated LMFBR fuel enough fissile material for one nuclear explosive has two alternatives. The first is to divert somewhere between one-half and one metric ton of LMFBR fuel and construct a device directly from this material. The second alternative is to process the diverted fuel and recover the contained plutonium.

Since, in theory, unirradiated LMFBR fuel may be employed directly in a nuclear explosive device, the LMFBR may be considered to be more attractive to potential subnational adversaries than other reactors. It should be noted, however, that a weapon constructed from such material would weigh several metric tons, up to one metric ton of that amount being LMFBR fuel.

In most circumstances, fresh, unirradiated reactor fuel would appear relatively less attractive a material to subnationals than other materials that are present elsewhere in nuclear fuel cycles. Nevertheless, an attractiveness hierarchy of sorts may be perceived from the foregoing, with those reactors fueled with low enriched or natural uranium the least attractive, and the LMFBR potentially the most attractive.

Spent Fuel

Spent fuel discharged from the cores of all these reactors is, of course, quite different in isotopic and elemental composition from unirradiated fuel.   Spent fuel is also highly radioactive, but the generally held assumption that the fissile material in spent fuel is protected from diversion by this radioactivity must be tempered by the consideration that after a decade or so, significant radioactive decay has occurred, and the problems of handling spent fuel somewhat reduced thereby. (7) LWR spent fuel storage pools have, for this reason, recently been described as "plutonium mines." (8)

Thus questions are raised concerning the attractiveness to subnational groups of long-term storage spent fuel; its attractiveness under conditions of retrievable storage in waste repositories; and its attractiveness in the transportation cycle between reactors; away-from-reactor storage, or waste repositories.

Spent fuel may be considered an attractive target for sabotage either in storage or in transport. The attractiveness of a spent fuel storage pool to subnationals for purposes of sabotage revolves around not only the previously discussed possible drawback of placing the general population at risk, but also around the question of the degree of technical competence required to successfully carry out such an act.

Most, but not all, spent fuel storage pools are below ground level. There are few acts of sabotage that could result in the release of significant radiation offsite from below-grade pools. If truly large quantities of explosives are detonated in such a pool in order to remove the cooling water, the residual heat in very recently discharged fuel may be sufficient to cause the fuel to partially melt and release radioactive gases. But such a scenario verges on the incredible for a couple of reasons. First, the quantity of high explosives required to remove the cooling water from the spent fuel pool is in the hundreds of pounds, and this loss of cooling water would not predictably result in a fuel meltdown. In addition, detonation of the explosives may alter the geometrical relationships of the fuel elements in such as way as to preclude any melting, irrespective of the amount of cooling water present.

With respect to above-grade spent fuel storage pools, some have walls that are common to the exterior walls of the buildings in which they are located. These concrete walls are approximately one meter thick, and can be penetrated with shoulder-fired antitank projectiles (9) - an attack requiring very little in the way of technical competence. Such projectiles would, however, create holes of only a few centimeters in diameter. Cooling water lost through such holes could be easily replaced by emergency water supplies, and there would be little or no danger of the contained fuel being uncovered. The small amounts of radioactivity lost in the leaking water could all be retained onsite.

One of the more technically difficult explosive attacks against an above-grade spent fuel storage pool involves the use of a platter charge. Platter charges can be quite simple devices. To design, fabricate, and place one that could penetrate a spent fuel storage pool containment would, however, require the possession of a considerable degree of sophistication in explosives technology. Even given that, it is far from certain that a platter charge would perform as desired without considerable testing.

In summary, although the spent fuel storage pool is inherently more accessible to some acts of sabotage than is the reactor core, it would appear nevertheless to be an unattractive target from the standpoint of causing a radiation release.

The requirements for, and the consequences of, effective sabotage of spent fuel in transport are largely unknown. The U.S. Nuclear Regulatory Commission presently assumes that sabotage that breaches a loaded spent fuel shipping cask would result in the release of all volatiles, and 1 percent of the contained solids would be released in the form of respirable particles. (10) These are very conservative estimates.

The preceding discussion deals with sabotage aimed at releasing radioactivity and the relative attractiveness of these targets to subnational groups for such purposes. It should be recognized that the potential attractiveness of these targets to subnational groups for sabotage may not lie in the release of radiation, but in disablement or damage which does not release radiation, and which may result in embarrassment to the regime, publication of the saboteurs' objectives, or some other result that may be perceived to advance subnational goals.

Finally, reactors and their attendant facilities, and the fuels necessary for their operation, appear to be relatively unattractive sources of fissile materials. Other fuel cycle facilities appear more attractive in this regard.

Fuel Enrichment Facilities

Two enrichment technologies are of current commercial importance: gas diffusion and gas centrifuge. A third technology, related to gas centrifuge technology, is the Becker nozzle process and its variants. A pilot nozzle enrichment facility is in operation in South Africa, and Brazil has contracted with the Federal Republic of Germany for an enrichment facility based on this technology. (11) The locations and characteristics of declared enrichment plants, existing, on order, and planned, are available elsewhere. (12)

Discussion of the potential involvement of subnationals with enrichment facilities dedicated to low enriched uranium production has revolved around the possibility of employment of these facilities in clandestine enrichment schemes. While this possibility cannot be dismissed out of hand, even for subnational groups, there exist other subnational activities in which enrichment technology figures prominently and which have not been examined in depth until recently. These will be touched upon following brief discussions of potential safeguards problems at enrichment facilities, and the potential attractiveness of enrichment facilities as sabotage targets.

The potential for subnational groups to attempt further enrichment of low enrichment uranium without reconfiguring the process stream of an enrichment facility has recently been examined. (13) This appears to be a most unlikely scenario for subnational acquisition or weapons-grade uranium, no matter what current enrichment technology is examined. The possibility of reconfiguring an enrichment facility would seem, on the other hand, to present an alternative possibility for subnational acquisition of high-enriched uranium. There are, however, a number of significant technology-specific and safeguards impediments to such schemes.

In a gas diffusion facility, the principal technological impediments to successfully reconfiguring such a facility to clandestinely produce high enriched uranium are:

- very low enrichment per stage;

- large separative capacity per unit;

- large in-process inventory of uranium hexafluoride (UF_6) gas; and

- a prolonged time (weeks to months) to reach isotopic equilibrium, and steady state operation.

A facility with large capacity stages in a single cascade connected in series to produce low enriched uranium (2 to 4 percent in ^{235}U) cannot be operated to produce high enriched uranium, nor reconfigured for that purpose. The enrichment could be extended under conditions of total reflux, but it is questionable whether high enriched uranium could be produced without construction of additional stages.

A facility constructed with two cascades that operate in parallel, both producing low enriched uranium, could in principle be reconfigured into one large cascade to produce high enriched uranium. A period of several weeks would be required for such a reconfigured facility to come into the new isotopic equilibrium. It would also take several months to reconfigure the facility. It is not clear how this could be done without the connivance of resident and visiting safeguards inspectors, and with a large number of operating and management personnel.

A third possibility for producing high enriched uranium in a gas diffusion cascade designed to produce low enriched uranium exists: the recycling of gaseous UF_6. Again, however, several weeks would be required to achieve isotopic equilibrium. The facility would be operating at inefficient and suboptimum levels, and the change in operating mode would become obvious to safeguards inspectors and operating personnel since, among other things, UF_6 feed would have been cut off.

Gas centrifuge facilities, in contrast to gas diffusion facilities, have a higher enrichment per stage, a low separative capacity per unit, and a smaller in-process gas inventory, and can reach isotopic equilibrium in about one day. They also have a number of cascades operating in parallel, as opposed to gas diffusion facilities, which generally consist of a single cascade.

Although it is in principle possible to produce high enriched uranium in a gas centrifuge facility dedicated to the production of low enriched uranium, by operating a cascade in a reflux or recycle mode, the most direct way would seem to be to reconnect the required number of cascade stages into a cascade of sufficient length to produce what is wanted. Some of the cascades could be connected to produce high enriched uranium, while the remaining cascades would produce the legitimate product. The in-process gas inventory in gas centrifuge cascades is very small compared to gas diffusion cascades, and the time for a centrifuge cascade to come into the new isotopic equilibrium between diffusion and centrifuge facilities may be important in an overall clandestine operation, since the operators would be likely to be less exposed to detection. Reconfiguring a centrifuge facility to produce high enriched uranium is, however, a time-consuming procedure. The existence of an adequate inspection strategy would probably expose the operators to detection during either reconfiguration or operation, unless the operators themselves were in collusion with the facility operators and managers. (14)

Although the Becker nozzle enrichment process is well on the way to the commercial stage, information concerning it is very tightly held by those marketing it and those either building facilities or committing themselves to do so in the future. (15) The basics of the generic nozzle enrichment process are well known, but the configuration and operating characteristics of enrichment facilities based on this process are known only in the most general terms; thus the attractiveness of such facilities to subnational groups for producing high enriched uranium, relative to other enrichment technology, cannot be assessed.

There is growing concern that laser isotope separation will prove to be commercially viable, and that if it does it may become the most attractive of all enrichment technologies for subversion to illicit purposes. (16) At issue is the apparently large isotopic separation factors that are at least theoretically possible with laser technology.

The seeming usefulness to nuclear weapons proliferators of an enrichment technology with a high separation factor may be illusory, however. It would seem that laser enrichment facilities dedicated to the production of low enriched uranium can be built in such a way that to alter their production to high enriched uranium would require resources in excess of those considered available to subnationals. (17)

All discussion to this point relative to potential clandestine employment of uranium enrichment facilities to produce high enriched uranium has dealt with facilities dedicated to production of low enriched uranium for use in LWR or other fuel cycles. If the HTGR or THTR fuel cycles were to become commercially viable, then large-scale production of high enriched (weapons-grade) uranium would ensue in order to suppor t them. In the United States, current production of high enriched uranium supports the military weapons program, propulsion reactors, and a demonstration HTGR. (The initial core loading at the Shippingport experimental LWBR employs ^{235}U enriched to about 13 percent. If this experiment continues, it may be expected that future core loadings will contain ^{235}U enriched to about 91 percent, that is, weapons grade.)

Commercial production of high enriched uranium for initial HTGR or THTR core loadings, or for makeup fissile material, places quite a different complexion on the potential of either gas or centrifuge enrichment facilities as sources of fissile material. Although HTGR and THTR fuels are considered to be relatively unattractive to subnationals, as was discussed earlier, the feed for HTGR and THTR fuel fabrication facilities coming from fuel enrichment facilities would probably be UF_6 highly enriched in 235_U. This material may be more easily converted to a form useful for nuclear weapons than is fabricated HTGR or THTR fuel; therefore, facilities producing high enriched uranium for HTGR or THTR fuel (or for any other purpose) can be considered inherently more attractive to potential subnational adversaries than enrichment facilities producing low enriched uranium.

Although safeguards measures such as, for example, isotopic correlation techniques (18) may lessen the attractiveness of enrichment facilities to subnational groups, such impediments to diversion of high enriched uranium may only be inconveniences to a mixed subnational-national effort.

With respect to the sabotage of fuel enrichment facilities, the potential consequences of such acts fall into three categories: chemical effects, radiological effects, and effects on national or regional nuclear energy programs.

Chemical effects would arise largely from flourine, which could be liberated upon explosive disruption of UF_6 feed cylinders (which contain up to 14 tons of UF_6) or penetration of anhydrous hydrofluoric acid (HF) tanks (which may contain up to 5 tons of HF). Sabotage of other parts of an enrichment facility could also result in fluorine releases, but releases potentially possible through sabotage of UF_6 feed cylinders or HF storage tanks appear to be the worst credible ones.

The maximum release of fluorine from such attacks could have an adverse, but transient, impact on man. Calculated concentrations from sabotage events of the nature being considered indicate that the tolerable but sublethal concentration of fluorine in air could be exceeded in the vicinity of the release. (19)

Agricultural effects could be significant, since green plants exhibit marked effects from rather low atmospheric fluoride exposures of a few hours. Other local, transient environmental effects could be expected, their extent dependent on site-specific factors.

Radioactive releases under these circumstances, if evenly distributed, would result in uranium ground concentration somewhat above that in average uranium ore. Calculated occupational exposures from worst-case sabotage would result in fractions of total body and critical organ (bone) exposure limits for uranium.

There is another aspect of enrichment technology, however, in which there could be subnational interest - the unregulated and illicit transfer of sensitive elements of enrichment technology. There is some suggestion this may already have occurred. (20)

In summary, fuel enrichment facilities appear marginally attractive to subnational groups for purposes of acquiring fissile material; moderately attractive to subnational commercial interests who may be influenced by prospects of sales, or motivated by extranational allegiances to transfer enrichment technology to unsafeguarded environments; (21) and moderately attractive as sabotage targets for purposes of embarrassing the regime.

Fuel Fabrication Facilities

Nuclear fuel fabrication facilities may take several forms, depending upon the reactor type or types serviced, and will therefore be variously attractive to a range of potential subnational adversaries. Fuel fabrication facilities which service LWRs only would not appear to be attractive to most subnationals as sources of fissile material for reasons previously discussed concerning unirradiated LWR fuel.

Fuel fabrication facilities that service research reactors, some propulsion reactors, and power reactors such as the HTGR and THTR, on the other hand, receive feed in the form of highly enriched uranium as either the hexafluoride, the dioxide, or the dicarbide. Prior to its processing into fuel, some of this uranium could be used directly in a nuclear weapon. Both uranium dioxide and uranium dicarbide can be used, although uranium hexafluoride would require processing before it could be used in a nuclear weapon. Fuel fabrication end products could also be attractive to a range of potential subnational adversaries.

As was indicated in the earlier discussion of uranium enrichment, civil production of high enriched uranium is currently limited to research reactors and demonstration power reactors (THTR fuel for the

West German reactor at Hamm-Uentrop is enriched in the United States). Should HTGR, THTR, or other power reactors utilizing high enriched uranium become commercially viable, however, the amount of weapons-grade uranium in fuel fabrication facilities would increase markedly. Under such circumstances it would have to be assumed that certain elements of fuel fabrication process lines, depending to some degree on the nature of the processes and the products, and the safeguards in place, could be attractive to potential subnational adversaries as sources of fissile uranium for clandestine weapons programs. Such programs could be entirely subnational or, as is more likely, mixed, in which subnationals act at the behest of national clients.

Fuel Reprocessing Facilities

In existing uranium once-through fuel cycles, the sources of uranium for fuel fabrication facilities are uranium enrichment facilities. In uranium (or plutonium) recycle, fuel fabrication feed would in many cases derive from fuel reprocessing facilities, with supplemental feed from uranium enrichment facilities.

As with fuel fabrication, fuel reprocessing can encompass a range of capabilities, either within the same complex or separately. In all cases, however, fissile material in the form of pluotonium or ^{233}U, depending on the fuel cycle being serviced, would be present. Uranium-235 would be present in significant enrichments (about 30 percent) from recycle HTGR fuel, (22) although it may not be in a form anywhere in the reprocessing cycle that would be attractive to subnational adversaries. It is assumed here that recycle THTR fuel would be of similar character to that of HTGR fuel with respect to first recycle residual ^{235}U.

Insofar as is known, reprocessing of HWR fuel takes place almost entirely within military programs, with the notable exception of India, which has reprocessed fuel from an HWR reactor, ostensibly for the purpose of developing a "peaceful nuclear explosive" technology. Descriptions of existing, past, and planned commercial and laboratory scale reprocessing facilities in support of LWR, HWR, and breeder reactor technology (outside the Warsaw Treaty Organization states) can be found elsewhere. (23)

The potential attractiveness of reprocessing facilities to sub-nationals lies in the large inventories of fissionable material present, either in storage or in process. At the receiving end of a reprocessing facility, fissionable material is present in a spent fuel matrix, that is, accompanied by fission products and transuranics, and is in an intensely radioactive environment. Intuitively, one would expect that if there were to be a subnational or mixed subnational-national effort to acquire fissionable material from a reprocessing facility, such an effort would be concentrated on the process stream, or at the storage facilities that receive separated fissionable material from the process stream.

Although there is at present no reprocessing of spent fuel from commercial HWR power reactors, nor from demonstration HTGR or THTR power reactors - which is to say that a recycle fuel cycle for these reactors has yet to be defined for commercial application - one may treat their reprocessing characteristics, as they relate to the presence of fissile materials, on a generic basis. That is, reprocessing per se may be discussed relative to its potential attractiveness to subnational adversaries irrespective of the type of reactor serviced.

Reprocessing is not, of course, limited to power reactors. Material test reactors, critical assemblies, and other research reactors can figure significantly in any subnational or mixed subnational-national reprocessing scheme, particularly in cases in which there may be an effort to construct unannounced facilities for purposes of reprocessing fuel from any of the above, including power reactors. (24)

In response to the inability to limit the spread of reprocessing technology, certain technological innovations have been suggested whose objectives are to reduce the immediate utility of reprocessing facility products for weapons purposes. These take a number of forms, depending somewhat on the nature of the fuel cycle involved.

Perhaps the most familiar of these are the so-called blending schemes proposed for reprocessing spent fuel from uranium-plutonium fuel cycles. These are summarized elsewhere, (25) and it is notable that they are not considered effective safeguards against national diversion schemes. It does not appear then, that these blending schemes would be effective safeguards measures against mixed subnational-national threats either.

Central to this issue is the presence in the open literature of information on selective dissolution techniques for recovering plutonium from blends of plutonium and uranium. (26) By employing such techniques, mechanical blends of plutonium and uranium could readily be separated; chemical blends (coprocessed materials) would require some additional treatment, but not much. It could be assumed that the hazards of illicitly reprocessing spent radioactive fuel would be taken into account, but there may arise circumstances in which subnationals would not consider it necessary to avoid these hazards, i.e., the processors could be considered expendable.

Other alternatives to blending schemes that have been considered, and largely dropped, include so-called spiking of reprocessed fuel with radioactive isotopes, and partial reprocessing, or partial stripping of fission products from reprocessed spent fuel. Both have the same objective: to make the reprocessed fuel so radioactive that extensive shielding is required for its safe handling. (27) For a variety of reasons, neither spiking nor partial reprocessing are viewed as either effective or practicable safeguards measures for reprocessing facilities.

An aspect of fuel reprocessing facilities that may appear to contribute to their attractiveness to subnationals as potential sabotage targets is their high-level waste storage facilities. The trend in spent fuel reprocessing, however (at least in the LWR fuel cycle), is to in-process vitrification of high-level wastes. It would be very difficult, perhaps impossible, to cause an offsite release of radioactivity from a facility storing such wastes.

Transportation

To many, transportation seems the weakest link in any fuel cycle in which fissile material, separated or not, is transferred among fuel cycle facilities. It is considered weak from the standpoint of safeguarding against theft, overt or covert, as well as from the standpoint of sabotage.

Several schemes have been proposed for transporting fissile material between fuel cycle facilities, including armed surface transport, air transport with dedicated aircraft operating from dedicated airstrips, and a number of other schemes that have been described elsewhere for a mixed oxide recycle LWR fuel cycle, and that are generally applicable to the transport options available to other fuel cycles in which fuel cycle facilities are dispersed. (28)

Popular wisdom has it that various transportation links could be eliminated, in particular those in which separated or separable fissile materials are transported, then such materials could be made as secure against misuse as anywhere else in the fuel cycle. On the other hand, it appears that if various safeguards innovations presently in the design stage were implemented, materials in transit would appear to be as well safeguarded as those in storage at fixed facilities.

The preceding applies principally to pure subnational threats. Mixed subnational-national threats are quite a different matter. There are more opportunities for subverting or neutralizing safeguards systems under the latter conditions, but this is as true for materials at fixed facilities as it is for materials in transport.

RELATIVE VULNERABILITIES OF NUCLEAR FACILITIES AND SAFEGUARDS INSTITUTIONS

The relative vulnerabilities of fuel cycle facilities and institutions to subnational threats, particularly mixed subnational-national threats, may be viewed almost entirely in terms of institutional vulnerabilities. That is to say, while the possibility of occurrence of physical attacks on fuel cycle facilities by subnationals must be taken into account in overall safeguards planning, experience seems to indicate that subnational threats are of more concern to institutions that support civil nuclear power programs.

Once this is accepted, then the subnational threat may be divided into two broad categories: subnationals acting in their own behalf, or at the behest of other subnationals; and mixed subnational-national activities in which subnationals act with the actual or tacit support of a national government - indeed, with a national government as a client. The situations whereby these arrangements may occur include:

Potential Subnational Threats

- Indigenous subnational group acting on its own behalf, or on behalf of another subnational group (indigenous, extranational, or transnational);

- Extranational subnational group acting on its own behalf, or on behalf of another subnational group (indigenous, extranational, or transnational);

- Transnational subnational group acting on its own behalf, or on behalf of another subnational group (indigenous, extranational, or transnational).

Potential Mixed Subnational-National Threats

- Indigenous subnational group acting on behalf of its own government;

- Indigenous subnational group acting on behalf of a government other than its own;

- Extranational subnational group acting on behalf of a host government;

- Extranational subnational group acting on behalf of a government outside the group's country of residence;

- Transnational subnational group acting on behalf of host or other government;

- Subnational group with formal ties to government, acting on behalf of another subnational group, its own or another government, or combinations thereof.

As can be perceived from the foregoing, terrorists may (and in fact do) play little part in subnational activities against nuclear facilities or institutions, insofar as the illicit transfer of nuclear materials or technology is concerned. This, at least, is borne out by the historical record to date. Who then are these subnationals?

They fall into two broad categories: those within government (which may not always mean they are working for the government) and those outside the government. Groups inside government that are alleged to have contributed to incidents involving illicit or irregular transfers of nuclear materials or technology, or clandestine nuclear weapons programs, include:

- The military establishment;

- The nuclear energy establishment (in a nationalized industry;

- Administrative elements of government.

Groups or individuals outside the government who are alleged to have made similar contributions to the proliferation of nuclear weapons technology include:

- The scientific and technological community;
- Management in nuclear industry;
- Other nuclear and nonnuclear commercial interests;
- Independent agents.

Space does not permit a discussion here of the characteristics (attributes, objectives, resources, capabilities, and access) of these and other groups that have the potential to subvert safeguards on the peaceful uses of nuclear technology.

The nuclear institutions some of the above groups may affect in adverse ways include the arrays of nuclear safeguards, domestic and international, that have evolved more or less parallel to the deployment of nuclear energy systems. The vulnerabilities of these institutions lie, as may be surmised, not so much in their physical safeguards (that is, physical security), but in the internal weaknesses of policies and procedures that may be exploited by subnationals in connivance with, or at the behest of, a national government.

It is not infrequently noted that the development or functioning, or both, of safeguards institutions is often impeded by the manner in which physical security, and material control and accounting safeguards are implemented; the degrees to which independent verification of safeguards is permitted or possible; the restrictions on third-party evaluations of safeguards programs; and other factors. (29) Much of the criticism of safeguards institutions is concerned with the nuclear policies of sovereign states, in spite of allegations of subnational activities that could contribute to both vertical and horizontal proliferation of nuclear weapons through resources associated with nuclear power programs. Thus many, perhaps all, safeguards programs fail to take into consideration mechanisms whereby 1) sovereign states may utilize subnational elements to foster a proliferation enterprise; or 2) subnational elements may themselves engage in activities that could have sensitive consequences.

The bases for these conclusions lie in the accounts of events alleged to have occurred from the mid-1960s to the present. (30) Some involved the alleged illicit transfer of fissile material in such forms that only minor processing would have been required to prepare it for nuclear weapons; others are suspected to have involved the illicit movements of substantial amounts of source materials; and still others are said to have involved the unregulated transfer of sensitive nuclear technology. Subnational elements are said to have been involved in each of these incidents. (31)

It would seem that nuclear safeguards institutions as presently constituted have worked to prevent direct illicit nation-to-nation dealings in nuclear materials or technology. These institutions, the intents of which are expressed in various conventions, seem to exert enough influence in the international community to prevent these kinds of dealings even among nations that have declined to accede to the Treaty on the Non-Proliferation of Nuclear Weapons (NPT). It would also seem, however, that these institutions have failed to prevent dealings at subnational levels in which nations become indirectly involved both as suppliers and as clients. Finally, it would appear that the vulnerability of nuclear fuel cycle materials or technologies to subversion by subnational or mixed subnational-national interests appears to be relatively insensitive to fuel cycle characteristics. That is to say, the small number of alleged events that are public knowledge involved materials or technology appropriate to a variety of fuel cycles.

This leads to the conclusion that optimum paths to the goal of preventing illicit subnational activities lies more in the domain of institutions than in existing or innovative fuel cycle technology - at least for the foreseeable future.

Vulnerabilities of Safeguards Institutions to Subnational Threats

There is no experience (at least there are no open accounts) with subnational efforts to acquire fuel cycle materials for use in developing a subnational nuclear weapons capability, and with the exception of a few hardly credible statements, (32) no announced intent of subnational groups to so utilize such materials. On the other hand, there are several accounts of the involvement of subnational elements in diversions of sensitive materials and technology at the behest of, or in cooperation with, national powers. (33)

Whether or not there is substance to any of the allegations concerning these events, the fact of such allegations and the scenarios suggested by them, raise some fundamental questions concerning the vulnerabilities of safeguards institutions to mixed subnational-national threats. For example:

● What subnational threats are least effectively safeguarded against by existing safeguards institutions?

● Can national participation in a subnational threat enhance the probability of avoiding safeguards?

● Are mixed subnational-national threats sensitive to the types of fuel cycles in operation under present safeguards institutions? Under some other safeguards institutions?

● Can technological controls, "fixes," or internationalization schemes result in resistance against mixed subnational-national threats?

● What sets mixed subnational-national threats apart from subnational or national threats?

This seems a minimum, but bounding, set of questions concerning the possible vulnerabilities of safeguards to potential subnational threats.

Safeguards Weaknesses

The inconsistencies and vagueness of some domestic nuclear safeguards regulations and the lack of implementation or inadequate implementation of some nondomestic safeguards may in themselves be considered evidence of some weakness in safeguards. The allegations of recent and past events are individually rather specific with regard to the nature of the subnational threat in each, including possible mechanisms and procedures employed in them. Common to all these events is the element of deception.

As was pointed out by Edelhertz and Walsh, (34) the implementation of so-called insider crime (or some internal threat to nuclear facilities) can be characterized as subtle, clandestine, and complex. Such qualities are not exclusively those of the insider, of course. It should be recognized, however, that each of the past occurrences of alleged illicit or irregular subnational activities (35) involved individuals directly associated with either some element of a nuclear fuel cycle, or elements of national governments, or both.

It may be observed that potential internal threats to nuclear fuel cycle facilities and institutions are, and continue to be, addressed defensively. It may also be observed that safeguards are only broadly applicable to technology transfer (although other measures may be more specific); they are only marginally effective for source materials; and there is evidence that their effectiveness to date in controlling and accounting for weapons-grade material is variable and potentially subject to manipulation. (36)

It seems fair to conclude that subnational activities characteristic of those of the subtle, clandestine, and complex insider threat are, in contrast to external forceful threats, least effectively safeguarded against.

In this regard, eminent safeguards authorities continue to treat the issue of protection against potential subnational threats as primarily one of improved physical security. (37) Perhaps a contributor to the failure to recognize the existence of safeguards requirements beyond physical security measures is the tendency to equate subnational threats with threats from terrorists; this notion appears much in the literature recently. While the potential threats posed by terrorists should not be minimized, subnational threats go quite beyond those that are considered to be characteristic of terrorists, threats which, in general, are mitigated by physical security measures.

In very broad terms, what past and existing safeguards seem not to cope with effectively are those mechanisms which arise in any controlled market in which there is trade in high-value commodities, i.e., mechanisms to avoid controls. It is these mechanisms which, it is alleged, have been exploited by subnationals in the past. There seems little reason to expect that allegations of similar activities will not arise in the future.

Effects of National Participation in Subnational Threats

Can national participation in subnational threats enhance the probability of avoiding safeguards? Historically, the answer would seem to be yes. It would also seem logical that a nation would engage subnationals in order to acquire nuclear materials or technology either not available to it, or that it wished to acquire clandestinely or in a nonattributable manner.

It is not quite that straightforward, however. For example, there may be considerable subnational activity in the conceptual design of nuclear explosives within the scientific and technological community of a nation. Such activity may proceed unofficially at the behest of some element of government or quite independently of any outside stimulus. At some point, scientific advisers may convince the government to pursue the program as a matter of national policy. Such a scenario has been suggested as having occurred in India and, perhaps, Sweden. (38) Any subsequent duplicity required to continue such a program would derive entirely from national policy.

In actuality, therefore, the question posed earlier never arises, since a mixed subnational-national threat never exists - not quite, anyway. It is not altogether clear how to categorize a situation in which the legally invested leaders of a nation are made aware of the activities of their scientists and encourage them, in a nonattributable way, to continue their studies until a decision can be made whether to bring them into the body of policy expressing national goals and objectives. Prior to such investment, a mixed threat could be viewed to exist.

A basis for the inevitability of national involvement in a subnational proliferation threat may be found in the perhaps more obvious need for a customer. This is particularly true of uncontrolled transfers of source materials and sensitive technology, since it is unlikely anyone but a national government would possess the resources to utilize either in a credible proliferation venture.

The same may not be said for fissibe materials, whether separated or not. It must be pointed out, however, that all public allegations concerning uncontrolled transfers of fissile material implicate subnationals acting with national governments as clients; there are no allegations involving purely subnational elements in such transfer, that is, subnational clients (terrorist or otherwise) for such materials.

Mixed Subnational- National Threat Activities

For purposes of illustration, two incidents with nuclear weapons proliferation potentials (out of about ten known to the author) are summarized briefly below. Both are alleged to have involved subnationals. From one, it may be concluded that a nation-state was the client; it is less apparent who the client may have been in the second incident. In neither incident, however, (nor in any other) is there evidence of a subnational client for nuclear technology.

The first of these incidents involved a loss of 200 metric tons (MT) of uranium. The chronology of events concerning this incident appeared to have proceeded on two parallel paths. This chronology is presented in table 7.1, and is reconstructed from several accounts concerning the incident. (39) Subnational involvements seem apparent, including the president of at least one firm in the Federal Republic of Germany, an attorney in Zurich, and a number of independent agents.

The critical maneuver in the entire operation was to evade Euratom safeguards. In 1968, when this occurred, the primary international safeguards instrument governing nuclear activities between European Economic Commission (EEC) nations, in particular the FRG, was the Euratom Treaty. Chapter 6, Article 75 of the Euratom Treaty states:

> The provisions of this Chapter shall not apply to undertakings in respect of the processing, transformation, or shaping of ores, source materials or special fissionable materials entered into between:
>
> (a) several persons or enterprises, in cases where the materials after being processed, transformed or shaped are subsequently to be returned to the person or enterprise of origin.

It would seem, then, that Euratom accepted at face value the representations of the FRG firm that the uranium ore was being shipped to an Italian firm for processing into a petrochemical catalyst, whence it would subsequently be returned to the FRG firm. The evidence that Euratom did indeed accept such representations is that the Italian firm had no capabilities whatsoever to so process the ore.

Thus the FRG operatives took advantage of an apparent lack of provision within the Euratom nuclear safeguards program for evaluating the bona fides of any intermediary in a chain of custody for uranium ore. The FRG firm merely had to represent to Euratom that the Italian firm was to process the ore as specified and then return it to the FRG firm. This permitted the people in the FRG to ship the ore to the putative processor when, in fact, the Italian firm was not the intended recipient. This, at least, is how the incident has been reconstructed elsewhere.

It should not be assumed from the foregoing, however, that the EEC was not at least hesitant about whether the safeguards provisions of the Euratom Treaty were enforced. There were, and are, such provisions. Chapter 7, Article 77 of the Euratom Treaty contains the following with respect to the safeguards responsibilities of the EEC:

> Within the framework of this Chapter, the Commission shall satisfy itself that in the territories of the Member States:

TABLE 7.1. Chronology of Events Leading to Loss of 200 Tons of Uranium

Date	The Ship	The Uranium	Date	The Ship	The Uranium
March 1968		Order placed by Asmara Chemie, Wiesbaden, with Societe General des Minerais (SGM) for 200 MT uranium oxide to be shipped to Morocco for processing into petrochemical catalyst.	Oct. 10, 1968		Contract for 200 MT uranium signed between Asmara Chemie and SGM.
			Oct. 30, 1968		Eurotom, by not intervening in sale, gives automatic approval for sale of uranium and its shipment from Antwerp to Genoa.
Aug. 20, 1968	Biscayne Traders Shipping Corp. (BTS) established in Zurich.	Asmara Chemie advised by SGM that uranium could not be shipped to Morocco, a non-EEC nation.	Nov. 6, 1968	Scheersberg A. leaves LaPallice, France, for Rotterdam.	
Aug. 21, 1968	All directors of BTS resign.		Nov. 11, 1968	Scheersberg A. arrives in Rotterdam. Entire crew, except captain, is fired.	
Aug. 21, 1968		Asmara Chemie approaches SAICA, Milan, for purposes of processing uranium. SAICA amends corporate constitution to permit it to do that. Italy is an EEC nation.	Nov. 15, 1968	Scheersberg A. sails from Rotterdam to Antwerp with new crew.	Uranium shipped from warehouse in Olen to dockside, Antwerp.
			Nov. 16, 1968	Scheersberg A. arrives in Antwerp. Uranium loaded on ship.	
Sept. 27, 1968	BTS purchases ship Scheersberg.		Nov. 17, 1968	Scheersberg A. sails from Antwerp, bound for Genoa.	
Sept. 28, 1968	Master and chief engineer of Scheersberg fired.		Dec. 2, 1968	Scheersberg A. arrives in Iskenderum, Turkey without uranium.	
Sept. 29, 1968	Scheersberg renamed Scheersberg A. Registry changed from West German to Liberian.		Jan. 17, 1969		EEC asks SAICA if it received uranium.
Oct. 2, 1968	Scheersberg A. leaves Rotterdam for Emden without captain or chief engineer.		May 1969		SAICA responds to EEC stating it did not receive uranium.
Oct. 7, 1968	Captain and chief engineer hired.		May 2, 1977		EEC states publicly that 200 MT uranium, shipped from Antwerp and bound for Genoa in 1968, is missing
Oct. 9, 1968	Scheersberg A. sails empty to Naples				

152

(a) ores, source materials and special fissionable materials are not diverted from their intended use by the users.

In the second incident it is less obvious whether subnational participation took place, and if it did, who they may have been, and who the client may have been as well. The essential elements of this incident are, first, the alleged continuation by the military, and perhaps by industrial interests as well, of a nuclear weapons research program in Sweden after the Swedish Parliament (Riksdag) instructed that all such research cease. (40) The second significant element was the apparent loss of three tons of uranium reactor fuel, as well as the loss of an estimated three kilograms of plutonium from the Eurochemic nuclear fuel reprocessing facility in Belgium, in which Sweden had an interest.

The nuclear weapons development (or feasibility) program had been underway for some period, with the apparent approval of the Swedish government, when in 1968 the Riksdag passed the Defense Act of 1968, which prohibited all such research. The Riksdag duly informed the military that the nuclear weapons research program must be brought to a halt forthwith. But the military apparently did not halt this research until sometime in 1972.

Elements of the Swedish armaments industry were said to have been brought into the program for purposes of designing and developing a nuclear weapon delivery vehicle. It is not clear whether this was done before or after the Riksdag ordered a halt to the program. If it was after this date then it would seem evident that the program was assuming a subnational character. It would seem equally evident, however, that subnational participation in the program would have involved not only the industrialists, but the military as well, including the scientists and technologists employed by them.

The disappearance of the three tons of reactor fuel, which was to have come from the ASEA's (Swedish General Electric Corporation's) nuclear fuel production facility in Vasteras, and was presumably intended for Sweden's only power reactor operating at that time (the Agesta reactor, a small power reactor built by the Swedes), as well as the loss of three kilograms of plutonium from the Eurochemic reprocessing facility at Mol, Belgium, occurred under circumstances even less well understood than the facts about the banned weapons research program.

The three tons of uranium disappeared from the Vasteras facility over a period of five years. It is conceivable that this discrepancy is entirely innocent, and not connected with the weapons research program. That is, all of it could have been lost as process waste, i.e., into air and water filters and elsewhere in the process system.

The loss of three kilograms of plutonium from reprocessed Swedish nuclear reactor fuel cannot be so easily explained away. When this plutonium was lost is not certain. Before 1968 a diversion could have been accomplished, with some help at the Eurochemic facility, by official Swedish representatives acting with official sanction. If it was lost after 1968, a diversion would not, it would seem, have occurred in quite the same way. Official Swedish representatives may have been involved, but would have been acting without the official sanction of their government (unless the government were clandestinely involved). Cooperation of Eurochemic personnel may have been required also.

Thus if subnational activities were involved in a diversion of plutonium, the potential range of actors includes the Swedish military and industrialists, Swedish technicians employed by them in Sweden and at the Eurochemic facility, and non-Swedish nationals at the Euro- chemic facility, perhaps including management and safeguards in- spectors.

The security chief of the Swedish Atomic Energy Board has been quoted as saying in 1978: "In the early 1970's I tried to learn the details about what happened to Agesta's plutonium, but I was not able to clear the matter up." (41)

Sensitivity of Mixed
Threats to Fuel Cycle Types

In the realm of potential subnational threats to fuel cycle facilities and institutions, are mixed subnational-national threats sensitive to fuel cycle characteristics? The initial impulse is to say yes, but again the issues do not seem so straightforward as to permit an unqualified response.

The record of alleged safeguards failures in the civil nuclear sector should be viewed in terms of the safeguards in place at those times, in terms of existing safeguards, and in terms of proposed safeguards regimes. Unfortunately, the nature and performance of safeguards programs outside the United States are matters of confidentiality; therefore evaluations of the ways in which safeguards may have been circumvented in these instances must be somewhat speculative. As a matter of fact, evaluations of events alleged to have occurred in the United States, since their particulars are not matters of public record, must also be speculative.

Some observations may nevertheless be made concerning the question at hand. It may be observed, for example, that all fuel cycles use source materials; all LWR fuel cycles employ sensitive enrichment technology, as do the HTGR and THTR fuel cycles, and in a derivative sense, the LMFBR fuel cycle; all fuel cycles employ fuel fabrication facilities; and so on. The point is, all fuel cycles contain materials or technology that may be employed for proliferation purposes, and the historical record suggests that several different fuel cycles have been exploited in the past to contribute to nuclear explosives programs. The question, then, is not whether subnational-national threats are sensitive to fuel cycle types, but whether they can be made sensitive to those fuel cycles that are deployed internationally.

To this, the answer seems to be perhaps. The goal seems to be worth pursuing, but the expectation that it will be achieved should be tempered by acceptance of the facts that:

- There exist nations with mature nuclear technological capabilities that are potentially isolated, threatened by external forces, outside the NPT, and capable of employing a variety of non-fuel cycle materials or technologies for a nuclear explosives development program;

- Isolation of a given fuel cycle in terms of restricting its deployment, or heavily conditioning it with safeguards and other measures, may increase threat pressures on alternative sources of materials utilizable in a proliferation program; and

- The employment, by a client state, of subnationals in an enterprise with proliferation potential is not a mechanism that has been, or seems to be now, specifically addressed by nuclear safeguards programs or research activities.

Sensitivity of Threats to
Technological Controls

The concept of technological control, independent of physical security or material control and accounting safeguards, includes restrictive control of technology, technological "fixes," and internationalization of technology.

Embargoing the transfer of technology, or unilaterally requiring renegotiations of already agreed-upon terms in existing agreements for cooperation, as was done by the United States with the 1978 Nuclear Non-Proliferation Act, may have several effects on national proliferation threats and their complexions. It is not clear whether such actions, unaccompanied by mechanisms to prevent their being circumvented by subnational activities, can in fact prevent the spread of sensitive technology. There already exist indications that subnational efforts were successfully applied to the unauthorized transfer of sensitive enrichment technology to a client state. (42)

The states participating in the Nuclear Suppliers Group (the London Club) have agreed among themselves that certain conditions must be met by recipient states prior to the transfer of technology or materials on a "trigger list,": and that the suppliers themselves agree to certain conditions which, broadly, acknowledge the proliferation potential of nuclear technology and materials and the necessity to accept the responsibilities associated with their transfer.

Although this agreement is not formalized in the form of a treaty, nevertheless its provision for sanctions against recipient states that violate agreed-upon terms would seem to provide inducements for such states to adhere to it. On the other hand, there appear to be no provisions for sanctions against supplier states should one of them not adhere to its guidelines. Of course, were a supplier state to engage subnationals to facilitate the transfer of sensitive technology to a client state which, for any number of reasons, would not be eligible to receive that technology, that state may avoid any opprobrium that could befall it were it to involve itself officially in such a transfer.

Since safeguards practice and research have, and do not emphasize, the potential for mischief through mixed subnational-national threats, it is difficult to believe that agreements that have no legal force are any more effective against such threats than existing treaties and agreements.

Technical "fixes," or modifications or materials or facility processes to raise the costs of using them for proliferation purposes, are likewise avoidable through the expedient of a mixed subnational-national enterprise. It is difficult not to accept the premise that in an environment in which there is no systematic application of resources against the mixed threat, there will somewhere at some time exist a nation that views the risks inherent in a mixed threat undertaking as less than the risks of not undertaking such an enterprise. It would appear that while so-called fixes may raise the threshold of risk in engaging in such threats, they may not discourage them. More importantly, there appear to be no qualities inherent in technological fixes alone that would increase the risk associated with a mixed threat effort except, perhaps, by reducing the number of options available to the threatener.

Internationalization is in a sense similar to restrictive control over transfer of technology or materials, in that controls are vested in an international body and not in sovereign states. Thus a supplier state would, in such a regime, transfer technology or materials to an international body that would retain permanent title to it. That, at least, is one proposal that is presently being examined among many proposed mechanisms for internationalization, which encompass various aspects of several fuel cycles.

Such proposals, if adopted, will not eliminate traditional supplier-client relationships in nuclear commerce. They will, of course, change the nature of those relationships for designated elements of particular fuel cycles. It is not apparent how internationalization can materially affect the basic problems that the mixed threat presents, however. In fact, there are some aspects of internationalization of fuel cycles or fuel cycle facilities that would seem to increase the potential for mixed subnational-national proliferation threats to be successful.

This observation is based in part upon the alleged circumstances surrounding at least one past event which involved close working relationships between elements of two governments. Of course, internationalization concepts may involve more than two governments, but it is not clear that that alone is sufficient to prevent collusive activities among subnationals and client states for purposes of proliferation, even in an international enclave.

Mixed Subnational-
National Threat Qualities

The mixed threat possesses a number of qualities that set it apart from either the purely subnational or the purely national threat. As was

suggested earlier, purely subnational threats of concern to nonproliferation goals are unlikely to occur except, perhaps, under circumstances
where they evolve into national programs. Such events may occur in
circumstances where subnational elements assume the reins of power,
or are in a position to favorably advise their governments to pursue a
nuclear explosives program which their analyses suggest to be feasible;
subsequent programs would be carried out as matters of national policy.

Purely national proliferation threats are, of course, situations which
international safeguards measures seek to prevent. In so doing, the
various agreements and conventions that address this problem do so in
terms appropriate to sovereign states and the relationships between
them as those concern commerce in nuclear technology and materials.

These and other safeguards mechanisms have been established to
prevent non-nuclear-weapons nations from acquiring civil nuclear
technology for noncivil purposes, or from converting civil nuclear
technology already in place to noncivil uses. They are predicated on a
defensive safeguards policy of adherence to agreed-upon conditions, and
assent not to acquire and subvert civil nuclear programs to the
development of nuclear explosives.

A nation that proceeds along a course obviously counter to the
intentions of the agreements it has entered into will very likely
sacrifice other options for proliferation available to it if it pursues
similar goals by employing subnationals. A client state that employs
subnationals to acquire materials or technology for a nuclear explosives
program may be able to shield itself from detection, or even suspicion,
for a significant period. Through the subtle, clandestine, and complex
mediations of subnationals, a nation may illicitly obtain materials or
technology with risks of exposure well within perceived limits of
acceptability.   With adequate planning and development of the
legitimate uses of nuclear energy, including research facilities, such a
mixed threat may lead to the establishment of an unannounced nuclear
weapons research program about which little can be done.

Such routes to a nuclear weapon capability would not be difficult to
pursue under all circumstances. Were a nation to pursue such a course,
it seems that engaging subnationals at some point in its accomplishment
decreases the risk of exposure, is less readily countered with existing
safeguards, and in general would contribute to the chances of achieving
the program goals.

THE IMPLICATIONS OF POTENTIAL SUBNATIONAL
ACTIVITIES FOR NUCLEAR SAFEGUARDS

Nuclear safeguards have been evaluated in exquisite detail with respect
to their national and international aspects. Only recently have the
implications of potential subnational activities for safeguards in global
environments come under consideration. Even so, these are yet to be
articulated much beyond the requirements for physical security

measures to mitigate potential subnational threats from groups that are, for the most part, external to the nuclear industry. (43)

So-called insider threats are beginning to receive generic treatment, (44) with certain subsets of this category receiving more systematic and specific attention. (45) To date, virtually all such work has perforce been related rather directly to domestic U.S. safeguards, with very little attention paid to potential international applications. In these matters it must be understood that analyzing potential insider threats external to the domestic U.S. nuclear industry would require access to foreign national safeguards programs. For the most part, such access is at present attainable only by the International Atomic Energy Agency (IAEA), which is bound to keep the particulars of such programs confidential.

Recently the possibility that subnationals could engage in illicit trade in nuclear materials has been suggested, (46) as has the possibility of subnational elements attempting to influence the politics of their country with nuclear resources acquired from the military. (47)

Potential subnational threats have most frequently been discussed as being terrorist or criminal in nature. Both within and without government the overt attack on facilities, or the covert attempt by employees to divert materials from facilities, continues to receive proportionately greater attention in the subnational arena than do potential threats by groups other than terrorist or criminal ones, groups which, because of their inherent capabilities, attributes, resources, and access to materials, facilities, or sensitive technology, appear to deserve at least equal attention.

Various of these groups possess characteristics which may make them particularly suitable for participation in mixed subnational-national ventures that could threaten the nonproliferation goals expressed in various international conventions and national safeguards programs. (48)

Some of these potential subnational threats have been articulated, but they are, in general, viewed as of less national concern than the potential for horizontal proliferation of nuclear weapons technology. Past events suggest, however, the possibility that subnational elements contributing to such proliferation may have been underestimated in the overall calculus of evolving nuclear safeguards policy. (49) This element of subnational threat to nuclear fuel cycles and institutions is examined from the perspective of its potential implications for domestic and international nuclear safeguards institutions.

Existing Safeguards Programs

Domestic Safeguards Programs

For the most part, domestic safeguards have been oriented toward protecting against the overt, forceful attempt at sabotage or theft of materials, and are exemplified by regulations set forth in Title 10 of the

Code of Federal Regulations, Part 73 (10 CFR 73). There the so-called insider threat is addressed in part by requiring licensees to protect, in unspecified ways, against one individual who may or may not be an employee, and in part in material control and accounting regulations (10 CFE 70). These regulations are to some extent performance-oriented, in that the nuclear licensee is given some latitude in choosing procedures, equipment, and methodologies to satisfy the intent of the regulations.

The history of safeguards in the United States has not been without its problems, of course. This applies both to the philosophiscal bases of nuclear safeguards measures in the United States and to some unresolved issues related to the alleged failures of domestic safeguards.

To the extent that history is a reliable indicator of the nature of future subnational activities that may be directed against domestic U.S. nuclear fuel cycle facilities, and to the extent that only domestic U.S. events are considered in evaluating the implications these events pose for safeguards policy for domestic commercial nuclear activities, some observations concerning these implications may be made.

It would seem there may have been two, perhaps three, domestic events (two of which may have occurred prior to the advent of a structured materials control and accounting safeguards program), involving subnational activities that could have contributed to nuclear proliferation. (50)

A sense of unease persists concerning these allegations; this unease concerns the integrity and competence of materials control and accounting safeguards to effectively counter subnational threats against them. This cannot be relieved until allegations of past safeguards failures are credibly disposed of and the relevant safeguards evaluated in that light.

Foreign Safeguards Programs

As was mentioned earlier, national nuclear safeguards programs are regarded as confidential by the nations that possess them, and their particulars are known to the IAEA only if a nation is a signatory of the NPT, or has made a safeguards agreement with the IAEA under INFCIRC/66/Rev. 2. (51)

Safeguards agreements implemented and still in existence under INFCIRC/66/Rev. 2 predate those entered into under the NPT and relate primarily to facility safeguards. Full fuel-cycle safeguards requirements under the NPT are described in INFCIRC/153 (corrected). (52)

The fact that the particulars of these national safeguards programs are kept confidential recently prompted the Office of Nuclear Material Safety and Safeguards of the U.S. Nuclear Regulatory Commission in the case of a pending report of nuclear material, to decline to certify that the safeguards program of the nation in question was adequate. The rationale, of course, was that the adequacy of a safeguards program the particulars of which were unknown could not be certified.

For similar reasons, it is not possible to evaluate here the implications that subnational activities may have for safeguards programs the nature and implementation of which are unknown. Nevertheless some inferences may be drawn concerning the effectiveness of these programs, based upon apparent past failures of safeguards (53) and upon the experiences of the IAEA with some of these programs as reflected in some of their recent reports.

In this light, it is difficult not to consider the possibility that some of the apparently less-than-adequate measures in some national safeguards programs are susceptible to subnational threats. It is interesting to note that aside from sabotage, subnational activities which are alleged to have occurred in the past in these nations have involved not fissile materials but source materials and sensitive technology. (54)

Implications for Existing Domestic and Foreign Safeguards Programs

When safeguards research and safeguards implementation programs are contrasted with the instances of alleged diversions of materials or sensitive technology in the United States and elsewhere, one is struck by the fact that the emphasis is put on the development of safeguards systems to cope with the overt threat, while all those alleged events, all of which had proliferation overtones, have been covert operations.

The implications seem obvious: systematic programs for dealing with covert threats must be given at least as much attention as those for overt threats. To be sure, the insider threat has in recent times been the subject of safeguards research. (55) That research would seem, however, to lack the coherence of an integrated research program.

The generic insider threat problem, and its implications for safeguards, were recognized by Edelhertz and Walsh some time ago. (56) Their exposition of this problem provides guidelines to insider threat safeguards research perhaps as good as any available to date, and is particularly pertinent to the problem at hand - that is, the subnational threats to national safeguards programs. To understand some of these implications, it may be useful to review some basic elements of the insider threat:

● Intent to commit a wrongful act, or to achieve a purpose inconsistent with law or national policy;

● Disguise of purpose;

● Reliance by an adversary on a victim's ignorance or carelessness;

● Voluntary action by the victim which assists the adversary;

● Concealment of the act.

On the first of these points, a subnational adversary diverting material from a safeguarded facility would act to prevent facility operators or safeguards inspectors from 1) learning of a possible diversion; 2) inferring that there were circumstances indicative of the possibility of a diversion; 3) discovering materials missing in excess of permissible limits of error; or 4) discovering that materials accounting and control records and procedures were being manipulated to limit the facility operator or safeguards inspector's ability to determine that a diversion had taken place.

Disguise, the second point, may take several forms. It may be written or oral, and it may rest on the authority of the adversary or on a claim of derivative authority. Disguise of purpose must occur in an apparently legitimate context to assure the desired response from the victim or system.

The third point relates to target hardness, so to speak, or the potential for the victim to perceive deception, or for the system to correctly verify paperwork or other information handled verbally or through automatic data processing.

Edelhertz and Walsh (57) consider voluntary victim action to assist the adversary to be essential to the adversary's success. Safeguards systems must, therefore, be assessed in terms of their potential for actually being used by the adversary to further his aims.

The final point, concealment, is important to the adversary because his actions are open. Concealment requirements may be flexible, however, since it frequently may not be possible to conceal an action indefinitely. The important point here is not concealment of a subnational's identity, but concealment of the fact that a safeguards infraction has occurred. If an action is a continuing one, concealment and disguise may overlap. Concealment, however, should be expected to be a continuing element of an action, even after the original action occurs.

In each of these points, it is assumed the subnational adversary acts as an insider in the sense discussed by Edelhertz and Walsh. (58) It is instructive to evaluate these basic elements of insider threat in terms of the alleged instances of diversion recounted previously and elsewhere. (59)

This point, and the nature of alleged past events, are relevant to several areas of national safeguards programs and international inspection programs regarding subnational threats to existing fuel cycles and institutions. These include, in part:

- The extent to which redundancy operates in materials control and accounting safeguards with respect to materials (including source materials) and technology transfers in commerce;

- The nature of the formal arrangements between national and multinational organizations with safeguards responsibilities in the area of materials and technology transfer;

- The procedures by which the integrity of those safeguards arrangements are assured;

- The procedures by which performance standards are assured for national safeguards programs with respect to materials control and accounting;

- Procedures to evaluate the extent to which limits of error may be exploited to conceal diversions;

- The existence of mechanisms to delay determination of materials balance discrepancies in excess of allowable limits of error;

- The existence of data processing mechanisms or pathways permitting the manipulation of material balance records;

- The potential for accepting fraudulent documentation concerning materials handling;

- The existence of internal mechanisms for confirming the identity of authorized documentation issuers; and,

- The existence of mechanisms to prevent concealment, through administrative or political intervention, of illicit transfers of nuclear materials or sensitive nuclear technology.

The preceding observations are directed at the structure and dynamics of existing systems, in other words, at the nature of existing fuel cycles, fuel cycle facilities, and the safeguards institutions and conventions that support them and govern national and international commerce in nuclear materials, facilities, technology, and services.

It should be apparent that while innovative measures may be necessary for safeguarding future deployments of nuclear power systems against overt subnational activities, safeguarding against illicit covert subnational activities is no less important.

Subnational Threats and the Design of Safeguards Institutions Supporting International Deployment of Nuclear Energy Systems

Many institutional innovations have been suggested concerning future deployments of nuclear energy systems. While these suggestions are directed almost entirely at mitigating the potential for national activities that may result in horizontal proliferation of nuclear weapons, many are relevant to subnational issues in this area as well. Institutional measures designed to reduce potentials for national governments to utilize civil nuclear power technology to acquire nuclear weapons may be expected to have some impact on potential illicit subnational activities. It should not be assumed, however, that institutional innovations designed to operate at the national level will be adequate to prevent illicit subnational activities.

For example, a recent report on international fuel service centers (IFSCs) suggests that materials control and accounting safeguards be patterned after 10 CFR 70. (60) These regulations, written in performance-oriented language so that licensees can satisfy regulatory requirements with materials handling procedures most appropriate to the design and operation of a particular facility, are vague with regard to document verification, automatic data processing security, and other safeguards issues relevant to subnational threats.

Intuitively, of course, one can assume that an international facility, operated and managed by individuals from the nations with an interest in it, would be a more difficult environment for illicit subnational activities than would purely national facilities. While this may in fact be the case, it nevertheless does not in and of itself constitute a safeguard of sufficient consequence to obviate the need for safeguards oriented specifically toward subnational threats.

Internationalization suggestions aside, it is apparent that the most pressing issue concerning the adoption of institutions to safeguard against subnational threats is the implementation of full-scope IAEA safeguards. This adoption needs in turn to be followed with programs to assure that safeguards performance standards are being met both by safeguards equipment and the personnel responsible for implementing safeguards procedures, particularly in the area of materials control and accounting.

This latter point cannot be overemphasized, for full-scope IAEA safeguards, where they are presently in force, are not uniformly implemented. While recognizing the desirability of imposing full-scope IAEA safeguards as a condition, for example, of nuclear technology transfers or nuclear fuel assurance, it must further be recognized that there must exist mechanisms for assuring the adequate implementation of those safeguards and the adequate performance of personnel charged with materials control and accounting.

This may require major changes in the way national safeguards programs are evaluated, with perhaps a suppliers' group established within the IAEA with full authority to assure the adequate implementation of safeguards as a necessary precondition of the transfer of nuclear technology or materials.

Alternatively, a supplier's group within the IAEA could design safeguards appropriate for specific cases, then provide the intended recipient of the technology or materials with personnel training in the relevant safeguards measures, with performance evaluation left in the hands of the IAEA's Department of Safeguards.

Various arrangements may be conceived between a supplier's group, the IAEA, and nuclear technology client states which could provide supplier states with assurances they presently do not have concerning the adequacy of national safeguards programs. While significant questions concerning discrimination, sovereign rights, and the preservation of the confidentiality of information are likely to arise, these seem amenable to solution, and should not present insurmountable obstacles to the institution of safeguards programs possessing mechanisms for the independent assessment of their implementation and performance characteristics.

The nature of potential subnational threats, particularly mixed subnational-national threats, is such, based upon past events and analyses of subnational groups which could be threatening to nuclear power programs, (61) that mechanisms must be established to detect and interrupt these processes that may have previously led to the illicit transfer of materials and technology. Some of the implications these may have for safeguards were addressed earlier: the implications these may have for the institutions that administer or depend upon safeguards are not insignificant.

SUMMARY AND CONCLUSIONS

The relative attractiveness of nuclear fuel cycle facilities to subnationals as sources of fissile material and as potential targets for sabotage is a function of a variable number of factors which depend to some extent upon changes in political and social environments, and upon advances in and the implementation of new technology in nuclear fuel cycle processes and nuclear safeguards.

A rank-ordering of the attractiveness of fuel cycle facilities to subnationals, that is based principally on technological factors is in a sense defective, since it does not take into consideration national and international commitments to nonproliferation conventions, the social and political environments in which these conventions are entered into, or the evolution of social and political environments that may alter present perspectives concerning these obligations. It may be argued these are national and not subnational issues, and should not materially affect the potential exposures of fuel cycle facilities or materials to subnational threats. Such an argument, however, ignores the mixed subnational-national threat, which, for various reasons, is viewed as historically significant and potentially significant for existing and future international deployments of nuclear fuel cycle technology.

Fuel cycle facilities that possess unirradiated, undenatured, and separated fissile materials in storage or in process are frequently considered the most attractive to subnationals. Such facilities include uranium enrichment facilities producing high enriched ^{235}U for research and propulsion reactors, as well as initial and make-up fissile uranium for HTGR and THTR core loadings. Under some conditions, centrifuge enrichment facilities producing low-enriched uranium for LWR fuel cycles may be covertly reconfigured to produce high enriched uranium.

On a similar plane of presumed attractiveness may be placed fuel fabrication facilities, which would receive high enriched uranium and possess it both in storage and in process. Such facilities are assumed here to service research and propulsion reactors, as well as the HTGR and THTR fuel cycles. Similarly, in an LWR recycle economy where spent LWR fuel is reprocessed for recycle into LWRs, LWBRs, or LMFBRs, fuel fabrication facilities would possess in storage either pure plutonium, as the dioxide, or plutonium dioxide mixed with uranium dioxide as either a mechanical blend or a solid solution. No safeguards credit is assumed for these blends.

Finally, also considered of attractiveness equal to the previous two kinds of facilities are fuel reprocessing facilities that would reprocess LWR or HWR and HTGR or THTR fuel where, in the latter instance, no in-process provisions were made for denaturing separated ^{233}U with ^{238}U. Even this would be of marginal safeguards utility, since separated plutonium could be present in storage at all these fuel reprocessing facilities.

It is conceded that if all these facilities were placed in international nuclear fuel service centers, it might be possible to mitigate somewhat potential subnational threats to them.

Given that internationalization of such facilities may prove only marginally acceptable, other safeguards measures may be employed that might reduce the attractiveness of these facilities to subnational threats of various kinds. In some cases, however, even innovative safeguards measures may be merely inconveniences rather than impediments to mixed subnational-national threats. Should such safeguards measures be adopted for use in fuel enrichment, fabrication, and reproducing facilities, they would have the general effect of making all such facilities less attractive sources of fissile materials, with specific effects dependent on a variety of factors including frequencies of inspection, process technology, nature of access to discrete elements of process streams, and quality of overall national safeguards programs.

Fissile materials in transport are usually held to be more susceptible to overt or covert diversions or theft than are materials at fixed sites. In present circumstances that may be correct, but there is room for debate on that point. The institution of innovative safeguards technologies in the transportation cycle could, in principle at least, make such materials as secure as if in storage at fixed facilities. On the other hand, such safeguards measures are as vulnerable to mixed subnational-national threats in the transportation cycle as elsewhere in the fuel cycle.

At the lower end of attractiveness as sources of fissile materials are reactors. Within reactors, however, a hierarchy of attractiveness may be discerned. Most attractive could be LMFBRs with fresh fuel in storage. Next would be HTGRs and THTRs with fresh fuel in storage. Fresh fuels for all these would require some processing, with the least required for LMFBR fuel, and some rather difficult processing required for HTGR and THTR fuel. Least attractive would be fresh fuel in storage at LWR, HWR, GCR, AGR, and LWBR (initial core loading) power plants.

Not to be overlooked, however, is long-term storage spent fuel from any of the above reactors. After a few decades of storage, this irradiated fuel becomes relatively easier to handle than short-term storage fuel, since its radioactivity has decayed markedly. It all contains plutonium, and some of it contains ^{233}U. All of it requires processing to recover the fissile material.

Sabotage attractiveness presents a hierarchy somewhat different from that of fissile material source attractiveness.   While the attractiveness of a fuel cycle facility as a source of fissile material may depend on how much material there is and what form it is in, a facility's attractiveness as a potential object of sabotage is not dependent on a single major factor, but on a variety of objectives that sabotage may be employed to achieve. It would appear, however, that some sort of hierarchy is possible, although one based upon rather broad, imperfectly understood, and probably clustered motivations.

Radioactive inventory, in and of itself, is probably not a realistic criterion on which to base a hierarchy of potential sabotage attractiveness (putting aside the question of primary motivations for committing sabotage in the first place).   The large radioactive inventory of a power reactor core is, for example, inaccessible to most external acts short of efforts more in the nature of war than of sabotage. There are, on the other hand, methods available to reactor operators to cause the core to melt. Such a melt could have a range of consequences, including a significant offsite release of radiation. Above-grade spent fuel storage pools, with radioactive inventories in some cases approaching those of reactor cores, are somewhat more vulnerable to an act of sabotage that could release large amounts of radiation, but only marginally so.

Sabotage of fuel enrichment facilities presents more of a transient chemical health hazard than a radiological hazard. The compartmented nature and heavy shielding of a reprocessing facility would tend to reduce chances that sabotage could cause an offsite release of radiation.   With uranium and plutonium in the oxide form in fuel fabrication facilities (rather than in the pyrophoric metallic form), opportunities for sabotage to cause offsite releases of radiation also appear limited.

It is instructive to note, as regards sabotage of nuclear facilities, that no operating power reactor, no reactor/spent fuel storage pool, no nuclear fuel fabrication facility, no nuclear spent fuel reprocessing facility - in short, no operating nuclear facility of any kind - has ever been sabotaged so as to cause a release of radiation. Of the several acts of terrorism (bombings, arson, shootings, occupations, etc.) known to have occurred at nuclear facility sites, virtually all have occurred at construction sites. Only two such acts are known by the author to have occurred inside the exclusion area of an operating reactor: the damaging of a ventilation stack on an auxiliary building within a power reactor complex in France, and the damaging of fresh (unirradiated) fuel stored at a reactor in the United States.

Thus terrorists have been an insignificant component of all the types of subnationals that may exploit nuclear safeguards vulnerabilities. While this could change, the circumstances that may precipitate such a change are not that obvious.   In fact, there are several reasons, previously outlined, for arguing against the proposition that terrorists will engage in sabotage that will result in a harmful release of radiation.

To date, neither is there evidence of subnationals (terrorists included) acting as clients for nuclear materials or technology for purposes of acquiring a nuclear weapon capability. There is, on the other hand, substantial evidence for subnationals (terrorist not included) acting as agents for client governments interested in acquiring a nuclear weapons capability. Such subnationals may be characterized as corporate officers, members of government acting in quasi-official or unofficial capacities, members of the military, scientists and technologists, and independent agents.

The vulnerabilities of fuel cycle facilities and institutions to subnational threats are therefore expressible primarily in terms of the mixed subnational-national threat, not of the pure subnational threat. The subtle, clandestine, and complex insider adversarial activities that subnational entities are capable of carrying out, and against which safeguards have not been developed to the same degree of sophistication as in other areas, are available to sovereign governments to employ in proliferation programs based in civil nuclear materials or technology.

Mixed subnational-national threats would appear to be only marginally sensitive to types of fuel cycles. Specific nations may be discouraged from pursuing proliferation programs with subnational assistance due to the nature of their nuclear resources and the controls on relevant facilities or materials. Such controls would, however, tend to shift the threat emphasis to alternate materials and technologies that are exploitable for weapons development purposes. The large areas of commonality between fuel cycles, and the ultimate futility of attempting to prevent the spread of technology, also tend to diminish the sensitivity of mixed subnational-national threats to fuel cycle types.

Proposed schemes for internationalization of various aspects of disparate fuel cycles would appear to be little more effective against mixed threats than measures already in existence. In fact, circumstances may exist in such internationalization schemes that could promote proliferation through a mixed threat, rather than prevent it.

The mixed subnational-national threat 1) provides a national with mechanisms to pursue proliferation programs that are in general less sensitive to safeguards than a national weapons program; 2) permits nations more freedom of action in pursuing proliferation; and 3) provides the potential for masking its effort in such a manner as to avoid attribution altogether, or to delay it for periods sufficient for it to meet at least minimal goals.

Potential subnational threats to civil nuclear programs are usually held to be of subordinate concern to those of potential national threats. While there are legitimate reasons to preserve this priority relationship, the overall result has been to fail to integrate into safeguards institutions mechanisms for dealing with the pernicious nature of some subnational threats.

Reviews of past alleged mixed subnational-national events are instructive of how failures in safeguards could have occurred, and evaluations of existing domestic safeguards relations and the IAEA safeguards experience suggest how such events could occur again.

While it may be argued that some of these events are reported to have taken place prior to the implementation of formal materials control and accounting safeguards, it nevertheless appears that safeguards institutions may continue to be vulnerable to similar mixed threats due to:

● An emphasis on physical security measures of a nature to prevent overt, forceful attacks on facilities or materials; and

● A continuing diminished capacity to deal with covert mixed subnational-national threats against safeguards institutions.

It seems that institutional changes in international safeguards must inescapably occur, to provide assurances not only that effective safeguards against mixed subnational-national threats will accompany the future deployment of nuclear power systems, but that such safeguards are being adequately implemented.

It is hoped the international safeguards community will not ultimately have to resort to curses, spells, and incantations, as has been suggested elsewhere, to maintain the integrity and adequate performance of national and international safeguards programs. Rather, those institutional changes necessary to generate confidence in these programs, whether they are the kinds of changes suggested here, or others, will be brought about through mutually agreed-upon conventions that are recognized to be to everyone's advantage in that they reduce the potential of subnational threats to nuclear programs.

NOTES

(1) R.L. Bett, Illicit Diversion of Nuclear Materials, Australian Atomic Energy Commission, Information Paper IP6, n.d.; Deborah Shapley, "Plutonium: Reactor Proliferation Threatens a Nuclear Black Market," Science 172, April 9, 1971 pp. 143-146; Donald P. Gessaman and Dean E. Abrahamson, "The Dilemma of Fission Power," Bulletin of the Atomic Scientists, November 1974 pp 37-41; Harold A. Feiveson and Theodore B. Taylor, "Security Implications of Alternative Fission Futures," Bulletin of the Atomic Scientists, December 1976 pp.   14-18, 46-48; and U.S. Congress, Office of Technology Assessment, Nuclear Proliferation and Safeguards, June 30, 1977.

(2) B.J. Berkowitz, M. Frost, E.J. Hajic, and H. Redisch, Superviolence: The Civil Threat of Mass Destruction Weapons (Adcon Corporation, A72-034-10, September 29, 1972); Robert K. Mullen, The International Clandestine Threat (Gaithersburg, Md.:   International Association of Chiefs of Police, 1975); Robert A. Wohlstetter, "Terror on a Grand Scale," Survival 18, no. 3 (May/June 1976 pp. 98-104; Robert K. Mullen, "Mass Destruction and

Terrorism," Journal of International Affairs 32, no. 1 (1978) pp. 63-89; and U.S. Nuclear Regulatory Commission, Safeguarding a Domestic Mixed Oxide Industry Against a Hypothetical Subnational Threat, NUREG-0414, Office of Nuclear Material Safety and Safeguards, May 1978.

(3) International Energy Associates, International Cooperation on Breeder Reactors 2, p. 3, appendix I (Rockefeller Foundation, May 1978).

(4) F.L. Culler, "Simple, Quick Processing Plant" (Memorandum to D.E. Ferguson, Oak Ridge National Laboratory, August 30, 1977); Warren H. Donnelly, A Preliminary Analysis of the ORNL Memorandum on a Crude Nuclear Fuel Reprocessing Plant (Library of Congress, Congressional Research Service, November 4, 1977); Comptroller General of the United States, "Quick and Secret Construction of Plutonium Reprocessing Plants: A Way to Nuclear Weapons Proliferation?" In U.S. Senate, Committee on Government Affairs, Report to the Subcommittee on Energy, Nuclear Proliferation and Federal Services, October 6, 1978; and L.E. Bruns, Selective Uranium Dissolution Flowsheet and Prototype Equipment (Atlantic Richfield Hanford Company, ARH-2260, n.d.) 7p.

(5) Bob Seldon, Reactor Plutonium and Nuclear Explosives, Unclassified Briefing Charts, November 1976 (Mimeographed).

(6) Mason Willrich and Theodore B. Taylor, Nuclear Theft: Risks and Safeguards (Cambridge, Mass.: Ballinger 1974).

(7) Chauncey Starr, "The Separation of Nuclear Power from Nuclear Proliferation" (Address to the Fifth Energy Technology Conference, Washington, D.C., February 27, 1978 pp. 1-11).

(8) Nucleonics Week, February 24, 1978, p. 1.

(9) U.S Department of the Army, Fundamentals of Protective Design (Non-Nuclear), TM 5-855-1, July 1965.

(10) C. Vernon Hodge and James E. Campbell, Calculations of Radiological Consequences from Sabotage of Shipping Casks for Spent Fuel and High Level Waste, NUREG 0194 (Washington, D.C.: U.S. Nuclear Regulatory Commission, September 1976).

(11) U.S. Congress, Nuclear Proliferation and Safeguards.

(12) Ibid.; U.S. Congress, Nuclear Proliferation Factbook, Congressional Research Service, September 23, 1977.

(13) D.M. Bishop and D.W. Wilson, "Clandestine Enrichment of Low-Enriched Uranium by Sub-National Groups: A Perspective," Nuclear Materials Management, Spring 1977 pp. 25-33.

(14) A.M. Fishman, R. Frederickson, and A.T. White, "Safeguarding Enriched Uranium at a Centrifuge Enrichment Plant," (Address at the Institute of Nuclear Materials Management Annual Meeting, Centar Associates, June 1976).

(15) The Atlantic Council of the United States, Nuclear Power and Nuclear Weapons Proliferation 2, appendix A, 1978, pp. 1-83.

(16) Barry M. Casper, "Laser Enrichment: A New Path to Proliferation?" Bulletin of the Atomic Scientists, January 1977 p. 28-41; and Allan S. Krass, "Laser Enrichment of Uranium: The Proliferation Connection," Science 196 (May 13, 1977) pp. 721-731.

(17) Laser Enrichment Review Panel, Laser Isotope Separation: Proliferation Risks and Benefits (Jersey Nuclear-Avco Isotopes, Inc., February 27, 1979).

(18) D. Gupta, Isotopic Correlation for Accounting and Control of Nuclear Materials in a Fuel Cycle, (KFK 2400 Karlsruhe: Kernforschungszentrum, September 1976).

(19) National Academy of Sciences, Biological Effects of Atmospheric Pollutants: Fluorides, Washington, D.C.: 1971.

(20) Zdenek Cervenka and Barbara Rogers, The Nuclear Axis (New York: New York Times Books, 1978).

(21) Ibid.

(22) R.C. Dahlberg, R.F. Turner, and W.V. Goedell, HTGR Fuel and Fuel Cycle Summary Description, GA-A12801 (rev.), (General Atomic Company, January 21, 1974).

(23) U.S. Congress, Nuclear Proliferation and Safeguards; U.S. Congress, Nuclear Proliferation Factbook; and Stockholm International Peace Research Institute, World Armaments and Disarmament SIPRI Yearbook, 1978 (New York: Crane, Russak, 1978).

(24) Culler, Simple, Quick Processing Plant; Donnelly, A Preliminary Analysis of the ORNL Memorandum; Comptroller General of the United States, "Quick and Secret Construction of Plutonium Reprocessing Plants"; and Bruns, Selective Uranium Dissolution Flowsheet.

(25) U.S. Regulatory Commission, Safeguarding a Domestic Mixed Oxide Industry.

(26) K.H. Puechl, "The Case for Low Concentration Plutonium Recycle," Nuclear Engineering International, September 1975, pp. 687-692; and U.S. Nuclear Regulatory Commission, Final Generic Environmental Statement on the Use of Recycle Plutonium in Mixed Oxide Fuel in Light Water Cooled Reactors, NUREG-0002, vol. 3 (August 1976).

(27) D.E. Deonigi, E.A. Eschbach, S. Goldsmith, P.J. Pankaskie, C.A. Rohrmann, and R.D. Widrig, Some Alternatives to the Mixed Oxide Fuel Cycle, BNWL-2197 (Battelle Pacific Northwest Laboratories, February 1977).

(28) Hodge and Campbell, Calculations of Radiological Consequences.

(29) Comptroller General of the United States, "Role of the International Atomic Energy Agency in Safeguarding Nuclear Material," in U.S. House of Representatives, Report to the Committee on International Relations (July 3, 1975).

(30) Robert K. Mullen, Nuclear Safeguards Institutions and Subnational Threats (Report to the Office of Nuclear Material Safety and Safeguards, U.S. Nuclear Regulatory Commission, July 31, 1979).

(31) Ibid.

(32) Al-Watan, July 21, 1978, in Daily Communication Report, Israeli Foreign Ministry, August 1, 1978 (Mimeographed); and Jim Quinn and Ralph Flood, "Philadelphia Escalates Its Conflict with an Anarchist Group," Washington Post, March 17, 1978, p. 4.

(33) Mullen, Nuclear Safeguards.

(34) Herbert Edelhertz and Marilyn Walsh, The White-Collar Challenge to Nuclear Safeguards (Lexington, Mass.: Lexington Books, 1978), p. 1-101.

(35) Mullen, Nuclear Safeguards.

(36) Brookhaven National Laboratory, A Review of the Regulations Concerning the Control and Accounting of Nuclear Material, Technical Support Organization File No. 5.9.7 (July 16, 1976); and U.S. Energy Research and Development Administration, Report on Strategic Special Nuclear Material Inventory Differences, ERDA 77-68 (August 1977).

(37) Russell W. Fox and Mason Willrich, International Custody of Plutonium Stocks: A First Step Toward an International Regime for Sensitive Nuclear Activities, International Consultative Group on Nuclear Energy (Rockefeller Foundation/Royal Institute of International Affairs, November 1978).

(38) Onkar Marwah, "India's Nuclear and Space Programs: Intent and Policy," International Security 2, no. 2, (1977) pp. 96-121; and Foreign Broadcast Information Service, Early Swedish Atomic Weapons Research: Current Capabilities, Nordic Affairs, 7, no. 225 (November 22, 1978) p. 1.

(39) Elaine Davenport, Paul Eddy, and Peter Gillman, The Plumbat Affair (Philadelphia: J.B. Lippincott, 1978); Reuter's News Service, "Norwegian Reports Confession: Missing Uranium Linked to Israeli Agent," Los Angeles Times, April 19, 1977, p. 4; Gerard Bonnot, "The Case of the Missing Uranium," Atlas World Press Review, September 1978, pp. 25-27; Denis Eisenberg, Eli Landau, and Menachem Portugali, "Das Geheimnis der 'Scheersberg'," Spiegel August 14, pp. 110-118, 21, pp. 134-148, 1978; and William Drozdiak, "Odyssey of Nuclear Shipment Baffles Experts in Europe," Washington Post, May 17, 1977 p. 12.

(40) Foreign Broadcast Information Service, Early Swedish Atomic Weapons Research; and U.S. Joint Publications Research Service, Translations on Western Europe, no. 1338 (December 13, 1978) p. 106.

(41) Svenska Dagbladet, October 26, 1978, p. 15.

(42) Cervenka and Rogers, The Nuclear Axis.

(43) U.S. Nuclear Regulatory Commission, Safeguarding a Domestic Mixed Oxide Industry; Ted Greenwood, Harold A. Feiveson, and Theodore B. Taylor, Nuclear Proliferation: Motivations, Capabilities and Strategies for Control (New York: McGraw-Hill, 1977); and U.S. Energy Research and Development Administration, U.S. Nuclear Power Export Activities, ERDA-1542, (Washington, D.C., April 1976).

(44) Edelhertz and Walsh, The White-Collar Challenge; and G. Bray, T. Grozani, L. Harris, H. Kendrick, L. Kull, R. Ludwig, M. Mali, P. Melling, M. Mazur, and D. Rundquist, Integrated Safeguards Against Internal Threats in LWR Fuel Reprocessing and Mixed Oxide Fabrication Plants, SAI-76-536-LJ, La Jolla, Calif.: Science Applications, February 18, 1976.

(45) T.L. McDaniel, J.E. Glancy, and W.H. Horton, Safeguards Against Insider Collusion, NUREG/CR-0532, vol. 1 (U.S. Nuclear Regulatory Commission, October 1979).

(46) Lewis A. Dunn, "Nuclear 'Gray Marketeering'," International Security 1, no. 3 (Winter 1977), pp. 107-118.

(47) Lewis A. Dunn, "Military Politics, Nuclear Proliferation and the 'Nuclear Coup d'Etat'," Journal of Strategic Studies 1, no. 1 (May 1978), pp. 31-50.

(48) Mullen, Nuclear Safeguards Institutions; and Robert K. Mullen, Taxonomic Methods for Evaluating Potential Subnational Adversaries (Santa Monica, Calif.: Rand, November 1978, in draft).

(49) Mullen, Nuclear Safeguards Institutions.

(50) Ibid.

(51) International Atomic Energy Agency, The Agency's Safeguards System (1965, as Provisionally Extended in 1966 and 1968), INFCIRC/66/Rev. 2 (September 16, 1968).

(52) International Atomic Energy Agency, The Structure and Content of Agreements Between the Agency and States Required in Connection with the Treaty on the Non-Proliferation of Nuclear Weapons, INFCIRC/153 (corrected), (June 1972).

(53) Mullen, Nuclear Safeguards Institutions.

(54) Ibid.

(55) Edelhertz and Walsh, The White-Collar Challenge; Bray et al., Integrated Safeguards Against Internal Threats; and McDaniel et al., Safeguards Against Inside Collusion.

(56) Edelhertz and Walsh, The White-Collar Challenge.

(57) Ibid.

(58) Ibid.

(59) Mullen, Nuclear Safeguards Institutions.

(60) Burns and Roe Industrial Services Corporation, International Fuel Service Center Study 1 (May 1979).

(61) Mullen, Nuclear Safeguards Institutions; and Mullen, Taxonomic Methods.

8 Responding to Terrorism: Basic and Applied Research

Edward Mickolus
Edward S. Heyman
James Schlotter

This chapter surveys terrorism research to identify major research themes, point out promising areas for continued work, and suggest some neglected resources that offer potentially valuable information to researchers.

Terrorist targets in democratic societies include both government and corporate property and personnel, and private individuals. The diverse tactics and targets of political violence have spawned a variety of research approaches and techniques to combat the problem. This chapter does not claim to be exhaustive regarding either research directions or ongoing research within any of the identified approaches. Particularly sensitive or classified research being conducted by or for United States or foreign governments has been omitted. Additionally, the proprietary nature of much excellent work taking place in research organizations has excluded it from the collection.

A SUGGESTED TYPOLOGY OF TERRORISM RESEARCH

Any system purporting to organize the independent research of a large number of individuals must focus on an overarching aspect of the problem. The typology advanced here keys on the application of research products. In this chapter, general studies that address broad environmental and social conditions have been separated from those that examine specific aspects of terrorist incidents or groups. The former can yield insights into the underlying causes and long-term effects of terrorism, while the latter assist in formulating effective responses to either the expectation or fact of a terrorist incident. Figure 8.1 summarizes the categories into which research has been organized.

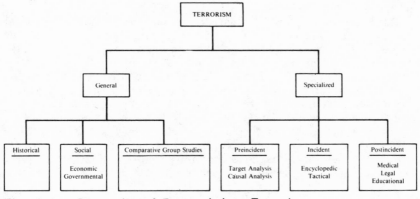

Fig. 8.1.   Categories of Research into Terrorism

GENERAL STUDIES

General studies seek the underlying social, economic, and societal conditions that foster political violence and search for systemic or strategic responses. These responses will tend to be preventive rather than tactical. General studies can be historical, social, or comparative.

Numerous studies have sought the causes of terrorism. The logical first step, defining terrorism, has unfortunately led to an often acrimonious and ultimately frustrating controversy. (2) Its resolution by researchers influences the direction of their studies in both scope and methodology. Definition of what constitutes a terrorist act or group in turn determines data collection and interpretation.

Historical Studies

By far the dominant number of intuitive general studies are historical. Histories of terrorist activity can cover thousands of years, as in the work of Laqueur, (3) date from the era of the Russian anarchists at the turn of this century, (4) or trace contemporary organizations.   Other historical studies focus not on terrorists themselves but on areas that have spawned indigenous terrorist violence over long periods of time, such as Israel, (5) Ireland, (6) and Italy. (7)   These studies have uncovered precedents for the current wave of terrorism, but the extent to which these trends have influenced the current generation is controversial. Walter Laqueur, for instance, notes that 19th-century Russian anarchists forecast current techniques such as letter bombs and manipulation of the press. Citing the obvious technological and social changes in the international arena, however, he qualifies the impact of the past upon the present.

Social Studies

Social studies of the general terrorist environment have taken a number of paths, including governmental and economic analysis. This work has been similar in many respects to that of traditional political scientists seeking sources of domestic civil violence. (8)   The compilation, ordering, and analysis of vast amounts of numerical data have offered a number of fruitful insights into political violence.

Gurr's study, a spinoff of his earlier concerns with mass political violence, seeks patterns in the types of governments and societies plagued by terrorism. (9)   Mickolus, using a similar events data approach, has examined international parallels to the local activities described by Gurr. (10)   These efforts have identified the following basic trends in terrorist behavior: it is engaged in by groups operating in essentially open, democratic societies; it is not sustained for lengthy periods by any group; and it has been adopted by a host of organizations.

Probe International is conducting research that combines political and economic perspectives to identify social milieus that foster terrorism. These analyses, conducted for private corporations, attempt to predict risk either to capital or personnel.

Comparative Studies

Comparative studies attempt to identify or predict key aspects of terrorist behavior across an incident type. Comparative group studies have focused on diverse aspects of terrorism, and include the efforts of Brian Crozier's Institute for the Study of Conflict to catalog the activities of groups worldwide in a search for sources of support (11) and inquiries into the imitative behavior of terrorists. (12)   These studies have led to the conclusion that terrorist motivations vary greatly and that there are large differences in the mechanisms for support and diffusion of terrorism among groups. They preclude any hope for simple or uniform responses to terrorist threats.

SPECIALIZED STUDIES

The findings of the general studies regarding the variegated nature of terrorist groups, tactics, and motivations underscore the importance of specialized studies that focus on characteristics of individuals and groups in differing incidents.   Research that is specialized can be categorized according to the phase of a terrorist incident that it addresses: preincident, incident, and postincident. (13)

Preincident Studies

Preincident studies focus on all stages of development and planning of an incident.   They are aimed at identifying patterns in behavior that may allow the interdiction of an event. Preincident study frequently takes one of two forms: target analysis or causal analysis.

Target Analysis

Target analysis is carried out by a number of firms in an effort to identify vulnerable facilities and terrorist preferences in target choice. Risks International, headed by a retired Air Force intelligence officer, uses a computerized data base of domestic terrorist incidents to

quantitatively predict clients' hazards. Several trade journals, such as
Intersearch (formerly Counterforce), give current information on
terrorist activities as they relate to American business interests. One
company offers its clients periodic reports on new and common terrorist
tactics as well as updated regional threat assessments. Clients are
allowed access to the firm's computerized data base to search answers
to specific questions or draw up personalized threat analyses.

Firms anxious about their vulnerability to terrorist attack are the
subjects of numerous security studies aimed at upgrading site and
personnel security in order to anticipate violence and discourage
attackers. Perhaps the most interesting techniques are those of the
"Black Hats" -teams using paramilitary techniques similar to those
employed by terrorists to attempt to breach whatever security
measures have been taken. Results of these operational simulations can
be used to shore up weaknesses in protective security. (14)

Other work in physical security has centered on controlling security
systems so that terrorists cannot lower protection levels either through
repeated hoaxes or distractions. Most security systems have at least
three levels of readiness: normal, alert, and crisis. The "normal"
status encompasses those situations not involving awareness of any
specific or generalized threat to facilities and personnel.   The alert
phase is characterized by a heightened readiness to respond, but is
usually too costly in terms of money, manpower, and guard stress to
maintain for prolonged periods.   Terrorists, aware of this fact,
frequently resort to hoaxes such as falsified bomb threats in order to tie
up resources at low terrorist risk and cost (a phone call). Repeated use
of this tactic establishes a "cry wolf" pattern that can eventually lull
the security forces or exhaust them, and distract attention from true
targets of attack. The ability to distinguish real threats from hoaxes
would allow decision-makers to respond properly, saving time and lives.
The development of such a capability, based on psycholinguistic analysis
of threat communications, is the goal of psychologist Murray Miron. (15)

Other preventive security studies center around altering targets'
patterns of predictable behavior. Strategies include frequently altering
routines, changing routes and times of travel to and from work, and
dropping company logos from official vehicles.

Enhanced preparedness is also the goal of research to develop
technical methods to detect armed terrorists, (16) and to create
methods to deal with attacks, such as offensive and defensive driving
for chauffeurs, and weapons practice for guards and potential
victims. (17)

Causal Analysis

Analyses of terrorism keyed to the motivations and requirements of the
terrorists attempt to preempt attacks from the opposite perspective.
They offer the potential to intercept the activities of established groups
as well as to detect potential new actors while they are still in a
developmental stage. Significant causal analyses have centered on the
effects of technological development, weapons availability, and the
interplay of tactical and motivational factors.

Several researchers have concentrated on what Martha Hutchinson has termed "permissive causes" of terrorism. (18)   These include the communications revolution, technological innovation and transportation advances,   and   the   proliferation   of   sovereignties   via   anticolonial violence by national liberation movements.   Also among these types of causes (alternatively viewed as facilitative aspects of the operational environment) are the general availability of conventional weapons for terrorists.   The characteristics of easily concealed weapons and devices have   been   recently   dealt   with   by   Dobson   and   Payne. (19)   The availability of ABC (atomic, biological, chemical) weapons and facilities for exploitation by terrorists has often been suggested by the press. The difficulties in actual implementation of these scenarios have been studied behaviorally by Rand, BDM, and Sandia. (20)   In sum, these studies have found that while it may be logistically possible to take over a facility, seize a weapon, or divert radioactive material to fabricate a lethal   device,   political,   moral,   and   behavioral   constraints   severely lessen the probability that terrorists will find mass destruction an attractive option.

New approaches question terrorists' capability to master the tactics of mass death and then systematically assess their willingness or motivation to do so.   Aside from black market purchase, acquisition of commercial or military SNM (Special Nuclear Material) is still beyond the capability of all but a handful of currently active terrorist groups. Some   groups   with   the   capability,   however,   have   demonstrated   a willingness to exploit these materials' terrorizing potential, as was evidenced by the German Red Army Faction's 1975 threat to destroy the population of Stuttgart with rockets and stolen mustard gas. (21)

Rather than actually using mass destruction techniques, however, some terrorist groups have taken to assaulting nuclear power plants that are under construction.   These actions still present a threat to society, but limit the actual risk to the terrorist.   Society is reminded of its vulnerability, and the terrorists advertise their "solidarity" with the antinuclear movement.   Such actions have been carried out by the Spanish ETA against the Lemoniz power plant being built by Babcock and Wilcox in Bilbao; the Argentine ERP; and the American New World Liberation Front, with its bombing of the Trojan nuclear facility in Northern California.

Incident Studies

A large body of work centers on studies of terrorist incidents as they occur.   These studies have focused on encylopedic treatments of groups or types of incidents and on tactical analyses of the handling of ongoing incidents.

Encyclopedic Analyses

Perhaps the earliest systematic research on terrorist behavior focused on aiding governmental responses to hostage incidents by providing comprehensive data on terrorist incidents. The path-breaking work was conducted at the Rand Corporation under the direction of Brian Jenkins, whose efforts included the compilation of a chronology of terrorist events from 1968 through 1974. (22)   The Historical Evaluation Research Organization, with the aid of BDM Corporation, used the same approach, going back to 1870 to give a historical context to contemporary terrorism. (23)   Mickolus (at Yale) and the Central Intelligence Agency synthesized these and scores of other compilations into a computerized data bank of international terrorist attacks occurring since 1968. (24) All of these efforts were designed to provide the crisis manager with easily retrievable information on incidents.   Further refinement of these information-handling systems has aimed at digesting the raw data and analyzing trends and likely behavior of adversaries. Rand's RITA system uses artificial intelligence modeling to derive probabilistic rules of behavior, which, in turn, can be used to give estimative inferences of terrorist responses to government or business crisis negotiation strategies. (25) Mickolus's ITERATE has attempted to utilize the capabilities of the Statistical Package for the Social Sciences (26) to draw similar historic parallels in terrorist behavior.

Other encylopedic studies have focused on inclusive histories of the tactics of individual groups.   Group-oriented studies have been undertaken on the Black September organization, (27) the Quebec Liberation Front, (28) and the Baader-Meinhof gang, (29) among others. Techniques in these studies vary, but have included interviews of terrorists in the field, (30) in prison, (31) or in retirement, (32) as well as studies of terrorists' writings. (33)

Tactical Analyses

Following these early encyclopedic efforts, research focused on improving strategy and tactics in bargaining for hostages.   The Rand Corporation led in this facet of research as well, conducting early empirical evaluations of contending theories of negotiation. (34)   These findings were later replicated quantitatively by Mickolus, (35) and in comparative studies by Evans of the "concessions-no concessions" debate. (36)   The lessons learned from these findings have been translated into operational gaming exercises; perhaps the best known is run by Stephen Sloan at the University of Oklahoma. (37)

Psychological studies have also been brought to bear. Margolin has attempted to apply well-established principles of human behavior to terrorist situations. (38) McClure has developed training programs for those officials who may some day become hostages based upon the psychological experiences of previous victims, (39) including Claude Fly, Ambassador Geoffrey Jackson, and Debbie Dortzbach. (40)

Among the actors involved in hostage situations are representatives of the news media. Their effect on the incident is largely unknown, however. A debate has raged over the proper role of the reporter covering terrorist incidents. Does media coverage incite other

terrorists to attack? Can the media's treatment of incidents threaten
the lives of hostages? Should the media consciously edit its news to aid
governments in dealing with terrorists? These and similar issues have
been the subjects of several conferences (41) and professional
papers. (42) Work continues on empirical assessment of the effects of
media coverage on terrorist behavior.

Finally, research has been devoted to the jurisdictional difficulties
in resolving terrorist incidents. Events in federally organized nations
can involve a clash of overlapping responsibilities among federal, state,
and local authorities, and international attacks can result in legal
conflicts between affected nation-states. The locus of responsibility in
turn affects the appropriateness of suggested responses to crises; for
example, paramilitary rescue teams available to national leaders may
not have been developed by local police departments. Work in this area
has focused on sorting out these jurisdictional ambiguities, as well as
transferring the technology and tactics developed at higher levels to
local authorities.

Postincident Studies

Perhaps the greatest immediate interest in the wake of an incident is
the medical treatment of those injured. Work in this area has been led
by Elliott Silverstein, who deals with these incidents in much the same
way as those charged with handling disaster response. (43) Use of the
disaster response model can also serve as a tool in planning for possible
future terrorist depredations.

Of similar urgency is the psychological well-being of victims,
particularly hostages. Abraham Miller has surveyed the total response
of governments to hostage situations, and has called for several
improvements, including a greater concern for the postincident
experiences of victims, (44) a view seconded by Frank Ochberg of the
National Institute of Mental Health. (45)

The legal community has not lagged behind in suggesting methods of
responding to terrorism. The American Society of International Law,
under contract to the U.S. Department of State, surveyed the existing
laws related to numerous forms of terrorism and suggested several
areas of potential improvement. (46) A similar effort, concentrating on
local measures, was undertaken for the Law Enforcement Assistance
Administration by the National Advisory Committee on Criminal
Justice Standards and Goals, (47) which drafted scores of suggestions on
the judicial handling of terrorist cases and the goals to be sought by
penal institutions. The work in the international legal sphere is too vast
to detail here, but generally has attempted to evaluate the effectiveness of existing international legal regimes and to suggest future
directions for regional and global cooperation. (48)

One last area of research has focused on methods of public
education. This has led to the development of various private
newsletters and professional journals; (49) a host of local, national, and

international gatherings of scholars and policymakers; and several adaptations of innovative teaching techniques, including role-playing simulations. (50)

OBSERVATIONS

All of the research approaches surveyed have resulted in valuable contributions to our current understanding of terrorism and potential ways to combat it. They are not, however, without drawbacks or areas of controversy.

The case studies trace organizational developments over time, but often lack generalizability across groups and societies. Frequently global surveys suffer from being pitched at such a high level of generality that their conclusions are of limited utility to policy- and lawmakers. Thus, while useful, traditional case studies and normative treatments offer only islands of insight into the overall process of terror. The recent infusion of quantitative analyses into terrorism research marks an important step forward in a field long mired in unproductive debates over the a priori utility of statistical techniques. Quantitative analysis and automated data collection facilitates wider analyses of the phenomenon.

NEGLECTED RESOURCES

Several sources of valuable intelligence generated by terrorists themselves appear to be woefully underutilized.

One resource that could profitably be mined is regular communiques and terrorist-produced newsletters. As political organizations, terrorist groups must stay in contact with their political followings. Many groups have gone so far as to publish regular periodicals, such as the Argentine ERP's Combatiente and Estrella Roja. Other groups have resorted to using previously established journals or magazines to air their statements. The Red Army Faction, for instance, published its early tracts in Agit 883.

Several books have been written by terrorists. These fall into three broad categories: autobiography, tactical and operational manuals, and political philosophy. Michael "Bommi" Baumann's self-criticism is a short tour through the West Berlin underground in the days before the emergence of the June 2 Movement. It depicts the ease with which a disaffected working-class youth can be drawn into underground terrorist circles and learn how to build and plant bombs. It is also a powerful statement on the loose organization and almost ad hoc nature of some terrorist groups. (51)

Both the Uruguayan Tupamaros and the Basque ETA have published books on how and why they carried out certain operations. (52)   In another vein, Carlos Marighella's Mini-Manual and Che Guevara's Guerrilla Warfare have joined The Anarchist's Cookbook as "must" reading for the would-be urban guerrilla. (53) Finally, the works of Frantz Fanon, Regis Debray, General George Grivas, Menachim Begin, General Giap, and Ho Chi Minh, among others, provide both insider's views of the motivations and theory of terrorism and guerrilla warfare and their personal views of politics and society. (54)

Yet another internally produced information source is the directive or history of the movement. The Sandinistas, recently successful in deposing Anastasio Somoza in Nicaragua, published in 1977 the massive 50 Anos de Lucha Sandinista. (55) Similar works have been undertaken by the Colombian M-19 and the Red Brigades. (56) Changes in strategy and tactics or group splinterings, usually lead to the publication of a new group manifesto, apology, or other explanation of activities. Regular efforts to maintain some public contact are exemplified by the Argentine Montoneros' clandestine newsletter News of the Resistance. (57) A rift in the ranks of the Red Brigades led, predictably, to the publication of a 20-page explanation in the left-wing Rome newspaper Lotta Continua. (58)

Their propaganda value aside, these self-generated works provide an excellent window to the particular terrorist group's motivation, thinking, goals, and ideology. They also offer unique insight into how terrorist groups deal with such orgnizational problems as logistics, recruitment, discipline, and leadership. Such material is invaluable for those wishing to understand the internal dynamics of terrorist movements.

NOTES

(1) This article has been reviewed by the CIA's Publications Review Board to assist the author in avoiding the unauthorized disclosure of classified information; however, neither that review nor the author's affiliation with the CIA either constitutes or implies CIA authentication of factual material or endorsement of the author's views.

(2) Perhaps the best discussions are found in Martha Crenshaw Hutchinson, "The Concept of Revolutionary Terrorism," Journal of Conflict Resolution 16 (September 1972); 383-96; Paul Wilkinson, Political Terrorism (New York: Wiley, 1975); Jordan J. Paust, "Terrorism and the International Law of War," Military Law Review 64 (1974); 1-36; and Brian Jenkins, "International Terrorism: A New Mode of Conflict" in International Terrorism and World Security, ed. David Carlton and Carlo Schaerf (London: Croom Helm, 1975), pp. 13-49. The authors have found the most empirically useful operational definition to be Milbank's synthesis of the above works. See David Milbank, International and Transnational Terrorism: Diagnosis and Prognosis (Washington, D.C.: Central Intelligence Agency, April 1976).

(3) Walter Laqueur, ed, The Terrorism Reader: A Historical Anthology (New York: New American Library, 1978).

(4) Edward Hyams, Terrorists and Terrorism (London: J.M. Dent, 1975).

(5) J. Bowyer Bell, Terror Out of Zion: Irgun, LEHI, and the Palestine Underground, 1929-1949 (New York: St. Martins, 1977); Yasumasa Kuroda, "Yount Palestinian Commandos in Political, Socialization Perspective," Middle East Journal 26 (Summer 1972): 253-70; and Bard O'Neill, Armed Struggle in Palestine: An Analysis of the Palestinian Guerrilla Movement (Boulder, Colo.: Westview, 1978).

(6) J. Bowyer Bell, "Societal Lessons and Patterns: The Irish Case," in Civil War in the Twentieth Century ed. Robin Higham (Lexington: University of Kentucky, 1974), pp. 217-28; Derek Birrell, "Relative Deprivation as a Factor in Conflict in Northern Ireland," Sociological Review 20 (August 1972); 317-43; and Timothy Patrick Coogan, The IRA (London: Pall Mall, 1970).

(7) See the 1979 special issue of Terrorism: An International Journal, which is devoted to terrorism in Italy. Also consult Alberto Ronchey, "Guns and Gray Matter: Terrorism in Italy," Foreign Affairs, spring 1979 pp. 921-40; G. Manzini, Indagine su un Brigatista Rosso: La Storia di Walter Alasia (Turin: Einaudi, 1978); Vittorfranco S. Pisano, Contemporary Italian Terrorism: Analysis and Countermeasures (Washington, D.C.: Library of Congress Law Library, 1979); and Alessandro Silj, Never Again Without Arms (Rome: Vallecchi, 1977).

(8) Ivo K. Feierabend and Rosalind L. Feierabend, "Systemic Conditions of Political Aggression: An Application of Frustration-Aggression Theory," Journal of Conflict Resolution 10 (September 1966): 249-71; Rudolph J. Rummel, "Dimensions of Conflict Behavior Within and Between Nations," General Systems Yearbook 8 (1963): 1-50; Raymond Tanter, "Dimensions of Conflict Behavior Within and Between Nations, 1958-1960," Journal of Conflict Resolution 10 (March 1966): 41-65; and Charles Lewis Taylor and Michael Hudson, World Handbook of Political and Social Indicators (New Haven: Yale, 1972).

(9) Ted Robert Gurr, "Some Characteristics of Political Terrorism in the 1960's" in The Politics of Terrorism, ed. Michael Stohl (New York: Marcel Dekker, 1979), pp. 23-49; Ted Robert Gurr "Proposals for Research on Political Terrorism," April 1973, available from the U.S. Department of State, INR/External Research, as FAR document 17081-N.

(10) Edward F. Mickolus, "Statistical Approaches to the Study of Terrorism" in Terrorism: Interdisciplinary Perspectives ed. Yonah Alexander and Seymour Maxwell Finger (New York: John Jay, 1977, pp. 209-69; Edward Mickolus, "Transnational Terrorism" in Michael Stohl, ed., The Politics of Terrorism, (New York: Marcel Dekker,

1979), pp. 147-90; and Edward Mickolus "Trends in Transnational Terrorism" in Terrorism in the Contemporary World, ed Marius Livingston (Westport: Greenwood, 1978), pp. 44-73. See also Russell L. Osmond, "Terrorism and Political Violence Theory: A Quantitative Examination" (Paper presented to the Joint National Meeting of the Operations Research Society of America and the Institute of Management Sciences, New York, May 1-3, 1978); and Lawrence C. Hamilton, Ecology of Terrorism (Ph.D. diss. University of Colorado, 1978).

(11) See their Annuals of Power and Conflict, as well as their Conflict Studies series, both published under their own London auspices. Also consult Richard Sim, "Research Note: Institute for the Study of Conflict" Terrorism: An International Journal (1978); 211-215.

(12) Manus I. Midlarsky and Martha Crenshaw Hutchinson, "Why Violence Spreads: The Contagion of International Terrorism" (Paper delivered to the annual meeting of the International Studies Association, Toronto, March 21-24, 1979); Edward Heyman, Monitoring the Diffusion of Transnational Terrorism (Gaithersburg, Md.: International Association of Chiefs of Police, 1979); and Edward Heyman and Edward Mickolus, "Imitation of Terrorists: Quantitative Approaches to the Study of Diffusion in Transnational Terrorism" in Terrorism: Behavioral Perspectives, ed. Yonah Alexander and John Gleason (forthcoming).

(13) Other treatments of the sequence of crisis situations are presented in Lincoln P. Bloomfield and Robert Beattie, "Computers and Policy-Making: the CASCON Experiment" Journal of Conflict Resolution 15 (1971): 33-46, and more formally spelled out in Lincoln P. Bloomfield, Robert R. Beattie, and G. Allen Moulton with Robert M. Mandel and John J. Spear, "CASCON II: Computer Aided System for Handling Information on Local Conflicts, User's Manual," C/72-14 (Cambridge, Mass.: MIT, September 1972).

(14) Don D. Darling, "The Inadvertent Adversary to Nuclear Security - Ourselves" in Joel J. Kramer, ed. The Role of Behavioral Science in Physical Security, Proceedings of the Second Annual Symposium, March 23-24, 1977 (Washington, D.C.: U.S. Department of Commerce, June 1978), n. 22, pp. 1-5; 27-33.

(15) Cited by Charles A. Russel, Leon J. Banker, Jr., and Bowman H. Miller, "Out-Inventing the Terrorist" in Terrorism: Theory and Practice ed. Yonah Alexander, David Carlton, and Paul Wilkinson, (Boulder, Colo.: Westview, 1979), pp. 3-42. Also see Murray S. Miron and Arnold P. Goldstein, Hostage (Kalamazoo, Mich.: Behaviordelia, 1978), 110 pp.

(16) See the chapter on airport security elsewhere in this volume, as well as John Dailey and Evan Pickrel, "Federal Aviation Administration's Behavioral Research Program for Defense Against Hijackings," Aviation, Space, and Environmental Medicine, April

1975, pp. 423-27; and Richard Shultz, "Responding to the Terrorist Threat: The State of the Operational Art" (Paper presented to the annual convention of the International Studies Association, March 1979).

(17) This has become a highly profitable business in southern Africa, where embattled whites attempt to avoid becoming the next headline.

For examples of suggested physical security arrangements, see C.S. DelGrosso and John C. Short, "A Concept for Antiterrorist Operations," Marine Corps Gazette 63 (June 1979): 54-59; and Basic Guidelines for the Executive (Denver, Colo.: Williams and Associates, 1979).

(18) Martha Crenshaw Hutchinson, "The Concept of Revolutionary Terrorism," Journal of Conflict Resolution 16 (September 1972): 383-96.

(19) Christopher Dobson and Ronald Payne, Weapons of Terror (London: Macmillan, 1979). For the terrorists' version of this book, see W. Powell, The Anarchist Cookbook (New York: Lyle Stuart, 1971).

(20) Brian Jenkins, The Impact of Nuclear Terrorism (Santa Monica, Calif.: Rand, September 1978); Brian Jenkins, "The Potential for Nuclear Terrorism" (Address to the Conference on Nuclear Arms Proliferation and Nuclear Terrorism at the Arms Control Association, Washington, D.C., May 8, 1977: reprinted Santa Monica, Calif.: Rand, May 1977, P-5876); Brian Jenkins and Joseph Krofcheck, "The Potential Nuclear Non-State Adversary" (Report prepared for the U.S. Congress, Office of Technology Assessment, May 1977); Russell William Mengel, Terrorism and New Technologies of Destruction: An Overview of the Potential Risk, Report prepared for the National Advisory Committee Task Force on Disorder and Terrorism, W-76-044-TR (Vienna, Va.: BDM Corporation, May 25, 1976).

(21) London Times, May 12, 1975.

(22) Brian Jenkins and Janera Johnson, International Terrorism: A Chronology, 1968-1974 R-1597-DOS-ARPA (Santa Monica, Calif.: Rand, March 1975).

(23) "The Terrorist and Sabotage Threat to U.S. Nuclear Programs: Phase One Final Report," prepared for Sandia Laboratories under Contract No. 82-9139 by the Historical Evaluation and Research Organization (Dunn Loring, Va., August 1974).

(24) Edward F. Mickolus, Codebook: ITERATE (International Terrorism: Attributes of Terrorist Events) (Ann Arbor: Inter-University Consortium for Political and Social Research, University of Michigan, 1976); and Edward F. Mickolus, "An Events Database for Studying Transnational Terrorism" in Quantitative Approaches to Political Intelligence: The CIA Experience, ed. Richards J. Heuer,

Jr. (Boulder, Colo.: Westview, 1978), pp. 127-63. Summaries of the incidents comprising the ITERATE data base can be found in Edward F. Mickolus, Transnational Terrorism: Chronology of Events (Westport: Greenwood, 1980).

(25) R.H. Anderson and J.J. Gillogly, "Rand Intelligent Terminal Agent: Design Philosophy, R-1809-ARPA (Santa Monica, Calif.: Rand, February 1976); and Donald A. Waterman and Brian Jenkins, "Heuristic Modeling Using Rule-Based Computer Systems" (Paper presented to the panel on Applications of Artificial Intelligence and Cognitive Psychology in International Relations of the 18th annual convention of the International Studies Association, St. Louis, Missouri, March 16-20, 1977).

(26) For a description of these analytical capabilities, see Norman H. Nie, C. Hadlai Hull, Jean G. Jenkins, Karin Steinbrenner, and Dale H. Bent, Statistical Package for the Social Sciences, 2d ed. (New York: McGraw-Hill, 1975); as well as the handbook's updates.

(27) John K. Cooley, Green March, Black September: The Story of the Palestinian Arabs (London: Frank Cass, 1973); and Christopher Dobson, Black September: Its Short, Violent History (New York: Macmillan, 1974).

(28) J.A. Frank and Michael J. Kelly, "Etude Preliminaire sur la Violence Collective en Ontario et au Quebec, 1963-1973" Canadian Journal of Political Science 10 (March 1977): 145-57; Gustave Morf, Terror in Quebec: Case Studies of the FLQ (Toronto: Clarke, Irvin, 1970); and Amy Sands Redlick, The Impact of Transnational Interactions on Separatism: A Case Study of the Quebec Separatist Movement (Ph.D. diss., Tufts University, 1978).

(29) Jillian Beckert, Hitler's Children: The Story of the Baader-Meinhof Terrorist Gang (Philadelphia: J.B. Lippincott, 1977); John D. Elliott, "Action and Reaction: West Germany and the Baader-Meinhof Guerrillas" Strategic Review 4 (Winter 1976): 60-67; and Hans Josef Horchem, "West Germany's Red Army Anarchists" Conflict Studies 46 (June 1974).

(30) J. Bowyer Bell, The Secret Army: The IRA, 1916-1974 (Cambridge, Mass.: MIT, 1974); and Gerald McKnight, The Terrorist Mind (Indianapolis: Bobbs-Merrill, 1974 are good examples.

(31) Patricia G. Steinhoff, "Portrait of a Terrorist: An Interview with Kozo Okamoto" Asian Survey 16 (September 1976): 830-45. Jeanne Knutson has suggested continuing this type of study.

(32) Ernest Evans, "Terrorism and International Politics" (Paper presented at the annual convention of the Northeast Political Science Association at South Egremont, Massachusetts, November 11-13, 1976.

(33) Jay Mallin, ed., Terror and Urban Guerrillas: A Study of Tactics and Documents (Coral Gables, Fla.: University of Miami, 1971).

(34) Brian Jenkins, Janera Johnson, and David Ronfeldt Numbered Lives (Santa Monica, Calif.: Rand, July 1977), reprinted in Conflict 1 (Fall 1977); Brian Jenkins, Hostage Survival: Some Preliminary Observations (Santa Monica, Calif.: Rand, April 1976); Brian Jenkins, Terrorism and Kidnapping (Santa Monica, Calif.: Rand, June 1974); Brian Jenkins, Should Corporations Be Prevented from Paying Ransom? (Santa Monica, Calif.: Rand, September 1974); Brian Jenkins Hostages and Their Captors: Friends and Lovers (Santa Monica, Calif.: Rand, October 1975).

(35) Edward F. Mickolus, "Negotiating for Hostages: A Policy Dilemma," Orbis 19 (Winter 1976); 1309-25, reprinted in Contemporary Terrorism: Selected Readings, ed. John D. Elliott and Leslie K. Gibson (Gaithersburg, Md.: International Association of Chiefs of Police, 1978) pp. 207-21.

(36) Ernest Evans, "The Failure of U.S. Policy," Counterforce 1 (February 1977): 9; and Ernest Evans, Calling a Truce to Terror: The American Response to International Terrorism (Westport: Greenwood, 1979).

(37) See Stephen Sloan, "Simulating Terrorism: Behavioral, Tactical, Administrative, Policy, and Issue Dimensions," (Paper presented to the annual convention of the International Studies Association, Toronto, March 1979); Stephen Sloan, "International Terrorism: Academic Quest, Operational Art and Policy Implications" Journal of International Affairs 32 (Spring-Summer 1978): 1-6; and Stephen Sloan, "Simulating Terrorism: From Operational Techniques to Questions of Policy" International Studies Notes 5 (Winter 1978): 3-8.

(38) Joseph Margolin, "Psychological Perspectives in Terrorism," in Terrorism: Interdisciplinary Perspectives, ed. Yonah Alexander and Seymour Maxwell Finger (New York: John Jay, 1977), pp. 270-82.

(39) Brooks McClure, "Hostage Survival" in International Terrorism in the Contemporary World ed. Marius Livingston (London: Greenwood, 1978), pp. 276-81; as well as Frank Bolz, "Strategies in Negotiation" (Paper presented to the conference on Terror: The Man, the Mind and the Matter, held at the John Jay School of Criminal Justice, New York City, October 15-16, 1976).

(40) Claude Fly, No Hope But God (New York: Hawthorn, 1973); Geoffrey Jackson, Surviving the Long Night: An Autobiographical Account of a Political Kidnapping (New York: Vanguard, 1974); and Karl and Debbie Dortzbach, Kidnapped (New York: Harper and Row, 1975).

(41) Summaries of two major conferences held in Oklahoma and New York can be found in Terrorism 2 (1979).

(42) Michael J. Kelly and Thomas H. Mitchell, "Transnational Terrorism and the Western Elite Press" (Paper presented to the annual meeting

of the Canadian Political Science Association, Saskatoon, Saskatche-
wan, May 30, 1979); Neil Hickey, "Terrorism and Television: The
Medium in the Middle" TV Guide, August 7, 1976; Yonah Alexander,
"Communications Aspects of International Terrorism" International
Problems 16 (Spring 1977); Marvin E. Leibstone, "Terrorism and the
Media" (Paper presented to the Conference on Moral Implications of
Terrorism, UCLA, March 14-16, 1979); H.H.A. Cooper "Terrorism
and the Media" Chitty's Law Journal 24 (September 1976): 226-32;
and Michael Sommer, Terrorism and the Media (forthcoming).

(43) Martin Elliott Silverstein, "The Medical Survival of Victims of
Terrorism" (Prepared for the Office of the Chief Scientist, U.S.
Arms Control and Disarmament Agency, 1976); and "Emergency
Medical Preparedness" Terrorism: An International Journal 1 (1977):
51-69, also available in Political Terrorism and Business: The Threat
and Response, ed. Yonah Alexander and Robert Kilmarx (New York:
Praeger, 1979), pp. 219-25.

(44) Abraham H. Miller, "Negotiations for Hostages: Implications from
the Police Experience" Terrorism 1 (1978): 125-46; Abraham H.
Miller, "Hostages as Victims: Research and Policy Issues" (Paper
presented to the International Studies Association annual
convention, Toronto, March 21, 1979); Abraham H. Miller, "SWAT
(Special Weapons and Tactics) - The Practical Link in Hostage
Negotiations," in Alexander and Kilmarx Political Terrorism, pp.
331-56; and Abraham H. Miller, "Hostage Negotiations and the
Concept of Transference," in Terrorism: Theory and Practice, ed.
Yonah Alexander, David Carlton, and Paul Wilkinson (Boulder, Colo.:
Westview, 1979), pp. 137-58.

(45) Frank Ochberg "The Victim of Terrorism: Psychiatric Considerations" Terrorism 1 (1978): 147-68; Frank Ochberg, ed., Victims of
Terrorism (Boulder, Colo.: Westview, 1979).

(46) Alona Evans and John F. Murphy, eds, Legal Aspects of
International Terrorism (Washington, D.C.: American Society of
International Law, 1977). Also see Lois McHugh, "International
Terrorism: Legal Documentation" (Washington, D.C.: Library of
Congress, Congressional Research Service, January 20, 1978); and
German Information Center, "A Comparative Study of the Anti-
Terrorist Legislation in the Federal Republic of Germany, France,
England, and Sweden, and an Overview of the Legal Situation in the
United States" Relay from Bonn 9 (January 16, 1978).

(47) Report of the Task Force on Disorders and Terrorism (Washington,
D.C., U.S. Department of Justice, National Advisory Committee on
Criminal Justice Standards and Goals, 1976).

(48) A summary of the relevant international conventions can be found
in Edward Mickolus, "Multilateral Legal Efforts to Combat Terrorism: Diagnosis and Prognosis," Ohio Northern University Law
Review, 1979. Also consult the writings of Robert A. Friedlander,
especially "Coping with Terrorism: What is to be Done?" in

Alexander et al., Terrorism: Theory and Practice, pp. 231-45;
"Reflections on Terrorist Havens," Naval War College Review 32
(March-April 1979), pp. 59-67; and "The Origins of International
Terrorism: A Micro Legal-Historical Perspective" Israel Yearbook
on Human Rights 6 (1976).

(49) Perhaps the best known journal is Terrorism, published by Crane-
Russak and edited by Yonah Alexander.

(50) Douglas   W.   Simon   "Policy   Recommendation   Exercises"
International Studies Notes 2 (Spring 1975): 19-21.

(51) Michael Baumann, Terror or Love? (Originally Wie Alles Anfig)
trans. Helen Ellenboogen and Wayne Parker (New York: Grove
Press, 1977).

(52) MLN, Actas Tupamaras (Buenos Aires: Shapire, 1971); and
Julienne Aguirre, Operation Ogro: The Execution of Admiral Luis
Carrero Blanco, trans. Barbara Solomon (New York: Quadrangle
Books, 1975).

(53) Marighella's Mini-Manual may be found on pp. 61-97 of his For the
Liberation of Brazil, trans. Rosemary Butt and John Sheed (London:
Penguin Books, 1971). Che Guevara, Guerrilla Warfare, trans. J.P.
Morray (New York: Random House, 1969).

(54) Frantz Fanon, The Wretched of the Earth, trans. Constance
Farrington (New York: Grove Press, 1968); Regis Debray, Revolution in the Revolution? (New York: Grove Press, 1967); George
Grivas, Guerrilla Warfare and EOKA's Struggle (London: Longman's,
1964); Menachim Begin, The Revolt (New York: Henry Schumer,
1951); Vo Nguyen Giap, People's War, People's Army (New York:
Praeger, 1967); Ho Chi Minh, On Revolution (New York: Praeger,
1967).

(55) Humberto Ortega, (member of the National Directorate of the
FSLN), 50 Anos de Lucha Sandinista (Managua, 1977).

(56) M-19, Los Testigos (Bogota: Editorial Presencia, 1977); Brigate
Rosse, Risoluzione della Direzione Strategica delle Brigate Rosse
(February 1978).

(57) News was a clandestine, mimeographed sheet that the group
mailed regularly to newspapers. The last issue was apparently
distributed in September 1978. See David Belnap, "Montoneros, In
Exile, Claim to Have Aided Sandinistas," Los Angeles Times, August
15, 1979.

(58) See "Dissent Splits Italy's Red Brigades," New York Times, July 28,
1979.

The Diffusion of
Transnational Terrorism
Edward S. Heyman

As part of their war against the Argentine government, the Montoneros abducted ex-President Pedro Aramburu's corpse from its crypt in October 1974 and threatened to hold on to it until the government met certain political demands. (1)   Within weeks, a group of Burmese radicals stole U Thant's body from its resting place to secure their own set of political demands from the Burmese government. (2)

This is one example of a terrorist group adopting another's tactics. Terrorist tactics are spreading, affecting more nations and people than ever before.   Various analysts have voiced their concern over the apparent diffusion of terrorism, noting that terrorist tactics are being used throughout the world in a wide variety of situations.   No systematic examination of the diffusion problem exists, however.

This paper attempts to fill that gap in terrorism research, examining how and why terrorism has spread throughout the international community over the last ten years. It will:

- Present a conceptual framework for identifying and discussing diffusion processes;

- Introduce new techniques for monitoring diffusion;

- Suggest explanations of the diffusion of transnational terrorism; and

- Discuss the elements of transnational terrorism that have promoted its rapid spread throughout the world.

A CONCEPTUAL FRAMEWORK OF
DIFFUSION PROCESSES (3)

Spatial diffusion refers to the spread of a particular phenomenon or class of phenomena within an environment over time. The concept of diffusion has been implicit in a number of popularly held notions in international relations.   The "domino theory" underlying the policy of containment was based on the belief that unless effective barriers were built, communism would spread throughout the world.   The U.S. government's "no bargaining" policy in dealing with terrorist acts is another example.   The policy is based on the assumption that capitulation to terrorists encourages others to make similar demands. Both policies see ideas traveling or diffusing within the international system over time.

Types of Diffusion Processes

Diffusion studies focus on movement within an environment over time. They address the location of a phenomenon during various time periods, and monitor the frequency of its appearance at each location as it travels through the environment.   Lawrence A. Brown, a spatial geographer at Ohio State University, has identified four basic types of diffusion processes: relocation, expansion, hierarchical, and contagious. (4) Relocation and expansion diffusion concern the diffusing item's patterns of movement.   Hierarchical and contagious diffusion deal with the structure and mechanics of the process.

- Relocation diffusion refers to members of a population moving from one place to another over time.   This type of diffusion is "conservative" in that the size of the population does not change over time; what changes is the location of the members of the population.   Population here refers to the class of phenomena under investigation, and can be anything from individuals to military bases, religious groups, or terrorist cells.   Migration and travel are forms of relocation.

- Expansion diffusion occurs when new members join the population over time, and are located away from the old members in such a way as to alter the overall spatial distribution of the population. Expansion diffusion is not conservative.

An example of relocation can be found in the movement of the headquarters of the Latin American Junta for Revolutionary Coordination (JCR) from Buenos Aires to Paris.   In an attempt to escape total defeat at the hands of the Argentine military, members of the terrorist organization moved from Argentina to France and other European countries.   Only the location of the group's members changed as a result of the relocation, while the group's size remained relatively unchanged.

If, however, instead of moving its headquarters, a group seeking European representation established new cells and recruited additional members in a new location, diffusion would be the result of expansion.

The next two types of diffusion deal with the mechanics of the process:

- To say that diffusion is <u>hierarchical</u> implies that the diffusion process is structured, and the structure underlying the process is intelligible. One example of hierarchical diffusion would be the spread of an order throughout a bureaucracy. Those in command would receive the order first. They would then pass the order along to those lower down in the bureaucracy.

- <u>Contagion</u> is one form of structured diffusion. Here, distance plays the strongest role in determining the path of the diffusing item. Over time, the item moves from one location to the next nearest possible location. Effort, as a function of traveling distance, is minimized. Riots may be seen as contagious, especially if bystanders are drawn into the fray. The effect of distance is apparent in that people close to the riot scene are more likely to become involved than those across town.

The relationship between the different types of diffusion processes may be seen in Figure 9.1. It should be noted that a given diffusion process is not necessarily of one type or another. The types are not mutually exclusive. In a multistage diffusion process, such as the spread of news about a terrorist incident, word might be sent over the news wires to major cities in a hierarchical pattern. Once received, however, the news might be spread throughout the cities by word of mouth in a contagious fashion.

	contagion	hierarchical
expansion	ideas and innovations at local levels: riots, diseases, mass action, regional wars	ideas and innovations at places, elite actions, transnational phenomena
relocation	migration waves; refugees moving away from a spreading conflict	elite migration, that is, patterns of exile, movement of corporations or the location of military bases

Fig. 9.1. Relationships between diffusion processes.

Elements of the Diffusion Process

Each of the four types of diffusion processes shares six essential elements. The six, according to Brown, are the basic components of any diffusion process. They are: the environment, time, the item being diffused, the point of origin, the point of destination, and the path or channel along which the diffusing item travels.

The <u>environment</u> is where diffusion takes place. Diffusion may occur in a variety of environments, ranging from the international system to regional subsystems, cities, towns, and so on. The environments have important characteristics, in that they may be urban or rural, structured or unstructured, primitive or modern, developed or undeveloped. Identification of the environment is important, as it helps determine who the actors are, and what kind of behavior to expect from the diffusing item. For instance, news will spread more rapidly in a modern environment with newspapers and telephones than in a primitive environment where communication is strictly person to person, and the messenger travels by ox-cart. Transnational terrorism diffuses through a structured political environment saturated with technology and reliant on rapid communications.

Time is used as a measure to monitor the process. It is divided into equal intervals of minutes, days, months, quarters, years, or whatever period best suits the process. It is not enough to say that something has spread; it is important to note how long it took to spread, and whether the rate of spread is constant, increasing, or decreasing.

The item being diffused is one of the most important elements of the diffusion process. Items may be inanimate physical objects, people, or ideas - anything that can be seen as spreading. Behavioral patterns such as criminality, violence, or other tendencies may be seen as spreading, or even thought of as "contagious." We might be interested in the apparent diffusion of communism, or of terrorism; the spread of items such as strikes or riots; or the use of new technologies, such as communications devices, automated travel, airport security screening mechanisms, or a particular new weapon system.

The point (or node) of origin is the place or places where the diffusing item is located at the beginning of the diffusion process. It is "where the diffusing item came from." During the cold war, when political commentators believed in a monolithic communist bloc under Soviet control, the USSR was seen as the node of origin in the diffusion of communist systems.

The point (or node) of destination is the place where the diffusing item is located for the first time at the end of each time interval. It is the place to which the diffusing item has spread. It marks a location that did not have the item before, but has it now.

The paths of movement are the channels along which the diffusing item travels. They imply some relationship between the node of origin and the node of destination. Channels may be people, or technology that facilitates or aids communication. The type of channel usually depends on what kind of item is diffusing, and on the environment in which diffusion occurs. Paths in any particular diffusion process may be preexisting, or may be a result of the process.

These six elements combine to form a conceptual model of a basic diffusion process. Each is variable, and has some impact on the nature, direction, or rate of the diffusion process.

Certain characteristics of the nodes, the item being diffused, and the environment in which diffusion occurs will affect the diffusion process. Consider the relationship between the node of origin and the node of destination. What makes the node of destination a likely candidate to receive the diffusing item? What attracts or repels the item? Why, for example, does terrorism spread to some countries and not to others?

Environmental characteristics are also important. Different types of barriers within the environment will have an effect on the path of a diffusing item. (5) Absorbing barriers stop the diffusion process cold. Reflecting barriers channel the "energy" of the diffusion process and deflect it from its original path. Permeable barriers allow part of the diffusing phenomenon through, but slow the speed and intensity of the diffusion process. Barriers can be cultural, linguistic, political, religious, psychological, or ideological. Politicians referred to the "iron curtain" during the cold war; security procedures, quarantines, and censorship are all forms of effective barriers.

MONITORING THE DIFFUSION OF TRANSNATIONAL TERRORISM

A phenomenon, such as transnational terrorism, may be said to be diffusing if we can:

- Observe changes in the location of the phenomenon over time;

- Note changes in the intensity or frequency of the phenomenon's appearance at various locations; and

- Determine the factors or channels that facilitate the movement of the phenomenon.

Our focus is on the pattern of movement. If terrorism is, in fact, diffusing, it must be possible to chart its spread to new locations in the world.

The following sections discuss a technique for tracing and monitoring the diffusion of terrorism. Data on transnational terrorist incidents occurring between 1968 and 1977 are plotted on "adjacency maps" to display the movement of terrorism to new locations.

THE DATA: ITERATE II

The data on transnational terrorism are from ITERATE II, a computerized data system created by Edward Mickolus. (6) ITERATE II employs an events- data approach in the study of terrorism, taking the individual terrorist incident as its unit of analysis. (7)

The ITERATE II data consists of information on 3,329 incidents of transnational terrorism during the period from January 1, 1968 to December 31, 1977. The data are culled from over 200 sources, including the U.S. and foreign media, government reports, academic analyses, and official U.S. chronologies. Each event is coded for 107 distinct variables. (8)

There are, of course, certain problems and limitations in using an events- data approach. Altering the definition of terrorism and the types of events included may affect some statistical findings. A running count of incidents alone may not be a valid indicator of the level of terrorist activity. Rises in the number of reported incidents may reflect a real increase in terrorist activity, or may be the result of more comprehensive and systematic press reporting. On the other hand, important incidents may not have been reported. However, ITERATE has attempted to avoid these shortcomings by using a large number of sources, and drawing data from as wide a cross section of sources as possible. Nevertheless, the results presented in this analysis are subject to refinement.

The Adjacency Maps

Political maps of the world are usually drawn to depict a country's territory. To display other types of information about a state, such as the number of terrorist incidents it experienced, or the number of terrorist groups operating within it, each state is shaded according to its assigned value. This convention creates two problems. Small states are difficult to shade, while the size of large states tends to distort the overall picture.

The adjacency map is designed to remedy these problems and enhance the display of spatial patterns. As designed by Dr. Claudio Cioffi-Revilla at the University of North Carolina, it is based on two criteria. Each state, regardless of its size, is represented by a single point (node), and is linked to its neighbors by lines (edges) representing borders. The resulting map is well suited for displaying diffusion patterns, depicted as a series of contour lines.

An example of an adjacency map showing part of the European continent appears in figure 9.2. An example of an adjacency map with diffusion patterns is given in figure 9.3. If we were using the second map to display the diffusion of terrorism, the contour line surrounding Denmark (DN), West Germany (GF), France (FR), Switzerland (ST), and Austria (AT) would indicate that these states had experienced terrorist incidents.

The ITERATE data allowed an examination of four diffusion patterns: the cumulative diffusion of all types of transnational terrorist incidents; the diffusion of transnational terrorist kidnappings; the diffusion of transnational terrorist skyjackings; and the annual incidence of transnational terrorism in each state.

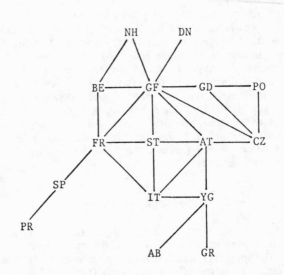

KEY

AB	Albania
AT	Austria
BE	Belgium
CZ	Czechoslovakia
DN	Denmark
FR	France
GD	East Germany
GF	West Germany
GR	Greece
IT	Italy
NH	Netherlands
PO	Poland
PR	Portugal
SP	Spain
ST	Switzerland
YG	Yugoslavia

Figure 9.2. Example of an adjacency map.

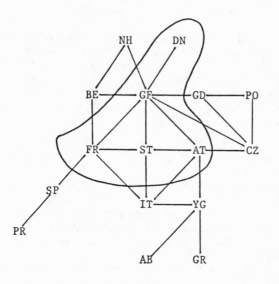

Inactive	AB	Albania
Country	AT	Austria
	BE	Belgium
	CZ	Czechoslovakia
Country New	DN	Denmark
to the	FR	France
Distribution	GD	East Germany
	GF	West Germany
	GR	Greece
	IT	Italy
	NH	Netherlands
	PO	Poland
	PR	Portugal
	SP	Spain
	ST	Switzerland
	YG	Yugoslavia

Figure 9.3.   Example of an adjacency map showing diffusion contours

The Diffusion Picture: Determining the
Location of the Phenomenon

The following analysis is drawn from the four sets of adjacency maps in
Appendix A. The first set of maps shows the cumulative diffusion of
transnational terrorism. The second set shows the diffusion of a
specific type of incident, transnational terrorist kidnappings, and the
third set depicts the spread of terrorist skyjackings. The final set of
maps displays the annual location and intensity of transnational
terrorist activity.

Reading the Maps

The contour lines on the first three sets of maps indicate which
countries have experienced incidents.   The squares mark states
experiencing incidents for the first time during the time period of the
map. The triangles mark states that may be considered inactive; once
the scene of activity, they have had no transnational terrorist activity
for at least two years.
    The contour lines on the fourth set of maps represent the number of
incidents each country experienced during the period of the map. This
allows a quick assessment of the annual frequency of terrorism.
    It should be noted that the maps do not distinguish or weigh the
various kinds of transnational terrorist events. Bombings, kidnappings,
assassinations, armed assaults, skyjackings, and barricade and hostage
incidents are treated equally. The only exception is when specific types
of incidents are isolated for display, as in the second and third sets of
maps, where only kidnappings and skyjackings are shown.

Observations from the Maps

Careful inspection of the maps allows a number of preliminary
conclusions. Taken as a group, the maps reveal the speed and extent of
the diffusion process.   The first map in Appendix A, of cumulative
diffusion of all incidents in 1968, indicates that 26 countries experienced transnational terrorist incidents that year. This map marks
the beginning of the diffusion process. The following nine maps show
that by the end of 1977, transnational terrorist incidents had occurred
in at least 98 countries. Similarly, the next two sets of maps reveal
that 40 countries were the location of skyjackings between 1968 and
1977, and that individuals were kidnapped in 49 countries.
    The first three sets of maps also indicate the extent to which
geographical proximity is a factor in the diffusion of transnational
terrorism.   Countries sharing borders with states that experienced
transnational terrorist incidents appear to have a high probability of
experiencing incidents themselves in the future. It is also interesting to
note the patterns formed by the entrance of new countries into the

distribution, and the pattern of countries that drop out of the distribution. Terrorism diffused rapidly throughout Latin America, Western Europe, and the Middle East, and slowly throughout Africa and Asia. African countries also had a tendency to drop out of the pattern soon after they entered.

The maps displaying terrorist skyjackings and kidnappings further highlight the rapid diffusion of incidents throughout Western Europe and Latin America. Kidnappings spread throughout the Middle East and southern Africa, but barely penetrated East Asia. Skyjackings spread little beyond the Americas, Western Europe, and the Middle East.

The fourth set of maps, showing annual intensity, indicates that Western Europe, Latin America, North America, and the Middle East were the hardest-hit regions. Sub-Saharan Africa and Asia experienced relatively few transnational terrorist incidents. The observable changes in the patterns over time indicate a marked shift in the location of high-frequency terrorism, which apparently moved from Latin America into the Middle East and then into Western Europe. After 1972, Western Europe became a sink for high levels of transnational terrorist activity.

The patterns that emerge from an analysis of the adjacency maps form the basis for a discussion of the diffusion of transnational terrorism over the last decade.

- The movement of the phenomenon is hierarchical between regions at first, and then becomes contagious within the regions.

- The rate of contagion varies according to region, and according to the type of incident.

- Transnational terrorism spread most rapidly throughout Latin America.

- Western Europe tended to have the highest levels of activity.

- Border contiguity appears to be a factor in diffusion. In 54 of the 72 cases of new countries experiencing transnational terrorism incidents after 1968, the country shared a border with a state that had previously experienced incidents. In two of these cases, the period of contagion was in excess of two years.

- The diffusion of transnational terrorism was particularly weak in certain regions of the world. Most of sub-Saharan Africa was unaffected by terrorism in general; Asia and Africa were left relatively unaffected by terrorist skyjackings. Kidnapping diffused little beyond Latin America, Western Europe, and Middle East and Southern Africa.

- Seventy-five percent of the diffusion occurred in the first half of the decade.

- The highest levels of activity, aggregated by region, moved over time from Latin America to the Middle East, and then to Western Europe.

A DISCUSSION OF THE DIFFUSION OF
TRANSNATIONAL TERRORISM

Transnational terrorism has diffused throughout the international system. Its spread to 98 countries over the past ten years is observable. Yet a number of questions remain to be answered. How and why has terrorism diffused? What factors account for the speed and extent of diffusion? What channels promote diffusion, and what barriers inhibit the spread of transnational terrorism? Is more than one type of diffusion process active?

Recalling the conceptual framework discussed earlier, we can isolate four hypotheses to account for the diffusion of transnational terrorism.

1. Spontaneous generation. This (null) hypothesis suggests that there is no connection between the various incidents or location of terrorist incidents. It rejects the very assumption of diffusion. Each affected area of country developed a problem with terrorism independently, and in isolation from every other affected area. All terrorist activity was in response to purely indigenous factors. Accordingly, terrorism did not diffuse, but developed spotaneously to create the observed spatial patterns. Although this explanation rejects the assumption of diffusion, it may account for very early activity in the system that occurred before contagion took effect. Or it may be a random component or residual or an overall diffusion process.

2. Cooperation between groups. The archetypical example of transnational terrorism is the Lod Airport massacre of May 1972. Japanese terrorists from the Japanese Red Army (JRA), acting in the name of the Popular Front for the Liberation of Palestine (PFLP), made their way through Europe with the aid of Western European connections, and used Czechoslovakian weapons to kill Puerto Rican pilgrims in an Israeli airport.

This hypothesis focuses on the links between various terrorist groups and cells, both within individual countries and throughout the world. The diffusion of terrorist tactics and strategies is accounted for by the free exchange of ideas, information, and assistance. Training centers, and central weapons caches, document forgery centers, and overt international alliances between groups, along with international terrorist conferences, provide readily exploited channels for the diffusion of tactics and terrorism.

3. Actual transport. Not all of the countries experiencing transnational terrorist incidents have spawned indigenous terrorist groups. Many of these countries are simply the victims of terrorists from other countries carrying their conflicts to new locations. Organizations may move to new areas for a variety of reasons. They may be driven out of their original staging grounds, as was the case with many Latin American groups that fled their native countries to other Latin American nations and to Western Europe. They may attack a government that they feel is an ally of their enemy, as with Palestinian attacks against supporters of Israel. They may also attack their own

countrymen on foreign soil, as is the case with Armenian terrorist attacks against Turkish targets. Or a group might decide to carry out an attack where it can best maximize the publicity and effect of the incident, or where the enemy is deemed weakest, as in the Black September Organization's assault on the Israeli Olympic team in Munich in 1972.

In terms of diffusion, this pattern is defined as hierarchical relocation. Terrorist cells move from place to place, with no necessary increase in the actual number of terrorists, yet carrying terrorism with them. Their movement alters the spatial distribution of the phenomenon.

4. Influence and imitation. This hypothesis focuses on groups that pattern their activities after the incidents they see, read, or hear about. The news and communications media provide the essential linkage between diffuser and adopter, and are the channels for the diffusion of tactics and ideas. In this case, the media provide an alternative to direct interpersonal contact between groups.

Factors Contributing to Diffusion

A number of factors contributing to the diffusion of transnational terrorism emerge from the four hypotheses. The most important factors are:

● General coordination of activities, such as:

   Training centers
   Joint operations
   Central weapons caches
   Coordinating councils

● Supporting governments

● International conferences

● Open air waves and travel

● Lack of legal barriers

● General political and ideological affinity between groups

General Coordination

There is ample evidence that different groups have gotten together to coordinate their terrorist activities. Two groups that have taken the lead in coordinating activities among a variety of terrorists are the Argentine People's Revolutionary Army (ERP) and the Palestinian PFLP.

The Latin American Infrastructure. The ERP was established in Argentina in 1969 as the armed wing of the Revolutionary Trotskyist Party (PRT). Its goal was to precipitate and lead the Second War of

Latin American Independence, to liberate Latin America from the "yoke of U.S. and West European imperialism." During its seven years of activity the ERP amassed a considerable war chest of money and arms, and shared its supplies and expertise with a number of neighboring guerrilla and terrorist groups. The group also made initial contacts with radical cells in Western Europe.

Examples of ERP involvement with other groups are numerous. The ERP learned the technique of kidnapping and holding victims in carcels del pueblo, or "people's prisons," from the Tupamaros in Uruguay. They trained Paraguayan terrorists in the technique in 1973, and taught them to operate a remote-controlled car that could be filled with explosives, a torpedo on wheels. (9) A member of the Basque ETA trained with the ERP in Argentina between January and March of 1974, and took part in at least one ERP mission. The Basque returned to Spain with plans for the construction and maintenance of "people's prisons." In December 1974 a female member of the ERP was arrested in Ezeiza Airport near Buenos Aires. She was carrying messages to French terrorists in Nice and Paris. (10)

Perhaps more important than these contacts was the ERP's role in the creation of the Revolutionary Coordinating Council (JCR) in 1974. The JCR consisted of leaders from the ERP, the Bolivian National Liberational Army (ELN), the Uruguayan Tupamaros, and the Movement of the Revolutionary Left (MIR) in Chile. The forming of the JCR marked the establishment of a central coordinating body to distribute funds, training, and weapons throughout Latin America. The ERP endowed the JCR with an initial stipend of $5 million. In 1975, Argentine police uncovered a JCR headquarters in La Plata, Argentina that contained a weapons factory for the construction of submachine guns, an underground firing range, printing presses for document forgery, and extensive files on JCR activities. (11)

The JCR's operational command in Buenos Aires oversees its activities throughout Latin America. The organization has front offices in Mexico, Venezuela, West Germany, France, and Portugal, and is also represented in Belgium, Holland, and Italy. A JCR affiliate, the Movement against Imperialism and for Socialism in Argentina (MASA), has offices in Los Angeles, San Francisco, and Miami. (12)

During its five-year existence the JCR has maintained close ties with Colombian guerrilla groups and has brought members of the Paraguayan FREPALINA into the council. Training for JCR members has been provided in Iraq and Libya and by the Cubans. The Angolan government has allegedly also trained JCR combatants. (13)

The Palestinian Connection. The JCR's activities notwithstanding, the Palestinians have provided the lion's share of terrorist training over the last decade. Al Fatah and the PFLP have had representatives recruiting trainees in Rio de Janeiro and Brazil (14) and throughout Europe. The PRLP has maintained training camps across the Middle East, notably the Tal Za'atar camp in Lebanon, and the Abu Ali Iyad camp in Iraq. Graduates of Camp Khayat, near the city of Aden, include six members of the Japanese Red Army; Rolf Pohle and Siegfried Haag of the Baader-Meinhof gang; Vereena Becker and

Gabrielle Kroecher-Tiedemann of the German Red Army Faction and June 2 Movement respectively; Wilfred Boese, who participated in the Entebbe skyjacking in July 1976; Zuhair Akkash, leader of the Mogadishu skyjacking of October 1977; two West Germans arrested near Nairobi's airport with surface-to-air (SAM-7) missiles supplied by the Libyans; and three members of the Dutch "Red Help" organization. (15)

Palestinian training is an important channel for the diffusion of terrorism. As Dr. Charles Russell has pointed out, terrorists who have shared training have effectively "studied with the same faculty and are graduates of the same academy." They are thus prone to the same camaraderie and support relationships that exist among any group of school classmates. The connections made at the camps promote the international quality of some terrorist teams; for example, some Germans and Palestinians who trained together later on worked together at Entebbe.

Training is but one form of contact. Weapons disbursement is another. The ERP's role in providing weapons to Latin American groups through the JCR has been noted. A case of American M-26 grenades stolen from a storage facility in West Germany fell into the hands of the Baader-Meinhof gang. They gave a number to "Carlos," who in turn distributed the grenades to a Parisian cell of the Turkish People's Liberation Army, and to members of the Japanese Red Army for use in their September 1974 barricade of the French embassy at the Hague. And it was an M-26 that "Carlos" dropped into Le Drugstore in Paris during that same JRA barricade of the French embassy to increase pressure on the French government to meet the JRA's demands. Weapons found in the possession of the German Socialist Patients Collective, the Red Army Faction, and the Italian Red Brigades have been traced to a cache stolen from a Swiss Army depot by the Petra Krause group. Krause allegedly was a member of the Italian Armed Proletarian Nuclei (NAP) before she moved to Switzerland. Weapons from her arsenal were allegedly used in both the Moro (Red Brigades) and Schleyer (RAF) kidnappings. (16)

Document exchanges form another link between terrorist groups. The passports the JRA team bound for Lod Airport used in 1972 were supplied by the Baader-Meinhof gang. And the Iranian passport used by Kristina Berster in her unsuccessful attempt to enter the United States in July 1978 was stolen from the Iranian consulate in Geneva by antishah radicals in June 1976. (17)

Government Support

Government interaction with terrorists provides yet another channel for diffusion. Governments may provide terrorists with safe-havens (perhaps saving the individual or groups from extinction), and disburse arms and funds. Government involvement helps to coordinate terrorist activities, offers a channel of communication between individuals and groups, promotes activity, and in some cases, maintains the terrorists' existence.

Training is one of the more common forms of government support for terrorists. During World War II, both the OSS and the Russians trained anti-Nazi forces in Europe in the art of subversion and insurrection. The Soviets reportedly continue to train terrorists in concert with their other activities at Patrice Lumumba University and in camps at Simferopol, Tashkent, Baku, and Odessa. (18) As early as 1960, the Cubans were running training camps for Argentine guerrillas, some in Cuba, others in Argentina. In July 1961, Argentina police uncovered two Cuban-run camps at Colonel Pringles and Lomas de Zamora in Buenos Aires Province. (19) The Cubans allegedly also run or have run training camps for skyjackers at Pine de Agua in Oriente Province, Cuba, and at Pinar de Rio in Cabayas. (20) The Egyptian government trained Al Fatah combatants in the late 1960s. Members of George Habash's PFLP received some training from the Chinese. (21) The North Koreans trained an estimated 2,500 terrorists between 1966 and 1973. (22) And recently there has been speculation in the press that members of Italy's Red Brigades train in Czechoslovakia.

Libyan money and arms have been channeled to the Black September Organization, the PFLP, the "Carlos" group, the JRA, the Baader-Meinhof group, and the Irish Republican Army (IRA). They have offered other forms of support to combatants in Chad, Chile, Corsica, Ethiopia, Iran, Lebanon, Morocco, Nicaragua, Panama, the Philippines, Sardinia, Thailand, Tunisia, Turkey, and Uruguay. (23)

International Conference

International conferences have also brought terrorists together. Conferences arranged by the IRA in 1972 and 1974 were attended by members of groups operating in the Middle East and Western Europe, including Welsh, Breton, Basque, and Corsican terrorists. A secret meeting in Zurich during September 1974 was attended by members of the JRA, the "Carlos" group, and the PFLP. Another meeting was held in 1972 at the PFLP-controlled Baddawi refugee camp. Participants included Andreas Baader, Fusako Shigenobu of the JRA, Abu Iyad and Fuad Shemali of the Black September Organization, and representatives of the IRA, the Turkish Peoples Liberation Army, the Iranian Liberation Front, and various Latin American groups. (24)

Open Air Waves and Travel

Terrorists also take advantage of the ever-expanding communications network and transport system. Not all terrorists are in direct contact with one another, but news broadcasts can provide terrorists with ideas and intelligence about terrorist activities in other countries. The air waves also inform terrorists about the movements of possible targets, and what precautions governments are taking. The transportation system allows them to travel and meet with other groups. It also affords them mobility in moving quickly to locations where their targets are most vulnerable, and where they can maximize the publicity and impact of their activity. The media and transport systems are thus crucial channels for the diffusion of terrorism.

Lack of Legal Barriers

There are countless stories in the press and the popular literature about nations letting known terrorists slip unpunished through their hands. Terrorists in the past have successfully planted the seeds of fear, making governments unwilling to prosecute them, hold them in prison, or extradite them to force punishment elsewhere. International legal conventions against terrorism are weak, and lack enforcement clauses. The recent trials and convictions in West Germany, Holland, and Italy are exceptions, rather than the rule.

Legal problems include the difficulty of distinguishing between political and criminal offenses, the intricacies of successfully extraditing the accused, and the right of nations to grant offenders political asylum. Ideological differences run deep, despite the common perception that terrorism must be subject to international law, complicating the transnational efforts required to stop the spread of a transnational phenomenon.

The Affinity Factor

Affinity is the least tangible factor affecting the diffusion of transnational terrorism, and perhaps the most important. Diffusion cannot occur unless there is some bond between the actors. The adopter must be sympathetic to the diffusing item in order to accept it.

Not all terrorist groups see eye to see. Nor do they all actively exchange information with one another. There is, as yet, no terrorist board of directors overseeing or controlling the activities of all transnational combatants. Nevertheless, as J. Bowyer Bell has pointed out,

> many active revolutionaries are convinced that a revolutionary comradeship exists. It may be a band of quarrelling brothers, but it is a band nevertheless ... Even the most parochial of rebels ... soon develop an international posture and feel akin to distant rebels who employ similar strategies and share the same heroes. (25)

Similarities in goals and philosophies, and the needs of many terrorist groups for training and advice, afford the necessary bonds for diffusion.

The rhetoric of transnational terrorism also weighs heavily in the affinity factors. Most terrorist groups at least pay lip service to the broad goal of continental or cinternational revolution. Adherence to the goal gives the movement a broader base, widens the focus of the struggle, makes it more meaningful to the terrorist, and supplants his search for identity. Terrorists derive from this a sense of joint purpose, solidarity, and support. They see themselves as members of a unique club, within which exchange and aid is almost inevitable.

The Other Side: When Terrorism Does
Not Diffuse

Certain areas of the world have not been affected by transnational terrorism. Others have been touched, but lightly. The question remains why terrorism does not diffuse in certain regions of the world with certain intensities. The answer to regional immunity is undoubtedly bound up in the basic causes of terrorism per se. An in-depth study of the fundamental causes and preconditions for terrorism is well beyond the scope of this paper. Nevertheless, the major points can be enumerated.

Terrorism is a form of communication. It is unlikely when people feel there are reliable alternatives for interest articulation or grievance resolution. At the same time, terrorism is also unlikely in situations where all channels of communication are tightly controlled. In essence, terrorism runs the middle ground between completely open and totally closed societies.

Within that middle ground, diffusion takes two forms. The first, between already existing groups, is the communication and exchange of the ideas, tactics, or hardware of terrorism. The second is the diffusion of the very idea of terrorism, and leads to the creation of new groups where none existed before.

For diffusion not to occur, some barriers must either exist or be erected which retard the establishment of groups, or inhibit communication between groups. Barriers to communication take two forms; natural and artificial. Natural barriers are expressed as a function of distance between the diffuser and the potential adopter. The distance may be physical, ideological, ethnic, cultural, religious, or political. Any circumstance that inhibits affinity between terrorist groups or increases the "distance" between them will inhibit the diffusion of terrorism. Artificial barriers such as censorship deny potential actors inspiration and ideas from the outside.

Cooptation and reform are methods governments may use to defuse the appeal of terrorism. When peaceful methods fail, authorities may resort to swift and effective reaction.

The question of intensities is more straightforward. David Milbank has suggested that very practical problems stand in the way of a group's ability to sustain high levels of activity over time. High-intensity terrorism, it seems, either depletes a group's resources, leads to factional divisions, causes an erosion of sympathy or support at the local and international levels, or precipitates more vigorous and effective countermeasures. In short, terrorism seems to be self-limiting. (26)

SUMMARY

We have seen that terrorism is diffusing. Its spread is observable in the adjacency maps. Four hypotheses were offered to account for the diffusion of terrorism. They suggest first that terrorists exchange ideas, weapons, funds, and share training, leading to a spread of tactical expertise and support. Second, terrorists travel to new locations in order to strike their enemy's weakest point, or where they may derive the greatest benefit from the act. Third, terrorists not in direct contact mimic one another's actions, believing that one group's success will rub off on the other if similar tactics are employed. Finally, a null hypothesis suggests that no connection between terrorists exists; however, this hypothesis is not supported by evidence. Terrorists are well connected, and apparently pay careful attention to what each has to offer the other.

A number of factors were also shown to contribute to the diffusion of terrorism. The coordination of terrorist activity, through the use of joint training centers, joint operations, central weapons caches, and coordinating councils such as the Latin American JCR, accounts for the lion's share of direct terrorist diffusion. These activities bring terrorists into contact with one another, allowing direct communications and exchanges. Government support to terrorists is another avenue of diffusion, as are conferences that bring together terrorists under nonoperational circumstances.

Less tangible factors were also identified. These include means for indirect contact between terrorists of different nationalities and from different groups. Terrorists read or hear about one another's exploits, and elicit ideas and tactics. Modern means of travel provide the terrorist the ability to move about the globe quickly. The general lack of legal barriers to terrorism, the classification of terrorism as a political crime (making the terrorist immune from extradition in many countries), and the unwillingness of many nations to ratify and uphold international treaties against terrorist crimes are other factors that allow the terrorist to act with impunity.

What implications does the study of the diffusion of terrorism hold for the future? There is much talk about "deterring" the terrorist. A deterrent, however, is little more than an effective barrier. We have already seen that there are few, if any, natural or artificial barriers to the diffusion of transnational terrorism. Without effective barriers, not only will old groups continue to travel to new locations, but new groups will appear where none were noted before. Ideas and tactics will continue to spread, raising the overall threat potential of groups that would otherwise be considered extraneous or unthreatening due to their apparently remote location.

NOTES

(1) Donald Hodges, Argentina, 1943-1976 (Albuquerque: University of New Mexico Press, 1976), p. 100. The Montoneros had kidnapped and killed Aramburu in 1970 as one of their first major terrorist actions.

(2) Ya (Madrid), December 12, 1974, p. 9.

(3) The following discussion relies heavily on the excellent works of two spatial geographers: Lawrence A. Brown, Diffusion Processes and Location: A Conceptual Framework and Bibliography (Philadelphia: Regional Science Research Institute, 1968); and Peter Gould Spatial Diffusion, Resource Paper 4 (Washington, D.C.: Association of American Geographers, 1969).

(4) See Brown, Diffusion Processes, ch. 2.

(5) Gould, Spatial Diffusion, p. 16.

(6) ITERATE stands for International Terrorism: Attributes of Terrorist Events. Mickolus began the ITERATE project while a Ph.D. candidate at Yale University. The pilot version of the data system (ITERATE I) contains information on 539 terrorist incidents between 1968 and 1974, and is available through the University of Michigan's Inter-University Consortium. The analysis here is based on an update and expansion of the pilot system.

(7) Mickolus defined transnational terrorism as "the use or threat of use, of anxiety-inducing extra-normal violence for political purposes by any individual or group, whether acting for or in opposition to established governmental authority, when such action is intended to influence a target group wider than the immediate victims and when, through the nationality or foreign ties of its perpetrators, its location, the nature of its institutional or human victims, or the mechanics of its resolution, its ramifications transcend national boundaries." See Mickolus, "Statistical Approaches to the Study of Terrorism," in Terrorism: Interdisciplinary Perspectives ed. Yonah Alexander and Seymour Maxwell Finger, "New York: John Jay, 1977) for a discussion of the ITERATE approach.

(8) The 107 variables are listed in ibid.

(9) Latin America Political Report 9, no. 4, p. 28.

(10) Charles Russell, "Transnational Terrorism" Air University Review 27, no. 2 (January-February 1976): 28.

(11) Kenneth Johnson, "Guerrilla Politics in Argentina," Conflict Studies 63 (1975): 13.

(12) Foreign Report, March 23, 1977, pp. 1-4.

(13) Ibid.

(14) Ibid, p. 1.

(15) Washington Post, November 6, 1977, p. C1-5; and Charles Russell and Bowman Miller, "Transnational Terrorism: Terrorist Tactics and Techniques," Group and Area Studies: Clandestine Tactics and Technology, (Gaithersburg, Md.: International Association of Chiefs of Police, 1977), p. 10.

(16) Christopher Dobson and Roland Payne, The Terrorists: Their Weapons, Leaders and Tactics (New York: Facts on File, Inc. 1979); pp. 114-15, 198-99. Also see Washington Star, August 22, 1978; and Vittorfranco S. Pisano, Contemporary Italian Terrorism: Analysis and Countermeasures (Washington, D.C.: Library of Congress Law Library, 1979); p. 95.

(17) To the Point (Johannesburg), October 27, 1978; p. 23.

(18) U.S. Senate, Committee on the Judiciary, Terrorist Activity: International Terrorism. 94th Cong., 1st sess., p. 5, p. 184.

(19) Hodges, Argentina, 1943-1976, p. 38.

(20) J. Sunberg, "Thinking the Unthinkable, or the Case of Dr. Tsironis," in Political Terrorism and International Crime, ed. M. Cherif Bassiouni (Springfield, Ill.: Charles C. Thomas, 1975; p. 451n. The existence of other Cuban training centers is documented in Cozean, Krymis, Hitt, and Arensberg, Cuban Guerrilla Training Centers and Radio Havana: A Selected Bibliography, CRESS-CINFAC R-1098 (Washington, D.C.: Center for Research in Social Systems, October 1968).

(21) Ovid Demaris, Brothers in Blood: The International Terrorist Network (New York: Scribner's Sons, 1977); pp. 177, 152.

(22) Annual of Power and Conflict, 1976-1977, p. 7. An article in the London Times, October 24, 1976, put the number as high as 5,000.

(23) New York Times, July 16, 1976, pp. A1, 6; and Raymond Cleveland et al., A Global Perspective on Transnational Terrorism: A Case Study of Libya, Report No. 25 (Maxwell Air Force Base: Air War College, Air University, April 1977) xerox; as well as Donald G. Campbell, The Growth of Transnational Terrorism (Maxwell Air Force Base: Air War College, Air University, April 1978), xerox.

(24) Christopher Dobson and Ronald Payne, The Carlos Complex: A Study in Terror (New York: G. Putnam and Sons, 1977), p. 22; and Demaris, Brothers in Blood, p. 38.

(25) J. Bowyer Bell, Transnational Terror Policy Study 17 (Washington, D.C.: American Enterprise Institute, 1975) p. 74.

(26) David Milbank, International Terrorism in 1976, RP77 10034U (Washington, D.C.: Central Intelligence Agency, 1977), p. 8n.

APPENDIX A: THE ADJACENCY MAPS *

This appendix is divided into four sections.

The maps in Section 1 show the cumulative diffusion of all transnational terrorist incidents according to the country in which they occurred. The squares indicate the countries in which incidents occurred by December 31 of the year indicated on the map. The triangles mark those countries, once active, that were inactive for a period of two or more years as of the date of the map.

The maps in Section 2 show the cumulative diffusion of terrorist kidnappings, and follow the same graphic format as the maps in Section 1.

The maps in Section ·3 show the cumulative diffusion of terrorist skyjackings, and also follow the same graphic format.

The maps in Section 4 show the actual spatial location and intensity of all incidents for the specific year indicated on the map. The contours represent gradients of five incidents. Thus a country circled once experienced between one and five incidents during the year of the map; a country circled twice experienced between six and ten incidents that year. The maps allow for five gradients or contours.

Number of Contours	Number of Incidents Experienced
1	1-5
2	6-10
3	11-15
4	16-20
5	21 or more

It should be noted that the adjacency map used here shows the International System of 1975: only those entities that were fully sovereign states as of January 1, 1975 appear on the map. Thus territories such as Hong Kong, Belize, and Puerto Rico do not appear, nor do countries such as Djibouti, which gained independence after January 1, 1975.

---

* Policharts and Adjacency Maps are used by permission of Professor Claudio Cioffi-Revilla, Department of Political Science, University of North Carolina, © C. Cioffi-Revilla. Source: ITERATE II

Appendix A, Section 1: Cumulative Diffusion of Transnational Terrorist Incidents of All Types

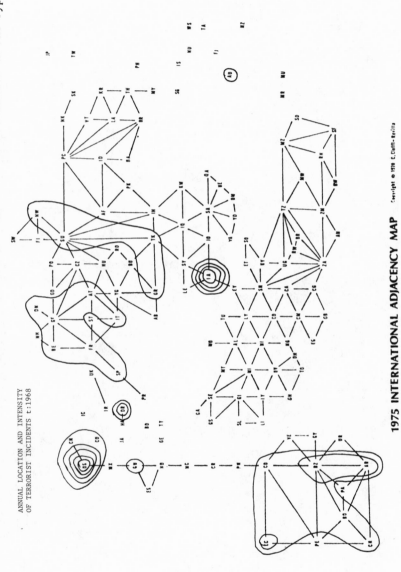

ANNUAL LOCATION AND INTENSITY
OF TERRORIST INCIDENTS t:1968

1975 INTERNATIONAL ADJACENCY MAP   Copyright © 1978 E.Claffin-Revilla

Appendix A, Section 1: (continued)

ANNUAL LOCATION AND INTENSITY
OF TERRORIST INCIDENTS t:1969

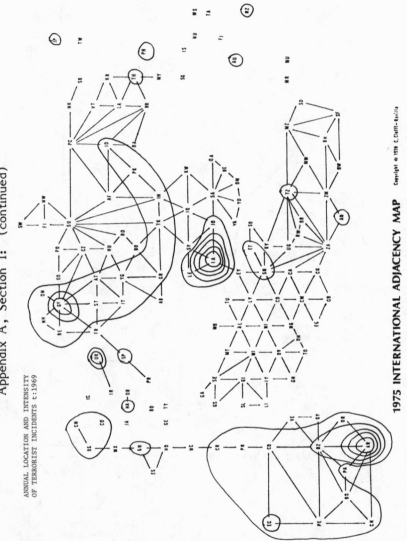

1975 INTERNATIONAL ADJACENCY MAP   Copyright © 1976 C.Ciuffi-Revilla

212

Appendix A, Section 1: (continued)

ANNUAL LOCATION AND INTENSITY
OF TERRORIST INCIDENTS t:1970

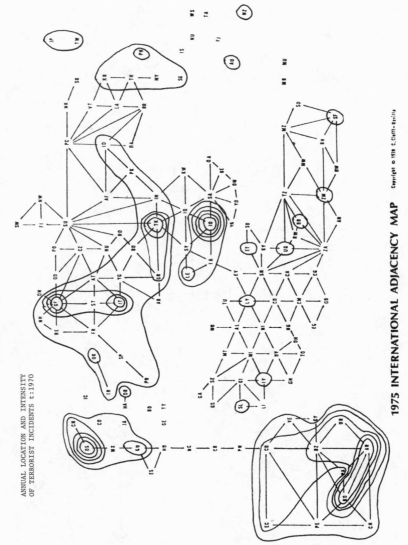

1975 INTERNATIONAL ADJACENCY MAP   Copyright © 1978 C.Cioffi-Revilla

213

Appendix A, Section 1: (continued)

ANNUAL LOCATION AND INTENSITY
OF TERRORIST INCIDENTS t:1971

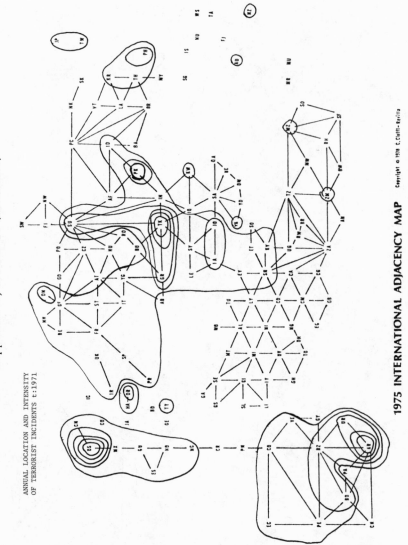

1975 INTERNATIONAL ADJACENCY MAP   Copyright © 1978 C.Ciotti-Revilla

214

Appendix A, Section 1: (continued)

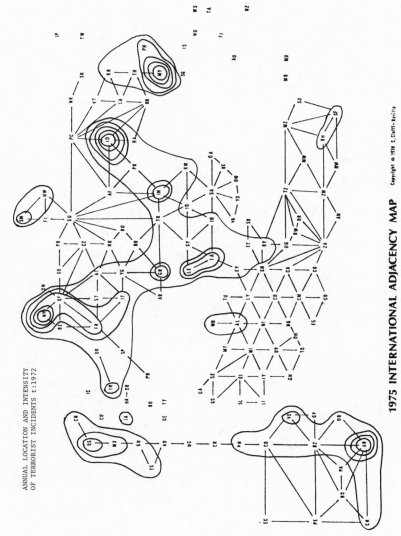

1975 INTERNATIONAL ADJACENCY MAP   Copyright © 1976 C.Cioffi-Revilla

Appendix A, Section 1: (continued)

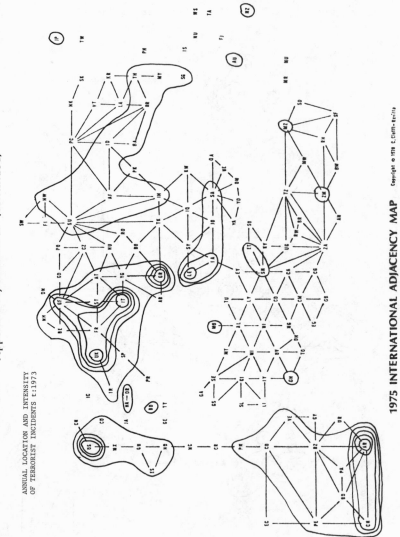

1975 INTERNATIONAL ADJACENCY MAP

216

Appendix A, Section 1: (continued)

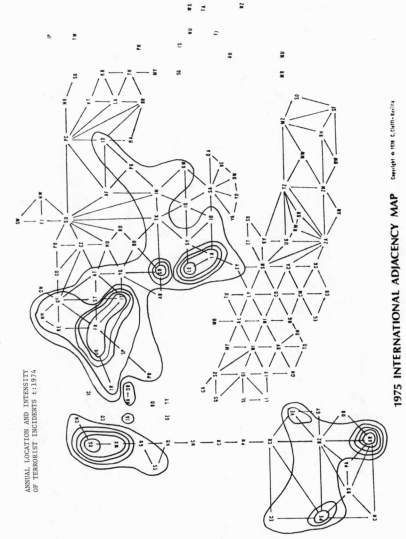

1975 INTERNATIONAL ADJACENCY MAP   Copyright © 1978 C. Cioffi-Revilla

Appendix A, Section 1: (continued)

ANNUAL LOCATION AND INTENSITY
OF TERRORIST INCIDENTS t:1975

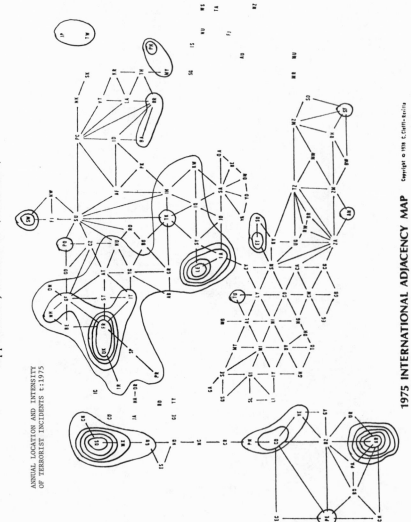

1975 INTERNATIONAL ADJACENCY MAP   Copyright © 1978 C.Cioffi-Revilla

218

Appendix A, Section 1: (continued)

ANNUAL LOCATION AND INTENSITY
OF TERRORIST INCIDENTS t:1976

1975 INTERNATIONAL ADJACENCY MAP Copyright © 1978 C.Cioffi-Revilla

219

Appendix A, Section 1: (continued)

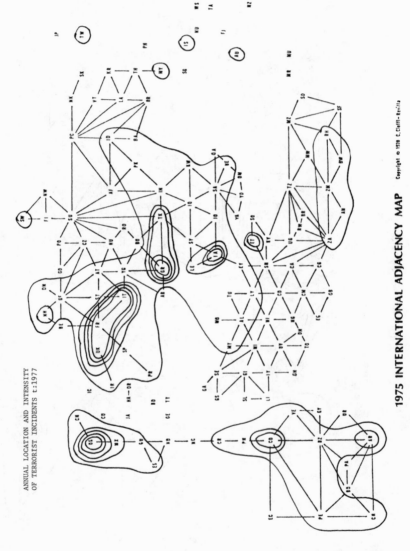

ANNUAL LOCATION AND INTENSITY
OF TERRORIST INCIDENTS t:1977

1975 INTERNATIONAL ADJACENCY MAP   Copyright © 1978 C.Cioffi-Revilla

Appendix A, Section 2: Cumulative Diffusion of Terrorist Kidnappings

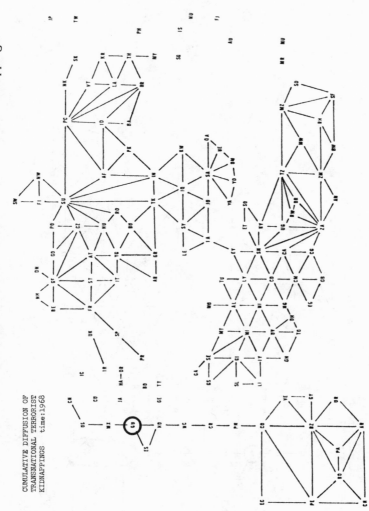

CUMULATIVE DIFFUSION OF
TRANSNATIONAL TERRORIST
KIDNAPPINGS   time:1968

1975 INTERNATIONAL ADJACENCY MAP   Copyright © 1976 C.Cioffi-Revilla

221

Appendix A, Section 2: (continued)

CUMULATIVE DIFFUSION OF
TRANSNATIONAL TERRORIST
KIDNAPPINGS   time:1969

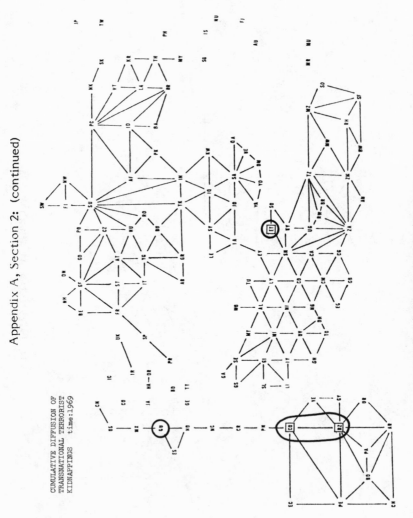

1975 INTERNATIONAL ADJACENCY MAP   Copyright © 1978 C.Cioffi-Revilla

Appendix A, Section 2: (continued)

CUMULATIVE DIFFUSION OF
TRANSNATIONAL TERRORIST
KIDNAPPINGS   time:1970

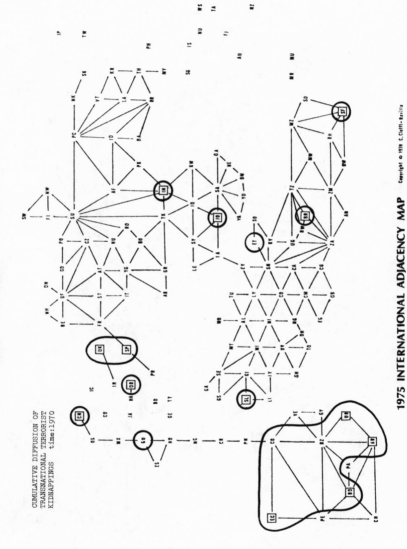

1975 INTERNATIONAL ADJACENCY MAP   Copyright © 1978 C.Cioffi-Revilla

223

Appendix A, Section 2: (continued)

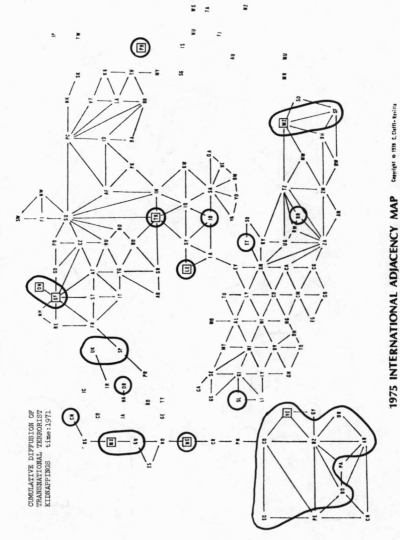

CUMULATIVE DIFFUSION OF
TRANSNATIONAL TERRORIST
KIDNAPPINGS   time:1971

1975 INTERNATIONAL ADJACENCY MAP   Copyright © 1978 C.Cioffi-Revilla

224

Appendix A, Section 2: (continued)

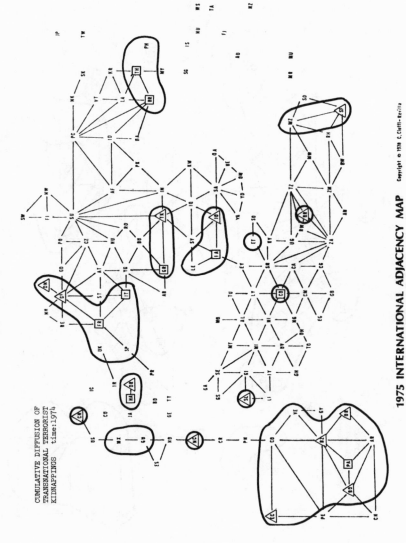

CUMULATIVE DIFFUSION OF
TRANSNATIONAL TERRORIST
KIDNAPPINGS   time:1974

1975 INTERNATIONAL ADJACENCY MAP   Copyright © 1976 C.Ciuffi-Revilla

225

Appendix A, Section 2: (continued)

CUMULATIVE DIFFUSION OF
TRANSNATIONAL TERRORIST
KIDNAPPINGS   time:1977

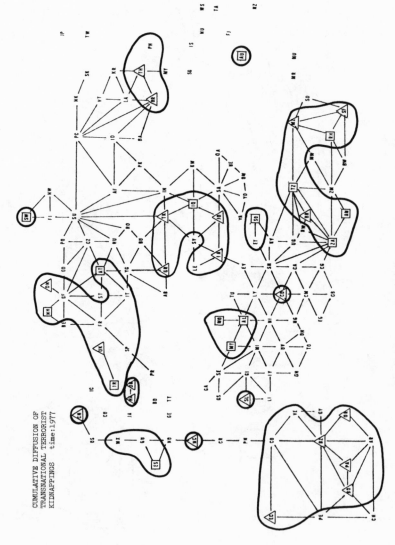

1975 INTERNATIONAL ADJACENCY MAP   Copyright © 1978 C.Ciaffi-Revilla

226

Appendix A, Section 3: Cumulative Diffusion of Terrorist Skyjackings

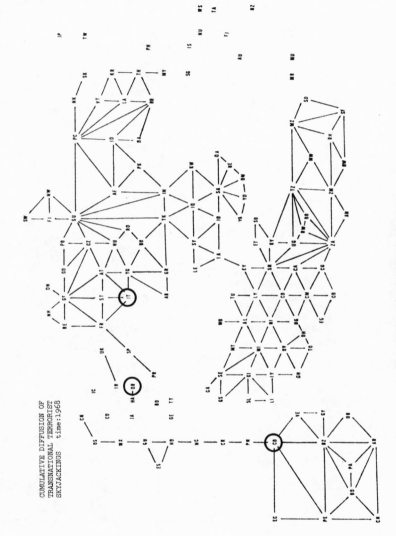

CUMULATIVE DIFFUSION OF
TRANSNATIONAL TERRORIST
SKYJACKINGS   time:1968

1975 INTERNATIONAL ADJACENCY MAP   Copyright © 1976 C.Cioffi-Revilla

227

Appendix A, Section 3: (continued)

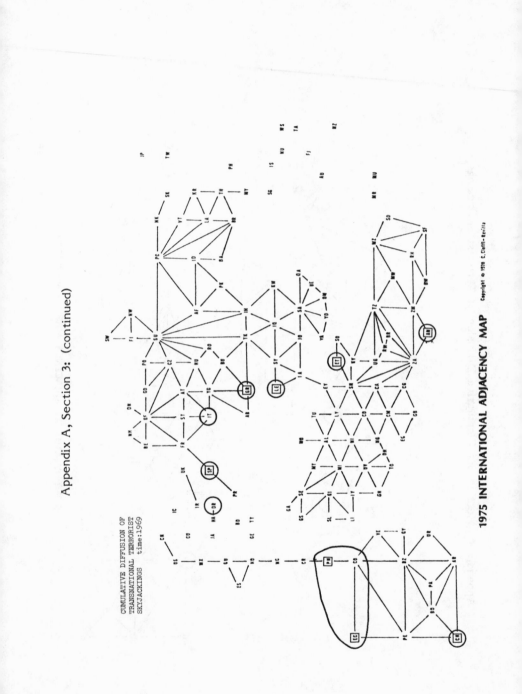

CUMULATIVE DIFFUSION OF
TRANSNATIONAL TERRORIST
SKYJACKINGS   time:1969

1975 INTERNATIONAL ADJACENCY MAP   Copyright © 1978 C.Cioffi-Revilla

228

Appendix A, Section 3: (continued)

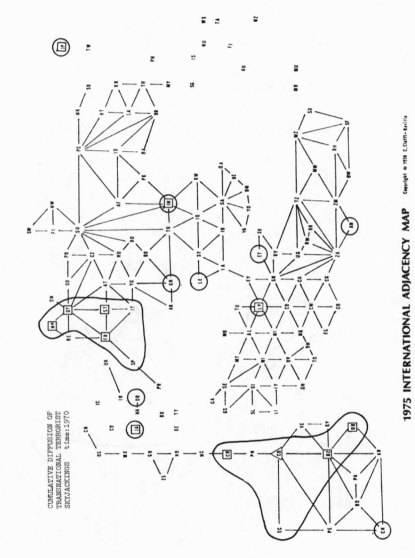

CUMULATIVE DIFFUSION OF
TRANSNATIONAL TERRORIST
SKYJACKINGS   time:1970

1975 INTERNATIONAL ADJACENCY MAP   Copyright © 1978 C.Ciotti-Revilla

229

Appendix A, Section 3:   (continued)

CUMULATIVE DIFFUSION OF
TRANSNATIONAL TERRORIST
SKYJACKINGS   time:1971

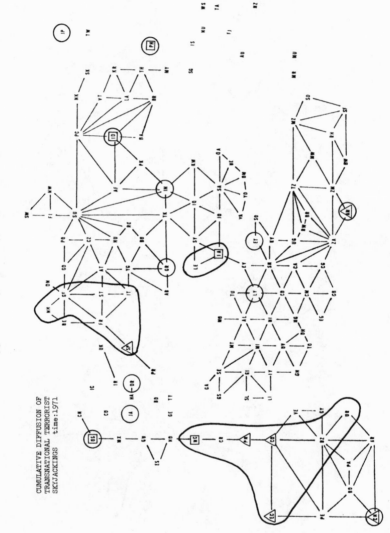

1975 INTERNATIONAL ADJACENCY MAP   Copyright © 1976 C.Cioffi-Revilla

Appendix A, Section 3: (continued)

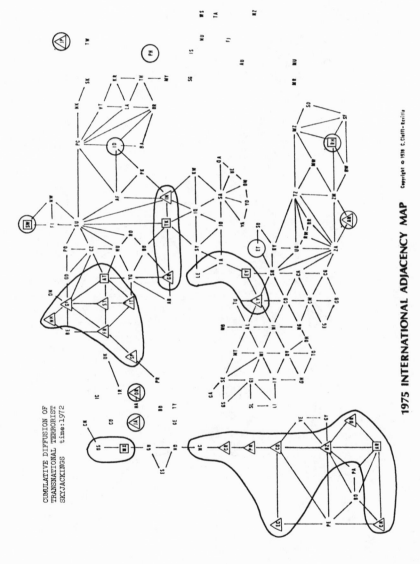

CUMULATIVE DIFFUSION OF
TRANSNATIONAL TERRORIST
SKYJACKINGS   time:1972

1975 INTERNATIONAL ADJACENCY MAP   Copyright © 1976 C.Cioffi-Revilla

231

Appendix A, Section 3:   (continued)

CUMULATIVE DIFFUSION OF
TRANSNATIONAL TERRORIST
SKYJACKINGS   time:1977

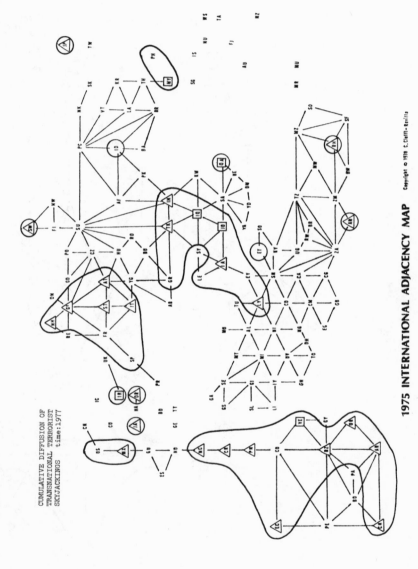

1975 INTERNATIONAL ADJACENCY MAP   Copyright © 1978 C. Ciotti-Revilla

Appendix A, Section 4: Location and Intensity of Transnational Terrorist Incidents

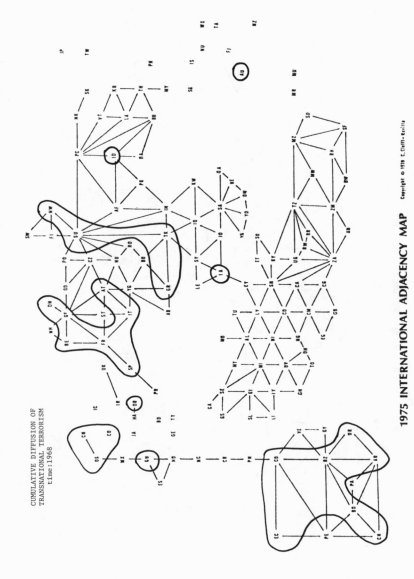

CUMULATIVE DIFFUSION OF
TRANSNATIONAL TERRORISM
time:1968

1975 INTERNATIONAL ADJACENCY MAP

Copyright © 1978 C.Cioffi-Revilla

233

Appendix A, Section 4: (continued)

CUMULATIVE DIFFUSION OF
TRANSNATIONAL TERRORISM
time:1969

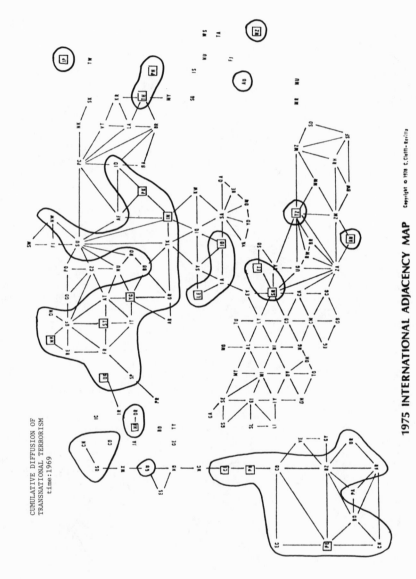

1975 INTERNATIONAL ADJACENCY MAP   Copyright © 1978 C.Cioffi-Revilla

Appendix A, Section 4: (continued)

CUMULATIVE DIFFUSION OF
TRANSNATIONAL TERRORISM
time:1970

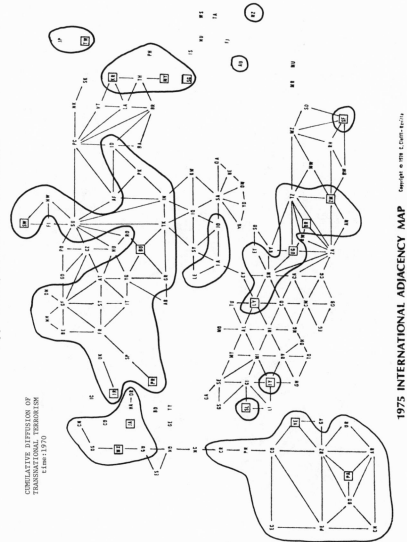

1975 INTERNATIONAL ADJACENCY MAP

Copyright © 1978 C.Cioffi-Revilla

235

Appendix A, Section 4: (continued)

CUMULATIVE DIFFUSION OF
TRANSNATIONAL TERRORISM
time:1971

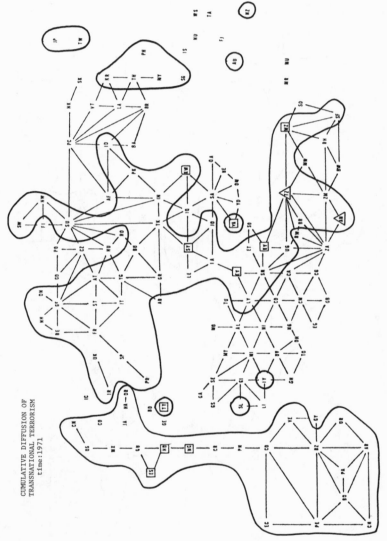

1975 INTERNATIONAL ADJACENCY MAP   Copyright © 1978 E.Cioffi-Revilla

236

Appendix A, Section 4: (continued)

CUMULATIVE DIFFUSION OF
TRANSNATIONAL TERRORISM
time:1972

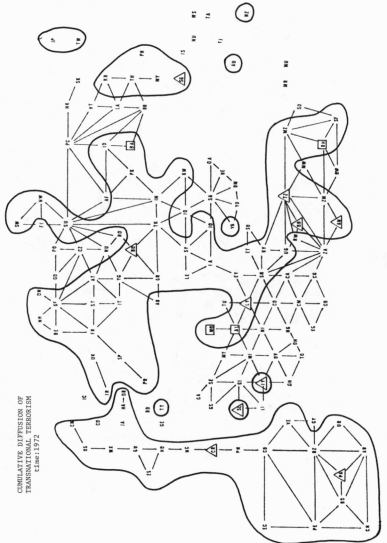

1975 INTERNATIONAL ADJACENCY MAP   Copyright © 1978 C.Cioffi-Revilla

237

Appendix A, Section 4:   (continued)

CUMULATIVE DIFFUSION OF
TRANSNATIONAL TERRORISM
time:1973

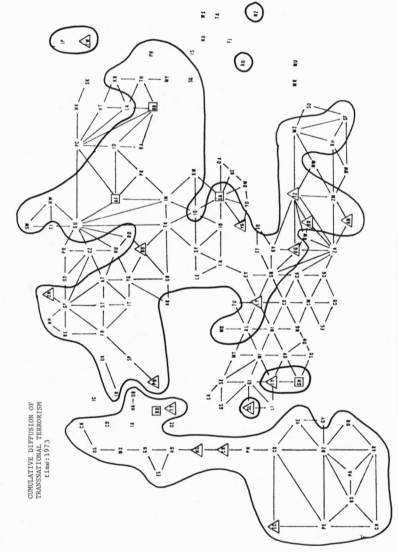

1975 INTERNATIONAL ADJACENCY MAP   Copyright © 1978 C. Cioffi-Revilla

238

Appendix A, Section 4: (continued)

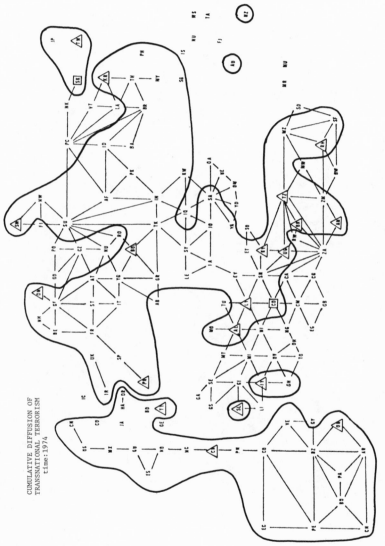

CUMULATIVE DIFFUSION OF
TRANSNATIONAL TERRORISM
time : 1974

1975 INTERNATIONAL ADJACENCY MAP   Copyright © 1978 E.Ciotti-Recilla

239

Appendix A, Section 4: (continued)

CUMULATIVE DIFFUSION OF
TRANSNATIONAL TERRORISM
time:1975

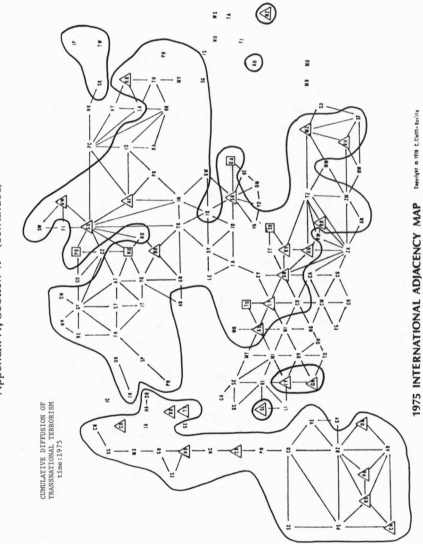

1975 INTERNATIONAL ADJACENCY MAP   Copyright © 1978 C.Cioffi-Revilla

Appendix A, Section 4: (continued)

CUMULATIVE DIFFUSION OF
TRANSNATIONAL TERRORISM
time:1976

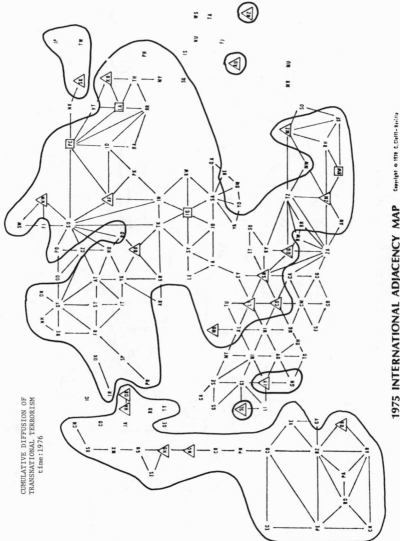

1975 INTERNATIONAL ADJACENCY MAP   Copyright © 1978 C.Cioffi-Revilla

241

Appendix A, Section 4: (continued)

CUMULATIVE DIFFUSION OF
TRANSNATIONAL TERRORISM
time:1977

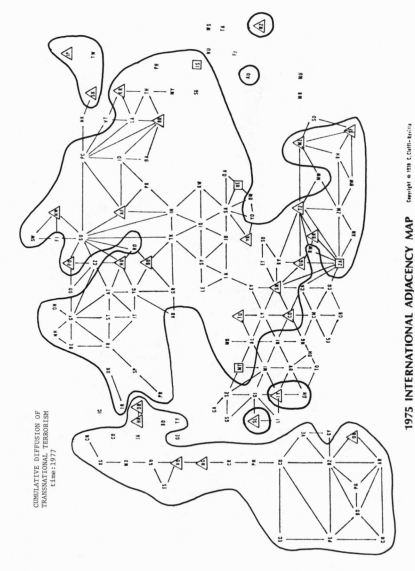

1975 INTERNATIONAL ADJACENCY MAP   Copyright © 1978 C.Cioffi-Revilla

Appendix B: Adjacency Map Country Codes

AB	Albania		GD	East Germany
AF	Afghanistan		GE	Grenada
AL	Algeria		GF	West Germany
AN	Angola		GH	Ghana
AR	Argentina		GI	Guinea
AT	Austria		GR	Greece
AU	Australia		GS	Guinea Bissau
			GU	Guatemala
BA	Bangladesh		GY	Guyana
BD	Barbados			
BE	Belgium		HA	Haiti
BH	Bahrain		HO	Honduras
BN	Bhutan		HU	Hungary
BO	Bolivia			
BR	Burundi		IA	Israel
BU	Bulgaria		IC	Iceland
BW	Botswana		ID	India
BZ	Brazil		IN	Iran
			IQ	Iraq
CA	Central African Republic		IR	Ireland
CD	Chad		IS	Indonesia
CG	Congo		IT	Italy
CH	Chile		IY	Ivory Coast
CM	Cameroon			
CN	Canada		JA	Jamaica
CO	Colombia		JO	Jordan
CR	Costa Rica		JP	Japan
CU	Cuba			
CY	Cyprus		KR	Cambodia
CZ	Czechoslovakia		KW	Kuwait
			KY	Kenya
DH	Dahomey			
DN	Denmark		LA	Laos
DR	Dominican Republic		LE	Lebanon
			LI	Liberia
EC	Ecuador		LY	Libya
EG	Equatorial Guinea		LX	Luxembourg
ES	El Salvador			
ET	Ethiopia		MI	Mali
EY	Egypt (UAR)		MO	Morocco
			MR	Malagasy Republic
FI	Finland		MT	Mauritania
FJ	Fiji		MU	Mauritius
FR	France		MW	Malawi
			MX	Mexico
GA	Gambia		MY	Malaysia
GB	Gabon		MZ	Mozambique

NC	Nicaragua	SO	Somalia
NG	Nigeria	SP	Spain
NH	Netherlands	ST	Switzerland
NI	Niger	SU	Soviet Union
NK	North Korea	SW	Sweden
NU	Nauru	SY	Syria
NW	Norway		
NZ	New Zealand	TA	Tonga
		TH	Thailand
OM	Oman	TK	Turkey
		TO	Togo
PA	Paraguay	TT	Trinidad and Tobago
PC	People's Republic of China	TU	Tunisia
PE	Peru	TW	Taiwan
PH	Philippines	TZ	Tanzania
PK	Pakistan		
PN	Panama	UE	United Arab Emirates
PO	Poland	UG	Uganda
PR	Portugal	UK	United Kingdom
		UR	Uruguay
QA	Qatar	US	United States of America
		UV	Upper Volta
RO	Rumania		
RW	Rwanda	VE	Venezuela
		VT	Vietnam
SA	Saudi Arabia		
SD	Swaziland	WS	Western Samoa
SE	Senegal		
SF	Union of South Africa	YA	North Yemen
SG	Singapore	YD	South Yemen
SK	South Korea	YG	Yugoslavia
SL	Sierra Leone		
SN	Sudan	ZA	Zaire
		ZM	Zambia

10 Terrorism: An Objective Act, A Subjective Reality

Richard H. Shultz, Jr.
Stephen Sloan

To the victims of terrorism the threat or the act of violence appears to be an irrevocable and searing experience. Held captive in a "peoples' prison" or a skyjacked plane, the hostage awaits an uncertain and often terrifying fate. The strains of incarceration impose severe tensions on the hostage's family that indirectly make them victims also. They too are held hostage. There is little need for discussion about what constitutes the act of terror among those who stand at the other side of the gun.

But despite the objectivity that characterizes the act, subjective factors intrude that have different implications to the immediate victim, the family, the organization he or she may represent, the public authorities who are charged with responding to the incident, and a broader audience that may or may not identify with the victim.

If terrorism is fraught with subjectivity, the gray areas that surround the act reflect the realization that this assault against the civil order represents a "new mode of conflict." (1) The line between combatants and noncombatants is either obscured or rendered meaningless by both the practitioners of terror and those who assume a relativistic position that seeks to weigh and measure potential justifications for even the most heinous resorts to carnage.

A great deal of this subjectivity can be readily observed in the continuous debates over what constitutes terrorism. The convoluted rhetoric that is often employed to justify the act of violence can often be heard in the United Nations and other international forums, where the debate has acted as a barrier to the development of an effective and coherent response to the resort to terror. While the diplomats and academics may be engaging in essentially semantic battles, they are battles that have thwarted the evolution of actions on the domestic, national, and international level that might have lessened the number of those who have become victims in an undeclared war.

But even more significant is the fact that the subjectivity and accompanying ambiguity that surround the act of terror have direct implications for those involved in an incident. The ambiguity has different implications to the immediate victim, the victim's organization, and the public authorities who must do more than simply discuss the threat. They must live with ambiguity or by their individual or collective miscalculation be responsible, along with the terrorists, for the death of the innocent. While the questions related to ambiguity may be limited when applied to the immediate victim, the farther one departs from being within the barricade, the more complex the development of a response strategy. The senior policymakers in both the public and private sectors must take decisive action despite the ambiguity that confronts them. They must develop responses in the face of the subjective aspects of a terrorist incident.

INDIVIDUAL RESPONSES AT THE OTHER SIDE
OF THE GUN

The ambiguities surrounding an act of terrorism are in part the result of the fact that there are no front lines in the continuing battle. Contemporary terrorists have not only declared a war against all but have enunciated a new and invidious form of "due process" - guilt by location, whereby the victim is held culpable because he was on an aircraft that was skyjacked or walked by a car-bomb when it was detonated.

Because there are no noncombatants there is a blurring of roles. It is difficult enough for a soldier to become a prisoner of war, but it may be even more traumatic for a civilian, who had no reason to anticipate that he would be at the other side of a gun.

This is not to suggest that the POW will not be traumatized, depending on his own personality or the behavior of his captors. But it can be contended that the civilian hostage has even less of an opportunity to prepare for potential incarceration, much less develop a role in the event of captivity. Moreover, even among civilian hostages, the question of appropriate role may also differ based on the organizational affiliation of the captive.

The tourist who happens to be on a skyjacked plane, the corporate executive who finds himself in a people's prison, the foreign service officer in an occupied embassy, and the military adviser kidnapped by an armed band in a disturbed area - for all four there are common threads to how they are expected to act or should act during the crisis. But because of their different positions, their different roles may not only affect their behavior but also affect the judgment of those who are seeking their release.

Are there suggested patterns of behavior that can assist the tourist held captive on a plane in dealing with the ordeal? Should some form of "survival training" be given to prepare travelers for an incident? (2) Does such a hostage have any obligation - a civilian code of conduct -to fellow passengers? Should such hostages relent to the demands of their captors, even if such concessions might compromise their own beliefs and their country? These questions have no simple answers, but it can be suggested that the nonaffiliated civilian traveler or tourist has an exceedingly broadly defined role, since he or she does not have institutional affiliations and subsequent obligations that may suggest how they should conduct themselves. In effect, they find themselves in a position where there are few norms to assist them in defining their roles. Is there a code of conduct for the passenger in seat 11A other than survival? And at what price?

Perhaps there are more norms of behavior for the corporate executive who might have been taken hostage precisely because he symbolized to the terrorists "an agent of the multinationals." In addition to the basic quest for survival, does the executive have a minimal obligation not to compromise the firm and its activities? Does some type of business ethic and loyalty exist, or is it negated by the threat of violence? The marketing manager does not have a duty to pay the final price for his firm, but does he have any obligations, however loosely defined?

The issue of role and subsequent obligation may become more defined in the vexing question of the duties of a foreign service officer held captive in a besieged embassy. Unlike the tourist who may have been randomly selected or the executive who was seized because he is a symbol, the diplomat - although a civilian - does represent his or her country. Does it therefore follow that the foreign service officer has an obligation - however informally stated - not to engage in various activities, even under the severest pressure, that could compromise the image and policies of the country he represents? Yet even if he does have more focused norms and attendant obligations than the tourist or the executive, the fact remains that the diplomat is a civilian, a noncombatant in an undeclared war which no longer even recognizes the basic obligation of protection of diplomatic personnel. Foreign service officers do not get combat pay.

Suggestions related to a code of behavior may be more strongly in focus, but also particularly complex, when one deals with how military personnel might be expected to act if they are held captive in nondeclared war. They do have a code of conduct, but how is it to be applied in a situation of neither war nor peace, when they are prisoners but not prisoners of war? At least in a POW camp there are clearly defined obligations to the other prisoners, a sense of professional loyalty, and a Geneva Convention that provides some standards that should be adhered to by the uniformed enemy. Does the military adviser or the marine sentry who is seized by terrorists have the ultimate obligation of paying the supreme sacrifice, as in the case of a declared war? Again, the choices are complicated in an outbreak of hostilities where an embassy office may become a new and also very dangerous type of foxhole.

THINKING THE UNTHINKABLE, AND PREPARING
TO RESPOND TO IT

If the position of different types of hostages suggests different
potential expectations of how they should behave, do the organizations
they use or represent have different obligations to make the potential
victim recognize the possibility of incarceration and training him or her
to deal with a potential incident? Again, subjectivity intrudes, but the
following may be used as a basis for a guideline: The greater the
likelihood that an individual may become a victim of terrorism as a
result of his or her duties, the greater the responsibility of the
organization he or she works for to sensitize the individual to the threat
and to provide effective training to deal with it. However, there may
also be a corollary that places a reciprocal obligation on a potential
victim: the greater the level of preparation to deal with an incident,
the greater the expectation for a more rigorous standard of conduct
during a hostage-taking. It will be noted below, however, that the
question of standards is in part based on the obligations the individual
might acquire based on his position within a particular type of
organization or profession.
    This guideline and its corollary suggest that it is essentially the
obligation of the tourist to recognize and be prepared for an incident,
since he does not represent any organization. However, the American
tourist should be able to obtain information provided from the State
Department and other concerned agencies, if he or she chooses to avail
himself of it, that can warn of potential threats in any particular
destination and also provide basic passive and active security suggestions. This does not mean to imply that the governmental role should be
totally passive. Since terrorism has indeed included tourists as if they
were soldiers, the Department of State should encourage travelers -
without overstating the threat - to recognize that terrorism is not
simply something that happens to other people.
    The obligation of commercial aviation to the passenger-tourist exist,
but it should be stressed that they essentially do not involve the direct
participation of the passenger. The airlines are and should be required
to increasingly refine their physical security measures and to train their
flight crews and attendants under the most realistic and rigorous
conditions to deal effectively with an incident. However, it should be
noted that since skyjackings are far rarer than malfunctions in
equipment, measures related to training in aviation safety, as contrasted to aviation security - although both are interrelated - should
still take precedence.
    It might be suggested that passengers be given a briefing - much like
the pretakeoff precautions - on how they should act in the event of a
disturbance aboard the aircraft. But given that skyjackings are
relatively rare, such an exercise would only create unnecessary alarm
and amplify the threat and moreover would probably not prove effective
in the event of a crisis. Finally, such a briefing would hardly be

supported by the airlines, who understandably do not wish to make their passengers think the unthinkable. Therefore the responsibilities for training and the development of an effective response should naturally be the obligation of the flight crew and the attendants.

For the corporate executive and his family who are symbolic targets, it can be suggested that the corporation has greater responsibilities in providing their employees with effective security. The difficulty here, in part, may be the reluctance of the corporation to sensitize its personnel overseas to the fact that they may become victims, and by so doing risk lowering the morale of the staff. Yet ignorance is not bliss. Most multinational executives are aware that they are increasingly likely to be targets, and therefore a realistic assessment of necessary security measures should be provided for vulnerable personnel. Such an assessment will not only indicate the organization's concern for its personnel but, realistically, will help to negate potential liability for the corporation in the event that a victim claims negligence on the part of the employer.

It should be stressed that such training is available, and varies in quality from superficial suggestions of personnel security measures to active programs related to defensive driving, surveillance techniques, and other steps. The judgment on the degree of training that should be given to personnel will, of course, depend on financial considerations, assessment of risk, and related factors. Irrespective of the degree of training, it is imperative that corporations meet their responsibility to their staffs in a war in which executives are often the most popular targets.

In conjunction with personal training of potential hostages, particularly vulnerable corporations should refine their crisis management techniques in recognition of the possibility of assaults on their personnel and facilities. Effective contingency plans should be drawn up that have the highest level of support within the hierarchy. But contingency plans lose their validity if they are not tested. Therefore, corporations should engage in developing a wide variety of gaming and, if necessary, more full-scale simulations as a means of preparing for a crisis that hopefully will not happen, but cannot totally be dismissed.

Given effective such presentations, the executive overseas might indeed avoid capture, since terrorists probe for the weakest link when selecting their targets. It does make a difference if adequate personal measures are effected. But what if the executive is captured? How should he or she behave? One can suggest that the obligations involved essentially deal with survival, not defending the activities of the corporation, a move which might in any case prove foolhardy and fatal. Yet if the employee knows that thanks to effective planning his affairs are in order, and that the corporation has consistently prepared to meet the contingency he finds himself in, the ordeal of captivity may be lightened, since concern for the victim has been indicated in the development of active security programs.

Questions of accountability and training come more into focus and therefore become more debatable when one deals with how foreign service officers should react if they are held hostage. Do they have a greater obligation than the tourist, the executive, and the clerical staff worker in the consulate? Should there be a code - however loosely defined - to adhere to in the event of a seizure? While they are civilians and noncombatants, they may have more stringent require- ments for behavior since they directly represent their country. The potential spectacle of a senior diplomat compromising classified information or his country cannot be dismissed, but it must also be realized that such individuals have not been trained for combat, nor is it their function. Any judgment must be tempered.

Yet since, regretably, foreign service officers have increasingly become victims, there is an obligation on the part of the foreign service to provide training to assist their personnel in avoiding captivity and obtaining some experience in hostage survival training. Much as pilots are put through POW training, key personnel and their families might experience in modified form how it feels to be at the other side of a gun. This program will make the entire family unit more cognizant of the need to practice security measures by providing, indirectly, the feeling of what it is like to have a member of the family held captive.

The need for effective and realistic training is vital. It can be contended that at this time it has not really been realized; the expectation may be that merely a short course can prepare the foreign service officer for potential captivity. (3) Yet as a result, members of the foreign service may claim that it has provided training and therefore place all responsibility for behaving properly on the victim. This is unfair: poor training may be worse than no training if it provides a means by which officers can say, "We trained you, and it's your responsibility to deal with an incident effectively." But the need for training is acute, for the diplomat is no longer a protected person but a potential victim.

On the surface, it would appear that there are more rigorous expectations in reference to a code of conduct for military personnel who are held in captivity. But below the surface assumption are many difficult issues, since the soldier may be a prisoner but is not a POW, and therefore the code, which is always subject to interpretation, may be in need of further refinement.

The issue of a code of behavior may be further clouded by what the assignment of the soldier is. Does a marine sentry who, as part of his obligations, must assist in providing security for an embassy have a greater responsibility than a military adviser who happens to be captured while touring in an unofficial position in a disturbed area?

While answers to these questions cannot be given in this short essay, it is strongly suggested that military personnel who might be posted to a dangerous area be given training to assist them, at least, in dealing with how to respond to captivity at the inception of an incident. (4) Hostage training modeled in part after POW programs for noncombatant soldiers may be a step in the right direction. Again, however, the training cannot be superficial. It must be realistic and provide a means for designated personnel to prepare for and accept the reality that they are, by dint of their professions, potential victims.

As soldiers, do these individuals have a higher standard of expected conduct than their civilian counterparts? There may be a more rigorous obligation, but judgment and compassion must be used in dealing with a soldier found in an unusual battlefield. Unfortunately it can be said that the professional soldier can ultimately say he or she may have to pay the supreme sacrifice, but what businessman would put the same premium on dying?

WHO STANDS IN JUDGMENT? - THE ISSUE OF ORGANIZATIONAL RESPONSE

In the final analysis, as one former hostage noted, "Once you are a hostage you are a hostage for the rest of your life. (5) The freed victims will display different responses to their captivity, from relatively painless adjustment to severe trauma; what obligations does the society at large and the individual's organization have in assisting the transition to the outside world? There are no clear axioms, but alternatives can be noted.

In the postcrisis phase, the hostage should be afforded more than a pat on the back. The authorities and (where appropriate) the airlines have an obligation to, at least, provide short-term assistance in contacting relatives, providing housing, and related essential services. But beyond such functions, the victim should be notified and given the opportunity to obtain psychological counseling to help them make an initial adjustment. Such techniques have been effectively employed by the Dutch, who realize that the trauma does not end when the hostages are released.

The obligation of the corporation to the former hostages may be fraught with ambiguity. There may be a temptation to provide a "business as usual" image, even while the victim attempts a readjust-ment. Far better is the view that in contingency planning, every effort is made to assist the returning victim in obtaining long-term psychologi-cal support if necessary, and any financial assistance that may be necessary. But perhaps even more complex is the issue of professional advancement in the organization after the incident, an area in which there may not have been sufficient sensitivity heretofore. The victim, like a rape victim, may be viewed to somehow be "damaged goods" and a living reminder that it can happen and has happened to "one of our own." Promising careers should not be sidetracked and individuals placed on the shelf, and yet it happens.

The need for support and enough sensitivity not to "accidentally" hinder a victim's career must also, most certainly, be kept in mind by foreign services. There may be a temptation to provide a slap on the back immediately after the incident, but followed it with an unwillingness and lack of sensitivity in understanding the victim's trauma, (6) a lack of sensitivity that may destroy a career. But, happily, events underscore the fact that there is a growing realization that a victim should not be accidentally victimized.

The question of judgment is even more sharply defined in the case of the freed officer or enlisted man. How are they to be treated? No code of conduct can be interpreted literally, but it should be added that even more flexibility must be employed in assessing the behavior of the military man held captive in an undeclared war, for it is all too easy to stand in judgment if one has not oneself lived through the primal experience of becoming a hostage.

CONCLUSION: THE HUMAN
CONDITION IN AN UNDECLARED WAR

In this concluding chapter the authors have chosen to return to the basic concerns of the training of and response to those who may become the terrorists' next victim. The fates of those who have been directly confronted by such acts of violence are often obscured by the attention paid to tactical responses to the continuing threat and related broad issues of public policy. These concerns are certainly vital, but we wish to keep at the forefront the need to protect the victims in a conflict that has often been characterized as a war against all. It is a war in which the battlefield is not drawn and where we all are to some degree unwitting and unwilling participants.

NOTES

(1) Brian Jenkins, International Terrorism: A New Mode of Conflict, (Los Angeles: Crescent Publications, 1974).

(2) For a brief list of suggestions that can be employed by a passenger confronted with an incident, see Christopher Dobson and Ronald Payne, "How to Survive a Hijack," reprinted from Business Traveler, n.d.

(3) The Department of State does conduct a one-day seminar for their personnel and other officials who will be on overseas assignments. Such a program is clearly a step in the right direction, but more extensive training should be given to particularly vulnerable personnel.   One expects that the Iranian crisis is leading to the development of more realistic and protracted training.   For a pamphlet that notes a number of the essentials presented at the current program see U.S. Department of State, Seminar on Terrorism, Washington Program, Foreign Service Institute.

(4) This article cannot deal in detail with the type of training measures that should be devised to assist potential victims. However, it should be noted that current realistic programs for the military suggest techniques by which civilian personnel can refine their

escape and evasion skills. The program also gives participants a feeling of how it is to be seized and held for a short period. Such programs cannot deal with the dynamics of long-term imprisonment, although they do discuss suggested patterns of individual and group behavior that can be employed during a long confinement.

(5) From an interview with a former hostage on the American Broadcasting Company Program Hostage, January 30, 1978.

(6) For an analysis of some of the problems of returning hostages see Brian Jenkins, Hostage Survival: Some Preliminary Observations (Santa Monica, Calif.: Rand, April 1976). Also see the chapter by Abraham Miller in this book.

Index

About the Contributors

RICHARD H. SHULTZ, JR. is an Assistant Professor of Political Science at The Catholic University of America. He is currently completing a book about American counterinsurgency strategy during the Vietnam War.

STEPHEN SLOAN, a Professor of Political Science at the University of Oklahoma, is the author of a forthcoming book titled Simulating Terrorism.

CLIVE C. ASTON is a leading authority on hostage-taking in England, and is currently completing his dissertation at the University of London.

EDWARD HEYMAN is currently a research associate at CACI, Inc.- Federal in Arlington, Virginia, where he is involved in research on transnational terrorism.

EDWARD MICKOLUS, who is with the Office of Political Analysis, Central Intelligence Agency, developed International Terrorism: Attributes of Terrorist Events Data, a comprehensive computerized information system on terrorism.

ABRAHAM H. MILLER, a Professor of Political Science at the University of Cincinnati, is the author of Terrorism and Hostage Negotiations.

ROBERT K. MULLEN is a private consultant to federal, state, and local agencies and industry with interests in nuclear safeguards and security; international trade in sensitive materials; and sabotage and allied threat assessments for major industrial, public utility, and military activity.

HARRY PIZER, head of Corporate Compliance for Braniff International Airlines, is a leading expert on both aviation and executive security.

JAMES SCHLOTTER is currently a research associate at CACI, Inc.- Federal, working on transnational terrorism.